GOD'S FORMULA FOR SUCCESS

GOD'S FORMULA FOR SUCCESS

AS REVEALED IN THE SCRIPTURES BY THE LORD

RANDY L. BOTT

CFI
An imprint of Cedar Fort, Inc.
Springville, Utah

ISBN 13: 978-1-4621-3870-8

Published by CFI, an imprint of Cedar Fort, Inc.
2373 W. 700 S., Springville, UT, 84663
Distributed by Cedar Fort, Inc., www.cedarfort.com

Library of Congress Control Number: 2020952250

Cover design by Courtney Proby

Printed in the United States of America

10 9 8 7 6 5 4 3 2 1

Printed on acid-free paper

CONTENTS

PROLOGUE

The story is told of a father who had two sons. He desperately wanted them to be successful in life, but it seemed their stubbornness and unwillingness to follow any other than their own way of thinking would destine them to less than optimal success. Deciding on a course of action, this wise father concocted a plan.

He called the two sons into his palatial study and explained the rules for the contest. Using only the resources within the study, they were to discover the combination to his safe within a certain time limit. If successful, each boy would win the contents of the safe. The father showed the boys the prizes: deeds to two large pieces of industrial property and two envelopes with a huge amount of cash. Only one deed and one envelope was to be placed in the safe at a time. Each boy could win. They were not competing with each other.

The rules of the contest allowed only one boy into the room at a time. No other person other than the observing father was allowed into the room during the contest. By the toss of a coin it was determined that the elder brother would go first. The hour time limit seemed to be ample for such an easy task.

With the younger son anxiously awaiting his turn in the hallway, the the father escorted the elder son into the study. Commencing at the desk, the elder son rifled through the papers, drawers, and files, looking for the combination to the safe. Minutes ticked away and frustration began to take its toll. Books from the study shelves were removed and examined for the elusive combination. As the hour began to wane, the boy frantically looked under the carpet, in the sofa, inside the lamp shade, and in every other conceivable hiding place. Not infrequently he verbally complained about the impossibility and stupidity of the contest. At last the hour concluded with him frantically trying to "feel" the clicks of the combination as he rotated the dial lock. Dejected and angry, he was escorted from the room. He had failed to win the prize.

The younger son was escorted into the study to the sound of warnings from the elder brother that it was a stupid contest and he may as well quit before he started because he would never find the combination. The search began in much the same manner with the younger son as it had with the elder son. The father stood quietly in the shadows with arms folded, watching the fruitless search of his younger son.

About fifteen minutes into the search it seemed as though a light bulb turned on in the mind of the searching son. He paused, looked at his father, and queried: "Did you say I could use any resource within the room?" The father answered in the affirmative. In an obvious voice of triumphant elation, the younger son asked, "Dad, what is the combination to the safe?" To his relief and joy, his father slowly repeated the combination. The dial on the safe's lock was rotated at the direction of the father, stopping precisely on the designated numbers. Gone was the frustration, the anxiety, and the hurry. Replacing the agitated dismay was a sense of peace and humble willingness to follow directions. As the father ceased speaking, the younger son reached for the handle. As he applied pressure, he felt the latch give, and with considerable effort he pulled open the safe's door to claim his prize.

With an embrace and tears of gratitude, he and his father exited the room to find the elder son still fuming over his defeat. In a voice of total unbelief, the elder son asked how the younger son had succeeded in opening the safe. Still beaming over his success, the younger son explained that he had asked his father for the combination. Now in total exasperation the elder son ranted and raved about the unfairness of the father. Why hadn't the father told him the combination? Without answering, the father turned to the younger son, who explained, "Dad said we could use *all* resources within the study. He was in the study and certainly was a knowledgeable resource, so I asked him. You never did ask!"

Such is the story. The application of the principle is probably self-evident. We are sent into mortality with a difficult task to perform. We have been promised by the Father that we may use all resources available to complete the task. He is not an absentee God but a loving, concerned, willing Father. He will not perform the task (opening the safe) for us, but He will, if we ask, give us the directions enabling us to open the safe ourselves. Inside the safe is far more than the deed to some real estate and an envelope with a huge sum of money. Inside is the promised deed: "All that my Father hath shall be given unto you" (see D&C 84:38).

Many a man and many a woman have exited the contest of mortality in total frustration, protesting the impossibility of the task. Others have defiantly raised their clenched fists toward the heavens, claiming favoritism because some have successfully asked the Father for the combination and have received positive confirmation of the promise: "Therefore, if you will ask of me you shall receive; if you will knock it shall be opened unto you" (D&C 6:5). What a disappointment to arrive at our final interview with the Father when our mortal lives will be reviewed in detail only to discover that we received from life exactly what we wanted and expected. How singularly beautiful the promise of the Father: "Verily, verily, I say unto you, even as you desire of me so it shall be unto you" (D&C 6:8).

While there is still time, we encourage all to "draw near unto [Him]" and receive the divine promise that "[He] will draw near unto you; seek [Him] diligently and ye shall find [Him]; ask and ye shall receive; knock, and it shall be opened unto you" (D&C 88:63). We testify from our own personal experiences that communicating with the Father is not only possible but achievable. The results of His constant answers to humble pleadings brings joy in this life and a lively hope of eternal life in the world to come. So "look to God and live" (Alma 37:47).

INTRODUCTION

During my high school experience, like everyone else, I was required to take geometry. To me, it was confusing and frustrating. However, a wise teacher taught us that all we needed to do was apply the step-by-step formula and the answer would be easily arrived at and always correct.

That started me thinking. Could the same thing be said of things other than math? It was surprising and gratifying to read what the Lord said in Doctrine and Covenants 130:20–21: "There is a law, irrevocably decreed in heaven before the foundations of this world, upon which *all blessings* are predicated—And when we obtain *any blessing* from God, it is by obedience to that law upon which it is predicated" (italics added).

As I pondered that statement, it became apparent that if I could identify the desired blessing, all I had to do was follow it back and discover the law upon which it was predicated. If I obeyed the law, then Heavenly Father (by His own declaration) was "bound" to give me the blessing. Note the Lord's statement in Doctrine and Covenants 82:10: "I, the Lord, am bound when ye do what I say; but when ye do not what I say, ye have no promise."

A general principle found in the scriptures is that all things must be certified to in the mouth of two or three witnesses (see 2 Corinthians 13:1). So, not surprisingly, this same principle is reiterated in Doctrine and Covenants 132:5: "For all who will have a blessing at my hands shall abide **the law which was appointed for *that blessing*, and the conditions thereof**, as were instituted from before the foundation of the world."

What a promise and a challenge. Obviously, it will require more than a passing familiarity with the scriptures and a desire to identify and follow the laws upon which the desired blessing is predicated.

Why consider a book like this? Thousands of years ago the Psalmist wrote: "Thy word *is* a lamp unto my feet, and a light unto my path. I have sworn, and I will perform *it*, that I will keep thy righteous judgments. I am afflicted very much: quicken me, O Lord, according unto thy word" (Psalm 119:105–107).

One must wonder whether one source of "afflictions" could be from our failure to follow the Lord's revealed word, causing us to stumble in the dark when His light is readily available.

In any such project such as this book, there are bound to be omissions that, in retrospect, should have been included. Perhaps there may be scriptures included that, upon deeper investigation, could have been left out. So, by definition, this will forever be a "work in progress" no matter when it is published. Rather than criticize, feel free to make marginal notes, cross out mis-applied scriptures, and use this work as a catalyst to get you thinking, pondering, and praying about blessings you desire from the Lord.

There is another caution to be given. It is obvious that the Lord does not wear a wristwatch. The scriptural phrase "in mine own due time" (see D&C 43:29 as one of twenty-five scriptural examples) is at times a source of frustration when the Lord's timing for bestowing the desired blessing does not coincide with our wishes. However, the Lord's promise is sure. He reaffirms:

> Verily I say unto you my friends, fear not, let your hearts be comforted; yea, rejoice evermore, and in everything give thanks;
>
> Waiting patiently on the Lord, for **your prayers** have entered into the ears of the Lord of Sabaoth, and are recorded with this seal and testament—**the Lord hath sworn and decreed that they shall be granted.**
>
> **Therefore, he giveth this promise unto you, with an immutable covenant that they shall be fulfilled**; and all things wherewith you have been afflicted shall work together for your good, and to my name's glory, saith the Lord." (D&C 98:1–3)

Some prayers are answered before we say "amen." Others may not be answered for years or even during our lifetime. But we can rest assured that the Lord will answer them "and it shall be in his own time, and in his own way, and according to his own will" (D&C 88:68). It can be a real test of our trust in God and faith in His promises when deadlines pass and the desired blessing hasn't been realized. However, we have discovered, if we live long enough, that He has our eternal welfare in mind. As Isaiah said so many years ago, "For my thoughts are not your thoughts, neither are your ways my ways, saith the Lord. For as the heavens are higher than the earth, so are my ways higher than your ways, and my thoughts than your thoughts" (Isaiah 55:8–9).

If the Lord withholds a blessing, it is *always* so He can bless you with a greater blessing in the future. In my own life I have witnessed time and again that when I humbly accept the Lord's timing and His method of blessing, it is always far superior to what I had originally asked for and *always* more appropriately timed to give me the maximum amount of growth and understanding.

Too often people want to counsel the Lord about the form the blessings are to be bestowed and the exact time they are to happen. Wisely the Lord said: "Seek not to counsel your God" (D&C 22:4).

We must develop the confidence in the Lord that He (an omnipotent, omniscient being) can accomplish His stated goal. Even if it seems impossible, the Savior taught: "With men *it is* impossible, but not with God: for with God all things are possible" (Mark 10:27). The Lord's objective for us is clearly outlined in Moses 1:39: "For behold, this is my work and my glory—to bring to pass the immortality and eternal life of man."

A WORD OF CAUTION: Although it would be foolish not to glean all we can from the inspiration and knowledge God has given to the people of the world, as well as the Latter-day Saints, we also need to be aware that "Satan fighteth against God continually" (see Moroni 7:12). Often his deceptive perversions of the truth are so subtle that without the inspiration of the Lord, even good people are deceived.

Paul saw our day and gave the following caution to Timothy about people in our day:

> Ever learning, and never able to come to the knowledge of the truth. . . .
>
> Yea, and all that will live godly in Christ Jesus shall suffer persecution.
>
> But evil men and seducers shall wax worse and worse, deceiving, and being deceived.
>
> But continue thou in the things which thou hast learned and hast been assured of, knowing of whom thou hast learned them;

> And that from a child thou hast known the holy scriptures, which are able to make thee wise unto salvation through faith which is in Christ Jesus.
>
> All scripture is given by inspiration of God, and *is* profitable for doctrine, for reproof, for correction, for instruction in righteousness:
>
> That the man of God may be perfect, throughly furnished unto all good works. (2 Timothy 3:7, 12–17)

There is a reason the Church calls scriptures "the standard works." They always have been and must continue to be the standard against which all philosophies are measured. Satan is the great counterfeiter. So closely does his deceptions mirror the truth that without the help of the Lord many are led astray. As we continue our quest for eternal life, the caution is to weigh very carefully everything we are bombarded with against the revealed word of the Lord found in the scriptures. Where there is a difference, wisdom would dictate that we "look to God and live" (Alma 37:47).

HOW TO USE THE BOOK

This book is not written as a story book where one chapter builds upon the previous one. Each chapter is designed to stand alone. You may choose to select from the table of contents a chapter of particular interest to you and go directly to that chapter. However, in so compiling the book, of necessity there will be some duplication of scriptures and thoughts that would be unnecessary if the book was designed to be read from beginning to end.

In many of the scriptures that I quote, I have put some words in bold and italicized others. Please note that the emphasis is my own and does not appear in the original scriptural text.

Encouragement is also given to you, the reader, to search out talks by prophets, apostles, Church leaders, and authors to complement what is written in this book. Perhaps someday one of you will get an irresistible urge to write the companion volume. In the meantime, I hope you have as much enjoyment and enlightenment in reading this volume as I have had in compiling it.

1

ACQUIRING WEALTH WITHOUT LOSING YOUR SOUL

Possibly no scriptural formula comes with more cautions and conditions than acquiring wealth without losing your soul. That shouldn't be very surprising given the adversary's demonic game plan to use the treasures of the earth to destroy mankind.

Starting with a statement from Moses, the Lord makes clear His intended use of riches or wealth: "But thou shalt remember the Lord thy God: for it is he that giveth thee power to get **wealth,** *that he may establish his covenant* which he sware unto thy fathers, as it is this day" (Deuteronomy 8:18).

Some mistakenly believe that "money is the root of all evil" and actually believe they can find a scripture to prove it. However, a more careful reading of 1 Timothy 6:10 clearly reveals a different definition: "For the **love of money** is the *root of all evil.*" It seems that over two thousand years ago the Apostle Paul realized that unstable man would use any and every means to satisfy the insatiable quest for wealth, putting temporary things before eternal principles.

Is there anything wrong with wanting to be temporally rich? In one of the greatest sections of the Doctrine and Covenants concerning the safety of His Saints in the latter days, the Lord defines the Father's objective for His children regarding eternal and temporal wealth: "And if ye seek the riches which it is the **will of the Father to give unto you**, ye shall be the richest of all people, for ye shall have the *riches of eternity*; and it must needs be that the *riches of the earth* are mine to give; but beware of pride, lest ye become as the Nephites of old" (D&C 38:39).

Even a casual reading of the Book of Mormon clearly reveals the basis for the warning. It has been called "the prosperity cycle." The Lord prospers the people, they become rich. There is a separation of those who have more abundantly from those with lesser means. Pride introduces itself into the society. Persecution and class distinction based on wealth becomes widespread. Failing to repent after repeated prophetic warnings, the people are brought into bondage by their enemies. Following a period of deprivation and servitude, the people humble themselves, the Lord prospers them, they become a free people (usually after much bloodshed), the Lord prospers them again, and the cycle starts all over again.

In an attempt to put the quest for wealth in proper sequence and perspective, after receiving his errand from the Lord, Jacob says:

> O that he would rid you from this iniquity (pride—see verse 13) and abomination. And, O that ye would listen unto the word of his commands, and let not this pride of your hearts destroy your souls!
>
> Think of your brethren like unto yourselves, and be familiar with all and free with your substance, that they may be rich like unto you.
>
> **But before ye seek for riches, seek ye for the kingdom of God.**
>
> And **after ye have obtained a hope in Christ ye shall obtain riches,** if ye seek them; and ye will seek them for the intent to do good—to clothe the naked, and to feed the hungry, and to liberate the captive, and administer relief to the sick and the afflicted. (Jacob 2:16–19)

Over many years of teaching, a large number of students have asked if I would define the formula for wealth. Usually these are young college-aged students. One only needs go to ancient scripture to find abundant evidence that "too much, too soon" can be soul destroying. So, without any attempt to prioritize elements of the Lord's counsel on acquiring wealth, here are some things to consider:

> And I have made the earth rich, and behold it is my footstool, wherefore, again I will stand upon it.
>
> And I hold forth and deign to give unto you greater riches, even a land of promise, a land flowing with milk and honey, upon which there shall be no curse when the Lord cometh;

> And I will give it unto you for the land of your inheritance, if you seek it with all your hearts.
>
> And this shall be my covenant with you, ye shall have it for the land of your inheritance, and for the inheritance of your children forever, while the earth shall stand, and ye shall possess it again in eternity, no more to pass away. (D&C 38:17–20)

Apparently, the Lord views the shortsightedness of man in accumulating wealth as an area that needs divine instruction. He reminds us that the earth is rich, He made it, and His objective is to share those riches with His Saints—even to granting them an eternal inheritance on the earth (the ultimate destiny of which is to become our celestial kingdom; see D&C 88:17–20, 25–26, and read the scriptural text at the end of the chapter). Since one of our objectives of mortality is to learn to become like our Heavenly Parents, this seems like a **poignant reminder to share.** Make your list of these principles as the scriptures reveal them.

Later in the Doctrine and Covenants the Lord castigates the selfish rich and issues a stern warning to the poor who harbor the "something-for-nothing" attitude. He revealed:

> And your hearts are not satisfied. And ye obey not the truth, but have pleasure in unrighteousness.
>
> **Wo unto you rich men, that will not give your substance to the poor**, for your riches will canker your souls; and this shall be your lamentation in the day of visitation, and of judgment, and of indignation: The harvest is past, the summer is ended, and my soul is not saved!
>
> **Wo unto you poor men**, whose hearts are not broken, whose spirits are not contrite, and whose bellies are not satisfied, and **whose hands are not stayed from laying hold upon other men's goods, whose eyes are full of greediness, and who will not labor with your own hands**!
>
> But blessed are the poor who are pure in heart, whose hearts are broken, and whose spirits are contrite, for they shall see the kingdom of God coming in power and great glory unto their deliverance; for the fatness of the earth shall be theirs.
>
> For behold, the Lord shall come, and his recompense shall be with him, and he shall reward every man, and the poor shall rejoice." (D&C 56:15–19)

No matter which category we fall into (rich, poor, or in between) how we handle the wealth the Lord puts into our hands plays a very important part in determining how successfully we are passing the tests of mortality.

Although there are many references directing the use of wealth, perhaps one more from the Doctrine and Covenants will suffice:

> That every man may give an account unto me of the stewardship which is appointed unto him.
>
> For it is expedient that I, the Lord, should make every man accountable, as a steward over earthly blessings, which I have made and prepared for my creatures.
>
> I, the Lord, stretched out the heavens, and built the earth, my very handiwork; and all things therein are mine.
>
> And it is my purpose to provide for my saints, for all things are mine.
>
> But it must needs be done in mine own way; and behold this is the way that I, the Lord, have decreed to provide for my saints, that the poor shall be exalted, in that the rich are made low.
>
> For the earth is full, and there is enough and to spare; yea, I prepared all things, and have **given unto the children of men to be agents unto themselves.**
>
> Therefore, if any man shall take of the abundance which I have made, **and impart not his portion, according to the law of my gospel, unto the poor and the needy, he shall, with the wicked, lift up his eyes in hell, being in torment.** (D&C 104:12–18)

Learning to use wisely the physical resources the Lord has put into our hands is once again elevated to an area of primary concern.

We, as a people, are not yet ready to be given the charge to live the law of consecration sometimes referred to as the United Order. However, certain elements of that law can help us prepare for that fast-approaching time when the faithful will be given the opportunity to participate in what the Lord terms "the law of the celestial kingdom." "And Zion cannot be built up unless it is by the principles of the law of the celestial kingdom; otherwise I cannot receive her unto myself" (D&C 105:5).

In a measured and rational way, we can get outside ourselves and show concern for our neighbors. The Lord revealed: "Every man seeking the interest of his neighbor, and doing all things with an eye single to the glory of God" (D&C 82:19).

Some scriptural citations concerning wealth are very familiar. In the last book of the Old Testament, the prophet Malachi issues this challenge and promise:

> Will a man rob God? Yet ye have robbed me. But ye say, Wherein have we robbed thee? In tithes and offerings.

> Ye are cursed with a curse: for ye have robbed me, even this whole nation.
>
> Bring ye all the tithes into the storehouse, that there may be meat in mine house, and prove me now herewith, saith the Lord of hosts, if I will not open you the windows of heaven, and pour you out a blessing, that *there shall* not *be room* enough *to receive it.*
>
> And I will rebuke the devourer for your sakes, and he shall not destroy the fruits of your ground; neither shall your vine cast her fruit before the time in the field, saith the Lord of hosts. (Malachi 3:8–11)

Certainly, a beginning point for accumulating wealth without losing our soul would be in **the faithful payment of tithes and offerings.** Jokingly, many members refer to tithing as "fire insurance" because of what the Lord revealed in Doctrine and Covenants 64:23: "Behold, now it is called today until the coming of the Son of Man, and verily it is a day of sacrifice, and a day for the tithing of my people; for he that is tithed shall not be burned at his coming." In a more serious moment of reflection one is prompted to ask: Why is paying of tithes a criterion for not being burned at the Second Coming? Perhaps one reason is that the tithe payer is well on the way to keeping his accumulated wealth in proper perspective. Money and possessions have not become an all-encompassing, all-consuming preoccupation.

Wise King Solomon, arguably the richest man of his generation (see 1 Kings 10:23) said: "By humility and the fear of the Lord are riches, and honour, and life" (Proverbs 22:4).

Amulek, in teaching the poor of the Zoramites, said: "Cry unto him over the crops of your fields, that ye may prosper in them. Cry over the flocks of your fields, that they may increase" (Alma 34:24–25).

As your wealth increases, acknowledge the Lord's hand. Thinking that you are having success because of your own genius may offend God and cause His blessings to cease. He said in these latter days: "And in nothing doth man offend God, or against none is his wrath kindled, save those who confess not his hand in all things, and obey not his commandments" (D&C 59:21).

A continent away, James emphasized again the necessity of having the right goal in mind in accumulating wealth: "Ye ask, and receive not, because ye ask amiss, that ye may consume it upon your lusts" (James 4:3).

During His mortal ministry, the Savior cautioned about putting trust in riches. He taught: "He also that received seed among the thorns is he that heareth the word; and the care of this world, and the **deceitfulness of riches, choke the word, and he becometh unfruitful**" (Matthew 13:22).

The more we read, the more evident it becomes that focusing too much attention on wealth has a spiritually lethal influence on successfully learning those essential lessons leading to eternal life.

When the rich young man who inquired about what one must do to gain eternal life turned away when instructed to divest himself of his riches and follow the Savior, the Lord shocked His disciples by teaching: "And Jesus looked round about, and saith unto his disciples, How hardly shall they that have riches enter into the kingdom of God! And the disciples were astonished at his words. But Jesus answereth again, and saith unto them, Children, **how hard is it for them that trust in riches** to enter into the kingdom of God!" (Mark 10:23–24).

The Apostle Paul gave more wise caution and direction concerning worldly wealth:

> But they that will be rich fall into temptation and a snare, and *into* many foolish and hurtful lusts, which drown men in destruction and perdition. . . .
>
> Charge them that are rich in this world, that they be not high-minded, nor trust in uncertain riches, but in the living God, who giveth us richly all things to enjoy;
>
> That they do good, that they be rich in good works, ready to distribute, willing to communicate. (1 Timothy 6:9, 17–18)

Apparently, the rich who are not alert to the attendant temptations find themselves stumbling because of "many foolish and hurtful lusts." Unless acknowledged and corrected, they can lead one to destruction—and for an endowed member of the Church, even to perdition. High-mindedness and putting too much trust in transitory riches, rather than keeping our focus on God and those mortal activities which will follow us into the eternal worlds, can become serious stumbling blocks to the rich. Being willing to share our wealth (distribute) and even willing to share our formulas for success (communicate) can be used as safety valves to help the rich avoid soul-destroying detours.

Another caution that is frequently overlooked is the desire for instant riches. Solomon gave the following warning:

> A faithful man shall abound with blessings: but he that maketh haste to be rich shall not be innocent.
>
> To have respect of persons *is* not good: for for a piece of bread that man will transgress.
>
> He that hasteth to be rich *hath* an evil eye, and considereth not that poverty shall come upon him. (Proverbs 28:20–22)

One need only watch the news or read the newspaper to see the number of wealthy people who die absolutely broke. A slow, calculated building of a solid financial foundation is much more likely to endure than hastening to be rich overnight.

King Solomon made some extremely wise observations: "He becometh poor that dealeth with a slack hand: but the hand of the diligent maketh rich" (Proverbs 10:4).

Many a rich person has lost it all when they stopped being diligent in managing their wealth. Accumulating wealth is one thing—managing and keeping it is another. Wise is the person who attends to his or her wealth all the days of his life.

As ancient Jerusalem was in the process of crumbling morally from within, Jeremiah the prophet said:

> Thus saith the Lord, Let not the wise *man* glory in his wisdom, neither let the mighty *man* glory in his might, **let not the rich *man* glory in his riches:**
>
> But let him that glorieth glory in this, that he understandeth and knoweth me, that I *am* the Lord which exercise lovingkindness, judgment, and righteousness, in the earth: for in these *things* I delight, saith the Lord. (Jeremiah 9:23–24)

Glorying in riches, wisdom, or might retards a person's quest to become like the Lord. What a great list of Christlike attributed to continually focus on: lovingkindness, judgment, and righteousness.

The Savior taught a powerful lesson in the following parable:

> And he spake a parable unto them, saying, The ground of a certain rich man brought forth plentifully:
>
> And he thought within himself, saying, What shall I do, because I have no room where to bestow my fruits?
>
> And he said, This will I do: I will pull down my barns, and build greater; and there will I bestow all my fruits and my goods.
>
> And I will say to my soul, Soul, thou hast much goods laid up for many years; take thine ease, eat, drink, *and* be merry.
>
> But God said unto him, *Thou* fool, this night thy soul shall be required of thee: then whose shall those things be, which thou hast provided?
>
> **So *is* he that layeth up treasure for himself, and is not rich toward God.** (Luke 12:16–21)

Nephi was so impressed with Jacob's teaching ability and insight that he quoted him in a powerful chapter which contains the following warning:

"But wo unto the rich, who are rich as to the things of the world. For because they are rich they despise the poor, and they persecute the meek, and their hearts are upon their treasures; wherefore, their treasure is their god. And behold, their treasure shall perish with them also" (2 Nephi 9:30).

It almost sounds like seeking for riches has more risks than rewards. However, if we analyze the opposites of each caution, it plots a course that will lead us to eternal life. For example, if you are rich and do not despise the poor or refuse to persecute the meek, and if your heart (focus) does not make wealth your god, then you can use your wealth to bless everyone and your wealth becomes one avenue for relieving the suffering of the beggar (see Mosiah 4:20, 22–27).

Alma punctuates in a very few verses the contrast between the righteous and the wicked and the influence that wealth had on them:

> And they did impart of their substance, every man according to that which he had, to the poor, and the needy, and the sick, and the afflicted; and they did not wear costly apparel, yet they were neat and comely.
>
> And thus they did establish the affairs of the church; and thus they began to have continual peace again, notwithstanding all their persecutions.
>
> And now, **because of the steadiness of the church they began to be exceedingly rich**, having abundance of all things whatsoever they stood in need—an abundance of flocks and herds, and fatlings of every kind, and also abundance of grain, and of gold, and of silver, and of precious things, and abundance of silk and fine-twined linen, and all manner of good homely cloth.
>
> And thus, in their prosperous circumstances, they did not send away any who were naked, or that were hungry, or that were athirst, or that were sick, or that had not been nourished; and they did not set their hearts upon riches; therefore they were liberal to all, both old and young, both bond and free, both male and female, whether out of the church or in the church, having no respect to persons as to those who stood in need.
>
> And thus they **did prosper and become *far more wealthy* than those who did not belong to their church.**
>
> For those who did not belong to their church did indulge themselves in sorceries, and in idolatry or idleness, and in babblings, and in envyings and strife; wearing costly apparel; being lifted up in the pride of their own eyes; persecuting, lying, thieving, robbing, committing whoredoms, and murdering, and all manner of wickedness; nevertheless, the law was put in force upon all those who did transgress it, inasmuch as it was possible. (Alma 1:27–32)

It seems as though these ancient Americans are crying to us from the dust "that ye may learn to be more wise than we have been" (Mormon 9:31). Unfortunately, many Church members' hearts have been turned away from full activity in their quest for worldly wealth. What a terrible mistake to trade our faith in God for a false reliance in unstable man. Jeremiah wrote: "Thus saith the Lord; Cursed *be* the man that trusteth in man, and maketh flesh his arm, and whose heart departeth from the Lord" (Jeremiah 17:5).

In our day, the Lord foretold the challenges we would face in raising our children: "Now, I, the Lord, am not well pleased with the inhabitants of Zion, for there are idlers among them; and their children are also growing up in wickedness; they also seek not earnestly the riches of eternity, but their eyes are full of greediness" (D&C 68:31).

Alma, counseling his errant son Corianton who had made some serious mistakes, said, "Seek not after riches nor the vain things of this world; for behold, you cannot carry them with you" (Alma 39:14).

What a poignant reminder: the rich and the poor will take the same amount of this earth's goods out of this life when their mortal test is completed. We'd better focus on things that we can take into the eternal worlds.

Regrettably, there are those who grow rich and think they have outgrown God and the Church. Here is yet another sad commentary from the Book of Mormon: "But they grew proud, being lifted up in their hearts, because of their exceedingly great riches; therefore they grew rich in their own eyes, and would not give heed to their words, to walk uprightly before God" (Alma 45:24).

"O Lord, how manifold are thy works! in wisdom hast thou made them all: the earth is full of thy riches" (Psalm 104:24). It would be a stretch of the imagination to believe that the Lord made the earth rich and then withheld those riches from His children. It is in learning to use Godly wisdom that we can prosper without riches becoming our pagan god.

In today's fast-paced world, it would be wise to follow this advice: "Be still, and know that I am God: I will be exalted among the heathen, I will be exalted in the earth" (Psalm 46:10). Although God will not make your decisions for you, He has given this promise: "Trust in the Lord with all thine heart; and lean not unto thine own understanding. In all thy ways acknowledge him, and **he shall direct thy paths**" (Proverbs 3:5–6).

Spend time pondering the direction you want to go. If you ask the Lord for direction, note the thoughts and impressions that come to you. Don't be in too big of a hurry. When you have hit upon the right course of action, you will enjoy that "peace that passeth all understanding" (see Philippians 4:7).

So as not to make this chapter too long, I will limit the commentary on the following parts of the formula. You will readily see that if you use the scriptures as a handbook and the Lord as a model, the entire volume of scripture becomes a formula for surviving and thriving life's challenges.

Broad appeal

Christ's gospel was intended to have universal appeal. If you want your business (or product) to succeed, ensure that is has broad appeal.

Well defined plan to roll out your product

The Creation story found in Genesis 1 outlines the divine pattern for executing a huge project. It would have been a huge mistake to put animals on earth before the plants and grasses!

Integrity

People have been willing to die for Christ because He was the absolute example of a person with unwavering integrity. If your employees or partners see that you have integrity, most will be true to you in return.

Stay focused on your business

Note how often the Jewish leaders attempted to get the Lord distracted, angered, frustrated, combative, and so on, only to have those devilish tactics reversed on themselves.

Don't rush to judgment

John 8:1–11 is the account of the woman taken in adultery. The Lord, who never condones sin, deferred to make a hasty judgment before every opportunity to repent and get back on track had been given. Get all the facts before making a summary (final) judgment. Make sure your timing affords time to recalibrate and refocus.

Don't let a mistake cripple you

Peter's denial of Christ is a prime example of giving a person a second chance. Even if you are the one who makes the mistake, it doesn't have to be fatal to your venture. Pick yourself up, dust yourself off, and try again—possibly many times!

Build others to build your business

The Lord said to Peter: "But I have prayed for thee, that thy faith fail not: and when thou art converted, strengthen thy brethren" (Luke 22:32). Paul further elaborated on this principle: "And the things that thou hast heard of me among many witnesses, **the same commit thou to faithful men, who shall be able to teach others also**" (2 Timothy 2:2). If you try to "go it alone" you are limiting the scope of what you can accomplish. Note how the Savior first chose the Twelve Apostles and then the Seventies (see Luke 10:1–2) to spread His gospel.

Believe in miracles

"For with God nothing shall be impossible" (Luke 1:37). Miracles can happen today as well as two thousand years ago.

Have faith in God and in yourself

"And Jesus said unto them, Because of your unbelief: for verily I say unto you, If ye have faith as a grain of mustard seed, ye shall say unto this mountain, Remove hence to yonder place; and it shall remove; and **nothing shall be impossible unto you**" (Matthew 17:20).

Keep employees productive or remove them

In Luke 19:16–26 the Lord gives the parable of the talents. Note that the ones who produced were promoted and given more responsibility. The one who hid his talent was dismissed.

Count the cost of your venture

The Lord counsels: "For which of you, intending to build a tower, sitteth not down first, and counteth the cost, whether he have sufficient to finish it? Lest haply, after he hath laid the foundation, and is not able to finish it, all that behold it begin to mock him, Saying, This man began to build, and was not able to finish" (Luke 14:28–30). If you need additional financing, make sure it is available. Counseling with those who have successfully launched a business or product can substantially reduce the likelihood of failure.

Be prepared for some opposition! Many Christians today deny or minimize the influence of the devil. But using Christ as the example, just before beginning His mission (like you beginning your business venture or launching your product), the devil used three areas which he considers most vulnerable or appealing to mankind: physical appetite, popularity, and possession (see Matthew 4:1–11). If you withstand the sometimes-overwhelming thought to abandon your quest, this counsel may carry you through to success: "Thou therefore endure hardness, as a good soldier of Jesus Christ" (2 Timothy 2:3).

To the newly liberated children of Israel, the unchangeable God said: "But I have said unto you, Ye shall inherit their land, and I will give it unto you to possess it, a land that floweth with milk and honey: I am the Lord your God, which have separated you from other people" (Leviticus 20:24).

In this day of trouble when Christians are being martyred in foreign lands and even persecuted in our land, the Lord has promised us if we will live as a "separated people"—not necessarily physically removed from others but separated from the worldly by our practice of handling, using, and sharing our wealth wisely—then the Lord will again give us a land flowing with milk and honey.

There is one more point to make before concluding this chapter. Six times in the scriptures the word "mammon" is used. The dictionary definition is "material wealth or possessions especially as having a debasing influence." Two times the Savior refers to it in the Sermon on the Mount (see Matthew 6:24 and 3 Nephi 13:24) where He states that "you cannot serve God and mammon." In Luke 16:9–13 the Savior commends the unfaithful steward, reiterates that one cannot serve God and mammon, and then makes the following observation:

> And the lord commended the unjust steward, because he had done wisely: for the children of this world are in their generation wiser than the children of light.
>
> And I say unto you, Make to yourselves friends of the mammon of unrighteousness; that, when ye fail, they may receive you into everlasting habitations.
>
> He that is faithful in that which is least is faithful also in much: and he that is unjust in the least is unjust also in much.
>
> If therefore ye have not been faithful in the unrighteous mammon, who will commit to your trust the true riches? (Luke 16:8–11).

All of these seem to have a negative connotation.

To the Saints in our day, the Savior said: "And now, verily I say unto you, and this is wisdom, make unto yourselves friends with the mammon of unrighteousness, and they will not destroy you" (D&C 82:22). We must learn to use our wealth according to the business practices of the world so that they will not destroy us.

It seems appropriate to end this chapter with the Lord's definition of rich: "Seek not for riches but for wisdom, and behold, the mysteries of God shall be unfolded unto you, and then shall you be made rich. Behold, he that hath eternal life is rich" (D&C 6:7).

"Seek not for riches but for wisdom; and, behold, the mysteries of God shall be unfolded unto you, and then shall you be made rich. Behold, he that hath eternal life is rich" (D&C 11:7).

Now consider that **YOU**, not the Lord, may be the one holding up your gaining wealth: "Therefore, be ye as wise as serpents and yet without sin; and I will order all things for your good, as fast as ye are able to receive them" (D&C 111:11).

POINTS FOR FURTHER CONSIDERATION

Perhaps with no other chapter is it as important to read carefully the cautions the Lord gives about wealth. We are blessed to have over six thousand years of examples of those who accumulated wealth and succeeded in blessing others with it, and those who accumulated wealth and it ended up destroying them, their families, the Church, and society.

Doctrine and Covenants 88:17–20, 25–26

And the redemption of the soul is through him that quickeneth all things, in whose bosom it is decreed that the poor and the meek of the earth shall inherit it.

Therefore, it must needs be sanctified from all unrighteousness, that it may be prepared for the celestial glory;

For after it hath filled the measure of its creation, it shall be crowned with glory, even with the presence of God the Father;

That bodies who are of the celestial kingdom may possess it forever and ever; for, for this intent was it made and created, and for this intent are they sanctified.

And again, verily I say unto you, the earth abideth the law of a celestial kingdom, for it filleth the measure of its creation, and transgresseth not the law—

Wherefore, it shall be sanctified; yea, notwithstanding it shall die, it shall be quickened again, and shall abide the power by which it is quickened, and the righteous shall inherit it."

Psalm 37:16

A little that a righteous man hath *is* better than the riches of many wicked.

Psalm 49:6–7

They that trust in their wealth, and boast themselves in the multitude of their riches;

None of them can by any means redeem his brother, nor give to God a ransom for him.

Psalm 52:6–7

The righteous also shall see, and fear, and shall laugh at him:

Lo, this is the man that made not God his strength; but trusted in the abundance of his riches, and strengthened himself in his wickedness.

Psalm 61:10

Trust not in oppression, and become not vain in robbery: if riches increase, set not your heart upon them.

Proverbs 11:28

He that trusteth in his riches shall fall: but the righteous shall flourish as a branch.

Psalm 112:1–2

Praise ye the Lord. Blessed is the man that feareth the Lord, that delighteth greatly in his commandments.

His seed shall be mighty upon earth: the generation of the upright shall be blessed.

Wealth and riches shall be in his house: and his righteousness endureth for ever.

Proverbs 28:6

Better is the poor that walketh in his uprightness, than he that is perverse in his ways, though he be rich.

1 Timothy 6:17–19

Charge them that are rich in this world, that they be not high-minded, nor trust in uncertain riches, but in the living God, who giveth us richly all things to enjoy;

That they do good, that they be rich in good works, ready to distribute, willing to communicate;

Laying up in store for themselves a good foundation against the time to come, that they may lay hold on eternal life.

2 Nephi 4:34–35

O Lord, I have trusted in thee, and I will trust in thee forever. I will not put my trust in the arm of flesh; for I know that cursed is he that putteth his trust in the arm of flesh. Yea, cursed is he that putteth his trust in man or maketh flesh his arm.

Yea, I know that God will give liberally to him that asketh. Yea, my God will give me, if I ask not amiss; therefore I will lift up my voice unto thee; yea, I will cry unto thee, my God, the rock of my righteousness. Behold, my voice shall forever ascend up unto thee, my rock and mine everlasting God.

Jacob 2:13–14

And the hand of providence hath smiled upon you most pleasingly, that you have obtained many riches; and because some of you have obtained more abundantly than that of your brethren ye are lifted up in the pride of your hearts, and wear stiff necks and high heads because of the costliness of your apparel, and persecute your brethren because ye suppose that ye are better than they.

And now, my brethren, do ye suppose that God justifieth you in this thing? Behold, I say unto you, Nay. But he condemneth you, and if ye persist in these things his judgments must speedily come unto you.

Alma 4:6–8

And it came to pass in the eighth year of the reign of the judges, that the people of the church began to wax proud, because of their exceeding riches, and their fine silks, and their fine-twined linen, and because of their many flocks and herds, and their gold and their silver, and all manner of precious things, which they had obtained by their industry; and in all these things were they lifted up in the pride of their eyes, for they began to wear very costly apparel.

Now this was the cause of much affliction to Alma, yea, and to many of the people whom Alma had consecrated to be teachers, and priests,

and elders over the church; yea, many of them were sorely grieved for the wickedness which they saw had begun to be among their people.
For they saw and beheld with great sorrow that the people of the church began to be lifted up in the pride of their eyes, and to set their hearts upon riches and upon the vain things of the world, that they began to be scornful, one towards another, and they began to persecute those that did not believe according to their own will and pleasure.

Alma 62:48–50

And the people of Nephi began to prosper again in the land, and began to multiply and to wax exceedingly strong again in the land. And they began to grow exceedingly rich.

But notwithstanding their riches, or their strength, or their prosperity, they were not lifted up in the pride of their eyes; neither were they slow to remember the Lord their God; but they did humble themselves exceedingly before him.

Yea, they did remember how great things the Lord had done for them, that he had delivered them from death, and from bonds, and from prisons, and from all manner of afflictions and he had delivered them out of the hands of their enemies.

Helaman 3:36–37

And it came to pass that the fifty and second year ended in peace also, save it were the exceedingly great pride which had gotten into the hearts of the people; and it was because of their exceedingly great riches and their prosperity in the land; and it did grow upon them from day to day.

And it came to pass in the fifty and third year of the reign of the judges.

Helaman 4:12–13

And it was because of the pride of their hearts, because of their exceeding riches, yea, it was because of their oppression to the poor, withholding their food from the hungry, withholding their clothing from the naked, and smiting their humble brethren upon the cheek, making a mock of that which was sacred, denying the spirit of prophecy and of revelation, murdering, plundering, lying, stealing, committing adultery, rising up in great contentions, and deserting away into the land of Nephi, among the Lamanites—

And because of this their great wickedness, and their boastings in their own strength, they were left in their own strength; therefore they did not prosper, but were afflicted and smitten, and driven before the Lamanites, until they had lost possession of almost all their lands.

2

RECEIVING REVELATION

Many people are almost incredulous at the idea of receiving personal revelation. However, without qualification the Lord said: "If thou shalt ask, thou shalt receive revelation upon revelation, knowledge upon knowledge, that thou mayest know the mysteries and peaceable things—that which bringeth joy, that which bringeth life eternal" (D&C 42:61).

While it is true that we cannot receive revelation for the Church unless we are the prophet, or receive revelation for the stake or ward unless we are the stake president or bishop, we can and must receive revelation for ourselves and for those over whom we have direct responsibility.

In the Book of Mormon, Jarom gave us a great starting point: "And there are many among us who have **many revelations**, *for they are not all stiffnecked*. And as many as are not stiffnecked and *have faith*, **have communion with the Holy Spirit**, *which maketh manifest unto the children of men, according to their faith*" (Jarom 1:4).

Have you ever wondered what the Lord meant when He labeled a people as "stiffnecked"? Here are a couple of examples so we can avoid falling under that same condemnation: "Ye stiffnecked and uncircumcised in heart and ears, **ye do always resist the Holy Ghost**: as your fathers did, so do ye" (Acts 7:51).

Nephi said: "And now I, Nephi, cannot say more; the Spirit stoppeth mine utterance, and I am left to mourn because of the unbelief, and the wickedness, and the ignorance, and the stiffneckedness of men; **for they will**

not search knowledge, nor understand great knowledge, when it is given unto them in plainness, even as plain as word can be" (2 Nephi 32:7).

The word "stiffneckedness" is used thirty-five times in the scriptures and never in a positive context. From these two references we can learn that if we resist the promptings of the Holy Ghost and if we will not search for true knowledge and understanding but look to the world and speculation rather than truth, we fall under that condemnation and cut ourselves off from receiving personal revelation.

From Jarom's account, we also learn that we need to increase our faith in order to qualify for revelation. Learning to trust in the Lord is a most rewarding experience that we can all benefit by engaging in.

There is another interesting part of the Lord's formula for receiving revelation. We must be clean from sin. Doctrine and Covenants 29:3 states: "Behold, verily, verily, I say unto you, that at this time *your sins are forgiven you,* therefore ye **receive these things**; but remember to sin no more, lest perils shall come upon you."

In the sad account of Korihor, one of the anti-Christs of the Book of Mormon, Korihor finally admitted his teachings were false when he came face to face with death:

> I know that I am dumb, for I cannot speak; and I know that nothing save it were the power of God could bring this upon me; yea, and I always knew that there was a God.
>
> But behold, the devil hath deceived me; for he appeared unto me in the form of an angel, and said unto me: Go and reclaim this people, for they have all gone astray after an unknown God. And he said unto me: There is no God; yea, and he taught me that which I should say. And I have taught his words; and I taught them because they were pleasing unto the carnal mind; and I taught them, even until I had much success, insomuch that I verily believed that they were true; and for this cause I withstood the truth, even until I have brought this great curse upon me. (Alma 30:52–53)

In the early days of this dispensation, Satan was at work giving false revelation. Hiram Page, a close associate of the Prophet Joseph Smith, had a peep stone through which he claimed to receive revelation. The Lord instructed Oliver Cowdery, who had been influenced by those false revelations, to instruct Hiram on the source of his revelations. The Lord said:

> And again, thou shalt take thy brother, Hiram Page, between him and thee alone, and tell him that those things which he hath written from that stone are not of me and that Satan deceiveth him;

> For, behold, these things have not been appointed unto him, neither shall anything be appointed unto any of this church contrary to the church covenants.
>
> For all things must be done in order, and by common consent in the church, by the prayer of faith. (D&C 28:11–13)

Far too many people are so anxious to receive revelation that they fail to realize that Satan, the great imitator, will do all in his power to get good people to believe his lies. That is why it is essential for Latter-day Saints to compare everything they receive by revelation against the standard works (which include the canonized scriptures and the teachings of the living prophets). If what they think they have received is at odds with what the Lord has revealed through His prophets, you can be assured that God is not the source of that revelation.

Sometimes the revelation does not come as quickly as we had hoped. Even the great prophet Jeremiah had to wait for his answer: "And it came to pass *after ten days,* that the **word of the Lord came unto Jeremiah"** (Jeremiah 42:7). Many people in the Church have reported that weeks, months, or even years pass before the sought-after revelation comes. One of the lessons we need to learn is that God does not wear a wristwatch, and the scriptural phrase "in mine own due time" may very well apply to our receiving revelation.

However, we need to be aware of the Spirit from the time we ask so that recognition of an answer is not delayed. We have all marveled at Daniel's ability to receive revelation to interpret dreams. However, note this exception: "In those days I Daniel was **mourning three full weeks**. . . . Then said he unto me, Fear not, Daniel: *for from the first day* that thou didst set thine heart to understand, and to chasten thyself before thy God, *thy words were heard,* and I am come for thy words" (Daniel 10:2,12).

To Oliver Cowdery who had received revelation but failed to recognize it, the Lord said: "Behold, thou knowest that thou hast inquired of me and I did enlighten thy mind; and now I tell thee these things that thou mayest know that thou hast been enlightened by the Spirit of truth" (D&C 6:15).

Part of our receiving revelation seems to depend on our being ready and able to receive it. In Doctrine and Covenants 67:11–14, the Lord revealed:

> And again, verily I say unto you that it is your privilege, and a promise I give unto you that have been ordained unto this ministry, that inasmuch as you strip yourselves from jealousies and fears, and humble yourselves before me, for ye are not sufficiently humble, the veil shall

> be rent and you shall see me and know that I am—not with the carnal neither natural mind, but with the spiritual.
>
> For no man has seen God at any time in the flesh, except quickened by the Spirit of God.
>
> Neither can any natural man abide the presence of God, neither after the carnal mind.
>
> **Ye are not able to abide the presence of God now, neither the ministering of angels; wherefore, continue in patience until ye are perfected.**
>
> Let not your minds turn back; and when ye are worthy, in mine own due time, ye shall see and know that which was conferred upon you by the hands of my servant Joseph Smith, Jun.

Several barriers are mentioned that retard our ability to receive the desired revelation. One is that we need to rid ourselves from jealousies. When our envy of others overrides our sensitivity to the promptings of the Spirit, we block our own ability to receive revelation. Next, we must get rid of the fears associated with coming into the presence of the Lord. Earlier in the same section the Lord revealed: "Ye endeavored to believe that ye should receive the blessing which was offered unto you; but behold, verily I say unto you there were **fears in your hearts, and verily this is the reason that ye did not receive**" (D&C 67:3).

The next admonition the Lord gave is the necessity of increasing our humility. After enumerating those conditions needing attention, He enjoins those early Saints to be patient until they had gained the experience and strength necessary to endure the presence of God and of angels. However, they were admonished not to turn back or return to their unbelieving ways.

Through the ancient Apostle Paul, the Lord revealed: "For God hath not given us the spirit of fear; but of power, and of love, and of a sound mind" (2 Timothy 1:7). It appears that "fear" is something that stands as a major stumbling block to receiving revelation.

Sounding almost a little disgusted, James, half-brother of the Lord, said, "Ye have not, because ye ask not. Ye ask, and receive not, because ye ask amiss, that ye may consume it upon your lusts" (James 4:2–3). We must also scrutinize our motives in asking for revelation. If those motives do not align with God's will, then it sounds as though we ask in vain.

It seems that for every revelation we receive we need to be prepared for the "equal and opposite" temptation from the devil. Then the greater the revelation, the greater the attempts by the adversary to destroy us. The trial may come before the revelation—as in the case of Joseph Smith's first vision. Or it may come immediately following, as you read in Moses 1:12–22. Far too many good people have failed to realize the "equal and opposite" principle. When they have their spiritual experiences, they let down their guard, and when the trial comes, they are swept away. This seems like such a vital point that I am putting a statement by Brigham Young in the section "Points for Further Consideration" at the end of the chapter.

The Spirit can reveal things to us in many ways. If we are not in tune with or aware of the variety of ways, we may miss some important divine communications. Below is a list (not comprehensive) of ways the scriptures teach us that God communicates with us.

Recognize how the Spirit impacts you

1. Gives feelings of love, joy, peace, patience, meekness, gentleness, faith, and hope (D&C 6:23; D&C 11:12–14; Romans 15:13; Galatians 5:22–23).
2. Gives ideas in the mind and feelings in the heart (D&C 8:2–3).
3. Occupies the mind and presses on the feelings (D&C 128:1).
4. Helps scriptures have powerful effect (Joseph Smith—History 1:11–12).
5. Gives good feelings to teach if something is true (D&C 9:8–9).
6. Enlightens the mind (Alma 32:28; D&C 6:14–15; 1 Corinthians 2:9–11).
7. Replaces darkness with light (Alma 19:6).
8. Strengthens the desire to avoid evil and obey the commandments (Mosiah 5:2–5).
9. Teaches truth and brings all things to remembrance (John 14:26).
10. Gives feelings of peace and comfort (John 14:27).
11. Guides to truth and shows things to come (John 16:13).
12. Reveals truth (Moroni 10:5).
13. Guides and protects from deception (D&C 45:57).
14. Glorifies and bears record of God the Father and Jesus Christ (2 Nephi 31:18; D&C 20:27; John 16:14).
15. Guides the words of humble teachers (D&C 42:16; D&C 84:85; D&C 100:5–8; Luke 12:11–12).
16. Recognizes and corrects sin (John 16:8).
17. Gives gifts of the Spirit (Moroni 10:8–17; D&C 46:8–26; 1 Corinthians 12).

18. Helps to perceive or discern the thoughts of others (Alma 10:17; Alma 12:3; Alma 18:16, 20, 32, 35).
19. Tells what to pray for (Romans 8:26; 3 Nephi 19:24; D&C 46:28, 30; D&C 50:29–30).
20. Tells what to do (1 Nephi 4:6; 2 Nephi 32:1–5; D&C 28:15; Helaman 5:18).
21. Teaches where to go (D&C 79:2; Helaman 5:18).
22. Helps the righteous speak with power and authority (1 Nephi 10:22; Alma 18:35).
23. Testifies of the truth (D&C 21:9; D&C 100:8; John 15:26).
24. Sanctifies and brings remission of sins (2 Nephi 31:17; Alma 13:12; 3 Nephi 27:20).
25. Carries truth unto the heart of the listener (1 Nephi 2:16–17; 2 Nephi 33:1; Alma 24:8).
26. Enhances skills and abilities (1 Nephi 1:1–3; Exodus 31:3–5).
27. Constrains or restrains (1 Nephi 7:15; 2 Nephi 28:1; 2 Nephi 32:7; Alma 14:11; Mormon 3:16; Ether 12:2).
28. Edifies both teacher and students (D&C 50:13–22).
29. Gives comfort (D&C 88:3; John 14:26).
30. Helps understand scriptures like never before (Joseph Smith—History 1:74).

After reviewing the above list, it is easy to see that God is eager to communicate with His spirit children. I have wondered if the reason we don't receive more revelation is that we do not recognize and thank the Lord for the ones He does give us. In Doctrine and Covenants 59:21 the Lord revealed, "And in nothing doth man offend God, or against none is his wrath kindled, save those who confess not his hand in all things, and obey not his commandments."

Perhaps one of the most productive activities we can engage in is to take time to look for, acknowledge, and thank the Lord for revelations we constantly receive.

The brother of Jared's faith was so strong that he not only broke through the veil separating him from the premortal Christ, but he also received a vision from the creation of the earth to the end of the Millennium. He wrote that vision and sealed it up—that is what is contained in the sealed portion of the Book of Mormon. However, the Lord made this promise: "And in that day that they shall exercise faith in me, saith the Lord, even as the brother of Jared did, that they may become sanctified in me, then will I manifest unto them the things which the brother of Jared saw, even to the unfolding unto them all my revelations, saith Jesus Christ, the Son of God, the Father of the heavens and of the earth, and all things that in them are" (Ether 4:7).

At the conclusion of one of the greatest visions of our time (D&C 76), the Lord told Joseph Smith and Sidney Rigdon:

> But great and marvelous are the works of the Lord, and the mysteries of his kingdom which he showed unto us, which surpass all understanding in glory, and in might, and in dominion;
>
> Which he commanded us we should not write while we were yet in the Spirit, and are not lawful for man to utter;
>
> Neither is man capable to make them known, for they are only to be seen and understood by the power of the Holy Spirit, which God bestows on those who love him, and purify themselves before him;
>
> **To whom he grants this privilege of seeing and knowing for themselves;**
>
> That through the power and manifestation of the Spirit, **while in the flesh**, they may be able to bear his presence in the world of glory. (D&C 76:114–118)

Combining the counsel from both of those expansive visions, the Lord tells us that increasing our faith, loving Him, and purifying ourselves through the sanctification process can help us enjoy like visions. Helaman 3:35 describes the sanctifying process: "Nevertheless they did fast and pray oft, and did wax stronger and stronger in their humility, and firmer and firmer in the faith of Christ, unto the filling their souls with joy and consolation, yea, even to the purifying and the sanctification of their hearts, which **sanctification cometh because of their yielding their hearts unto God.**"

Heavenly Father is anxious to open the lines of communication with His spirit sons and daughters. Now the burden lies with us. As we reach upward, we can rest assured that He is reaching downward. Noting the thirteen times in scripture where He said, "Ask and ye shall receive," it appears that if revelation is not being received, the blockage isn't on the heaven side.

POINTS FOR FURTHER CONSIDERATION

Revelation (oracles) given through the prophet to the Church (D&C 90:4)

Nevertheless, **through you shall the oracles be given** to another, yea, *even unto the church.*

Brigham Young: Equal and opposite temptations for each blessing

I ask, is there a reason for men and women being exposed more constantly and more powerfully, to the power of the enemy, by having visions than by not having them? There is and it is simply this--God never bestows upon His people, or upon an individual, superior blessings without a severe trial to prove them, to prove that individual, or that people to see whether they will keep their covenants with him, and keep in remembrance what He has shown them. Then the greater the vision, the greater the display of the power of the enemy. And when such individuals are off their guard they are left to themselves, as Jesus was. For this express purpose the Father withdrew His spirit from His Son, at the time he was to be crucified. Jesus had been with his Father, talked with Him, dwelt in His bosom, and knew all about heaven, about making the earth, about the transgression of man, and what would redeem the people, and that he was the character who was to redeem the sons of earth, and the earth itself from all sin that had come upon it. The light, knowledge, power, and glory with which he was clothed were far above, or exceeded that of all others who had been upon the earth after the fall, consequently at the very moment, at the hour when the crisis came for him to offer up his life, the Father withdrew Himself, withdrew His Spirit, and cast a vail over him. That is what made him sweat blood. If he had had the power of God upon him, he would not have sweat blood; but all was withdrawn from him, and a veil was cast over him, and he then plead with the Father not to forsake him. "No," says the Father, "You must have your trials, as well as others."

So when individuals are blessed with visions, revelations, and great manifestations, look out, then the devil is nigh you, and you will be tempted in proportion to the vision, revelation, or manifestation you have received. Hence thousands, when they are off their guard, give way to the severe temptations which come upon them, and behold they are gone (*Journal of Discourses* 3:205–206).

Harold B. Lee

Now the only safety we have as members of this church is to do exactly what the Lord said to the Church in the day when the Church was organized. We must learn to give heed to the words and commandments that the Lord shall give through his prophets "as he receiveth them, walking in all holiness before me;...as if from mine own mouth, in all patience and faith." There will be some things that take patience and faith. You may not like what comes from the authority of the Church. It may contradict your political views. It may interfere with some of your social life. But if you listen to these things, as if from the mouth of the Lord himself, with patience and faith, the promise is that the "gates of hell shall not prevail against you; yea, and the Lord God will disperse the powers of darkness from before you, and cause the heavens to shake for your good, and his name's glory."...Your safety and ours depends upon whether or not we follow the ones whom the Lord has placed to preside over his church. He knows whom he wants to preside over this church, and he will make no mistake. The Lord doesn't do things by accident. He has never done anything accidentally. And I think the scientists and all the philosophers in the world have never discovered or learned anything that God didn't already know. His revelations are more powerful, more meaningful, and have more substance than all the secular learning in the world.

Let's keep our eye on the President of the Church (Conference Report, October 1970, 152–53).

3

ACHIEVING HAPPINESS

The Prophet Joseph Smith said, "Happiness is the object and design of our existence; and will be the end thereof, if we pursue the path that leads to it; and this path is virtue, uprightness, faithfulness, holiness, and keeping all the commandments of God. But we cannot keep all the commandments without first knowing them, and we cannot expect to know all, or more than we now know unless we comply with or keep those we have already received" (*Teachings of the Prophet Joseph Smith*, 255).

To put to rest forever the idea that happiness can be captured through wickedness, here is what two Book of Mormon prophets have said:

> Do not suppose, because it has been spoken concerning restoration, that ye shall be restored from sin to happiness. Behold, I say unto you, **wickedness never was happiness**. (Alma 41:10).

> But behold, your days of probation are past; ye have procrastinated the day of your salvation until it is everlastingly too late, and your destruction is made sure; yea, **for ye have sought all the days of your lives for that which ye could not obtain; and ye have sought for happiness in doing iniquity**, which thing is contrary to the nature of that righteousness which is in our great and Eternal Head. (Helaman 13:38)

Before we even begin numbering the elements of this formula, this statement trumps all others: "Happy is that people, whose God is the

Lord" (Psalm 144:15). There may be temporary pleasure in pursuing or even worshipping worldly idols or things, but true happiness comes when we focus on the only true and living God. No matter what scriptural admonitions follow, without heeding God's own voice from Mt. Sinai, we will eventually give up in utter frustration:

> Thou shalt have no other gods before me.
>
> Thou shalt not make unto thee any graven image, or any likeness *of any thing* that *is* in heaven above, or that *is* in the earth beneath, or that *is* in the water under the earth:
>
> Thou shalt not bow down thyself to them, nor serve them: for I the Lord thy God *am* a jealous God, visiting the iniquity of the fathers upon the children unto the third and fourth *generation* of them that hate me. (Exodus 20:3–5)

The first element of this formula may sound a bit contradictory. Job said, "Behold, happy *is* the man whom God correcteth: therefore despise not thou the chastening of the Almighty" (Job 5:17). On further investigation, however, the Lord makes clear His purpose in chastising His Saints: "Verily, thus saith the Lord unto you whom I love, and whom I love I also chasten that their sins may be forgiven, for with the chastisement I prepare a way for their deliverance in all things out of temptation, and I have loved you—Wherefore, ye must needs be chastened and stand rebuked before my face." (D&C 95:1–2). Since perfection is our goal, and since "all have sinned come short of the glory of God" (see Romans 3:23), chastisement by the Lord only accelerates the perfecting process.

The next element to consider is one that many seem to disregard: "For thou shalt eat the labour of thine hands: **happy *shalt* thou *be***, and *it shall be* well with thee" (Psalm 128:2).

The idea of "something for nothing" may sound inviting. Certainly a growing number of people have adopted that philosophy, but what a terrible disappointment it will be when we arrive at the judgment seat to discover that we will be judged according to our works. Since God's command "six days shalt thou labour, and do all thy work" (Exodus 20:9) has never been repealed, any able-bodied person who is preparing for the final judgment needs to seriously consider the necessity of being "anxiously engaged in a good cause" (D&C 58:27).

The Lord flatly reprimanded the early Saints of this dispensation as He enumerated the responsibility of parents in teaching their children. He said: "Now, I, the Lord, am not well pleased with the inhabitants of Zion, for there are idlers among them; and their children are also growing up in wickedness; they also seek not earnestly the riches of eternity, but their eyes are full of greediness. These things ought not to be, and must be done away from among them" (D&C 68:31–32).

Ignorance, especially self-imposed ignorance of God and His plan for His children or when one accepts false theories, or is shackled by false traditions, renders it impossible to find true and lasting happiness. "Happy is the man that findeth wisdom, and the man that getteth understanding" (Proverbs 3:13).

In today's technologically advanced world, one has little excuse for not gaining knowledge which, hopefully, will lead to understanding. However, not all knowledge is of equal value. Paul saw our day and lamented as he described the final days before the Second Coming by saying that the masses are "ever learning, and never able to come to the knowledge of the truth" (2 Timothy 3:7).

Wise King Solomon has a lot to say about how to achieve happiness: "He that despiseth his neighbour sinneth: **but he that hath mercy on the poor, happy *is* he**" (Proverbs 14:21). "He that handleth a matter wisely shall find good: and whoso trusteth in the Lord, **happy is he**" (Proverbs 16:20). "Where *there is* no vision, the people perish: but **he that keepeth the law, happy *is* he**" (Proverbs 29:18).

During His mortal ministry, the Savior taught His disciples:

> For I have given you an example, that ye should do as I have done to you.
>
> Verily, verily, I say unto you, The servant is not greater than his lord; neither he that is sent greater than he that sent him.
>
> **If ye know these things, happy are ye if ye do them.** (John 13:15–17)

It isn't just in the hearing or knowing the principles that makes one happy—it is in the doing of them. He was teaching His disciples to serve one another without regard to rank or superiority. This is a great lesson for all of us.

In his final address to his people, King Benjamin taught this great principle: "And moreover, I would desire that ye should consider on the **blessed and happy state of those that keep the commandments of God.** For behold, **they are blessed in all things, both temporal and spiritual;** and if they hold out faithful to the end they are received into heaven, that thereby they may dwell with God in a state of never–ending happiness. O remember, remember that these things are true; for the Lord God hath spoken it" (Mosiah 2:41).

In abridging the record of the Nephites, Mormon makes the following observation: "But behold there never was a happier time among the people of Nephi, since the days of Nephi, than in the days of Moroni, yea, even at this time, in the twenty and first year of the reign of the judges" (Alma 50:23).

In reading the verses preceding this one and those following, one discovers that they were enjoying a brief interlude of peace sandwiched between seemingly endless accounts of wars. But they had learned how to "live after the manner of happiness" (see 2 Nephi 5:27). Some people think we must postpone happiness until the next life. However, at the end of the Nephite history, Moroni makes this summary statement: "And then cometh the judgment of the Holy One upon them; and then cometh the time that he that is filthy shall be filthy still; and he that is righteous shall be righteous still; **he that is happy shall be happy still; and he that is unhappy shall be unhappy still**" (Mormon 9:14).

After separating from his jealous and vengeful brothers, Nephi recorded: "And it came to pass that **we lived after the manner of happiness**" (2 Nephi 5:27). One might wonder what that means. Mormon, in abridging the Nephite record, particularly the first hundred years following the visitation of the resurrected Savior, said:

> And it came to pass that there was no contention in the land, because of the love of God which did dwell in the hearts of the people.
>
> And there were no envyings, nor strifes, nor tumults, nor whoredoms, nor lyings, nor murders, nor any manner of lasciviousness; and **surely there could not be a happier people among all the people who had been created by the hand of God.**
>
> There were no robbers, nor murderers, neither were there Lamanites, nor any manner of –ites; but they were in one, the children of Christ, and heirs to the kingdom of God.
>
> And how blessed were they! For the Lord did bless them in all their doings; yea, even they were blessed and prospered. (4 Nephi 1:13–18)

Although it may seem impossible to establish a society like that in today's world, the elements that caused their happiness are within reach of every marriage, family, neighborhood, ward, or stake.

In spite of the challenge and frustration often associated with raising children in these pre-millennial days, the Psalmist said: "Lo, children are an heritage of the Lord: and the fruit of the womb is his reward. As arrows are in the hand of a mighty man; so are children of the youth. **Happy is**

the man that hath his quiver full of them: they shall not be ashamed, but they shall speak with the enemies in the gate" (Psalm 127.3–5).

For many modern families struggling with wandering children, that may seem like a promise that is not capable of fulfillment. Perhaps waiting upon the Lord to fulfill His promise will necessitate waiting until the next life. But anyone who has that unwavering trust in the Lord must know that He who has all power can and will make that promise a reality.

To conclude this chapter, I would like to cite scriptural references to the list of prerequisites that the Prophet Joseph Smith gave at the beginning of the chapter.

Virtue

> Whereby are given unto us exceeding great and precious promises: that by these ye might be partakers of the divine nature, having escaped the corruption that is in the world through lust.
>
> And beside this, giving all diligence, add to your faith **virtue**; and to virtue knowledge;
>
> And to knowledge temperance; and to temperance patience; and to patience godliness;
>
> And to godliness brotherly kindness; and to brotherly kindness charity.
>
> For if these things be in you, and abound, they make you that ye shall neither be barren nor unfruitful in the knowledge of our Lord Jesus Christ. (2 Peter 1:4–8)

> Let thy bowels also be full of charity towards all men, and to the household of faith, and **let virtue garnish thy thoughts unceasingly**; then shall thy confidence wax strong in the presence of God; and the doctrine of the priesthood shall distill upon thy soul as the dews from heaven.
>
> The Holy Ghost shall be thy constant companion, and thy scepter an unchanging scepter of righteousness and truth; and thy dominion shall be an everlasting dominion, and without compulsory means it shall flow unto thee forever and ever. (D&C 121:45–46)

> Finally, brethren, whatsoever things are true, whatsoever things *are* honest, whatsoever things *are* just, whatsoever things *are* pure, whatsoever things *are* lovely, whatsoever things *are* of good report; if *there be* any **virtue**, and if *there be* any praise, think on these things.

Those things, which ye have both learned, and received, and heard, and seen in me, do: and the God of peace shall be with you. (Philippians 4:8–9)

A revelation I give unto you concerning my will; and if thou art faithful and walk in the paths of virtue before me, I will preserve thy life, and thou shalt receive an inheritance in Zion. (D&C 25:2)

And let every man esteem his brother as himself, and practise virtue and holiness before me.

And again I say unto you, let every man esteem his brother as himself. (D&C 38:24–25)

And again, I say unto you, all things must be done in the name of Christ, whatsoever you do in the Spirit;

And ye must give thanks unto God in the Spirit for whatsoever blessing ye are blessed with.

And ye must practise virtue and holiness before me continually. (D&C 46:31–33)

For intelligence cleaveth unto intelligence; wisdom receiveth wisdom; truth embraceth truth; **virtue loveth virtue**; light cleaveth unto light; mercy hath compassion on mercy and claimeth her own; justice continueth its course and claimeth its own; judgment goeth before the face of him who sitteth upon the throne and governeth and executeth all things. (D&C 88:40)

Clearly likes attract. If you want to be virtuous, associate with virtuous people. Opposites repel in the economy of God. Look at the list and make sure you are seeking out the companionship of those with like virtues.

We believe in being honest, true, chaste, benevolent, virtuous, and in doing good to all men; indeed, we may say that we follow the admonition of Paul—We believe all things, we hope all things, we have endured many things, and hope to be able to endure all things. If there is anything virtuous, lovely, or of good report or praiseworthy, we seek after these things. (Articles of Faith 1:13)

Uprightness

For all his judgments *were* before me: and *as for* his statutes, I did not depart from them.

> I was also upright before him, and have kept myself from mine iniquity.
>
> Therefore the Lord hath recompensed me according to my righteousness; according to my cleanness in his eye sight.
>
> With the merciful thou wilt shew thyself merciful, *and* with the upright man thou wilt shew thyself upright. (2 Samuel 22:23–26)

> O thou enemy, destructions are come to a perpetual end: and thou hast destroyed cities; their memorial is perished with them.
>
> But the Lord shall endure for ever: he hath prepared his throne for judgment.
>
> And he shall judge the world in righteousness, he shall minister judgment to the people in uprightness.
>
> The Lord also will be a refuge for the oppressed, a refuge in times of trouble.
>
> And they that know thy name will put their trust in thee: for thou, Lord, hast not forsaken them that seek thee. (Psalm 9:6–10)

In these very troubled times, when terrorists are destroying nations, it is comforting to know that the Lord will provide a refuge for the upright in times of trouble. This is indeed a time when we must learn to trust the Lord and His promises.

> In the Lord put I my trust: How say ye to my soul, Flee *as* a bird to your mountain?
>
> For, lo, the wicked bend *their* bow, they make ready their arrow upon the string, that they may privily shoot at the upright in heart.
>
> If the foundations be destroyed, what can the righteous do?
>
> The Lord *is* in his holy temple, the Lord's throne *is* in heaven: his eyes behold, his eyelids try, the children of men.
>
> The Lord trieth the righteous: but the wicked and him that loveth violence his soul hateth.
>
> Upon the wicked he shall rain snares, fire and brimstone, and an horrible tempest: *this shall be* the portion of their cup.
>
> For the righteous Lord loveth righteousness; his countenance doth behold the upright. (Psalm 11:1–7)

This entire psalm was written by a man whose life was surrounded by wars, evil, traitors, and enemies combined to destroy him. His insightful psalm is worth reading and pondering as we strive to find happiness and peace in a world in turmoil. In 1831 this prophecy was given by the Lord as something in the future. We live in the time of its fulfillment: "For I am no respecter of persons, and will that all men shall know that the day speedily cometh; the hour is not yet, but is nigh at hand, when peace shall be taken from the earth, and the devil shall have power over his own dominion. And also the Lord shall have power over his saints, and shall reign in their midst, and shall come down in judgment upon Idumea, or the world" (D&C 1:35–36).

> Lord, who shall abide in thy tabernacle? who shall dwell in thy holy hill?
>
> He that walketh uprightly, and worketh righteousness, and speaketh the truth in his heart.
>
> *He that* backbiteth not with his tongue, nor doeth evil to his neighbour, nor taketh up a reproach against his neighbour.
>
> In whose eyes a vile person is contemned; but he honoureth them that fear the Lord. *He that* sweareth to *his own* hurt, and changeth not.
>
> *He that* putteth not out his money to usury, nor taketh reward against the innocent. He that doeth these *things* shall never be moved. (Psalm 15:1–5)

Here is another very applicable list of vices to guard ourselves against: "The Lord knoweth the days of the upright: and their inheritance shall be for ever. They shall not be ashamed in the evil time: and in the days of famine they shall be satisfied" (Psalm 37:18–19).

Noting the calamitous times prophesied to precede the Second Coming, these verses give a lot of comfort and increase the urgency for us to be upright.

> The sinners in Zion are afraid; fearfulness hath surprised the hypocrites. Who among us shall dwell with the devouring fire (used to describe the fire at the Second Coming)? who among us shall dwell with everlasting burnings (used to describe the eternal presence of God)?
>
> He that walketh righteously, and speaketh uprightly; he that despiseth the gain of oppressions, that shaketh his hands from holding of bribes, that stoppeth his ears from hearing of blood, and shutteth his eyes from seeing evil (Isaiah 33:14–15, commentary in parenthesis added).

> But ye are commanded in all things to ask of God, who giveth liberally; and that which the Spirit testifies unto you even so I would that ye should do in all holiness of heart, walking uprightly before me, considering the end of your salvation, doing all things with prayer and thanksgiving, that ye may not be seduced by evil spirits, or doctrines of devils, or the commandments of men; for some are of men, and others of devils. (D&C 46:7)

Search diligently, pray always, and be believing, and all things shall work together for your good, if ye walk uprightly and remember the covenant wherewith ye have covenanted one with another. (D&C 90:24)

Faithfulness

He that is void of wisdom despiseth his neighbour: but a man of understanding holdeth his peace.

A talebearer revealeth secrets: but he that is of a faithful spirit concealeth the matter.

Where no counsel *is,* the people fall: but in the multitude of counsellors there is safety. (Proverbs 11:12–14)

A faithful man shall abound with blessings: but he that maketh haste to be rich shall not be innocent. (Proverbs 28:28)

And this was their faith, that by so doing God would prosper them in the land, or in other words, if they were faithful in keeping the commandments of God that he would prosper them in the land; yea, warn them to flee, or to prepare for war, according to their danger. (Alma 48:15)

And those who were faithful in keeping the commandments of the Lord were delivered at all times. (Alma 50:22)

And no unclean thing can enter into his kingdom; therefore nothing entereth into his rest save it be those who have washed their garments in my blood, because of their faith, and the repentance of all their sins, and their faithfulness unto the end. (3 Nephi 27:19)

And blessed is he that is found faithful unto my name at the last day, for he shall be lifted up to dwell in the kingdom prepared for him from the foundation of the world. And behold it is I that hath spoken it. (Ether 4:19)

If thou wilt do good, yea, and hold out faithful to the end, thou shalt be saved in the kingdom of God, which is the greatest of all the gifts of God; for there is no gift greater than the gift of salvation. (D&C 6:13)

Be faithful and diligent in keeping the commandments of God, and I will encircle thee in the arms of my love. (D&C 6:20)

Do this thing which I have commanded you, and you shall prosper. Be faithful, and yield to no temptation.

Stand fast in the work wherewith I have called you, and a hair of your head shall not be lost, and you shall be lifted up at the last day. (D&C 9:13–14)

Wherefore, be faithful, praying always, having your lamps trimmed and burning, and oil with you, that you may be ready at the coming of the Bridegroom. (D&C 33:17)

And if you are faithful, behold, I am with you until I come. (D&C 34:11)

But blessed are they who are faithful and endure, whether in life or in death, for they shall inherit eternal life. (D&C 50:5)

For verily I say unto you, blessed is he that keepeth my commandments, whether in life or in death; and he that is faithful in tribulation, the reward of the same is greater in the kingdom of heaven. (D&C 58:2)

And they shall also be crowned with blessings from above, yea, and with commandments not a few, and with revelations in their time—they that are faithful and diligent before me. (D&C 59:4)

He that is faithful and endureth shall overcome the world. (D&C 63:47)

And the inhabitants of Zion also shall remember their labors, inasmuch as they are appointed to labor, in all faithfulness; for the idler shall be had in remembrance before the Lord. (D&C 68:30)

Wherefore, be faithful; stand in the office which I have appointed unto you; succor the weak, lift up the hands which hang down, and strengthen the feeble knees.

And if thou art faithful unto the end thou shalt have a crown of immortality, and eternal life in the mansions which I have prepared in the house of my Father. (D&C 81:5–6)

And any man that shall go and preach this gospel of the kingdom, and fail not to continue faithful in all things, shall not be weary in mind, neither darkened, neither in body, limb, nor joint; and a hair of his head shall not fall to the ground unnoticed. And they shall not go hungry, neither athirst. (D&C 84:80)

And I give unto you a commandment, that ye shall forsake all evil and cleave unto all good, that ye shall live by every word which proceedeth forth out of the mouth of God.

For he will give unto the faithful line upon line, precept upon precept; and I will try you and prove you herewith. (D&C 98:11–12)

All victory and glory is brought to pass unto you through your diligence, faithfulness, and prayers of faith. (D&C 103:36)

For behold, I have prepared a great endowment and blessing to be poured out upon them, inasmuch as they are faithful and continue in humility before me. (D&C 105:12)

Holiness

But now being made free from sin, and become servants to God, ye have your fruit unto holiness, and the end everlasting life. (Romans 6:22)

Having therefore these promises, dearly beloved, let us cleanse ourselves from all filthiness of the flesh and spirit, perfecting holiness in the fear of God. (2 Corinthians 7:1)

That ye put off concerning the former conversation the old man, which is corrupt according to the deceitful lusts;

And be renewed in the spirit of your mind;

And that ye put on the new man, which after God is created in righteousness and true holiness.

Wherefore putting away lying, speak every man truth with his neighbour: for we are members one of another.

Be ye angry, and sin not: let not the sun go down upon your wrath:

Neither give place to the devil.

Let him that stole steal no more: but rather let him labour, working with *his* hands the thing which is good, that he may have to give to him that needeth.

Let no corrupt communication proceed out of your mouth, but that which is good to the use of edifying, that it may minister grace unto the hearers.

> And grieve not the holy Spirit of God, whereby ye are sealed unto the day of redemption.
>
> Let all bitterness, and wrath, and anger, and clamour, and evil speaking, be put away from you, with all malice:
>
> And be ye kind one to another, tenderhearted, forgiving one another, even as God for Christ's sake hath forgiven you. (Ephesians 4:22–32)

> And the members shall manifest before the church, and also before the elders, by a godly walk and conversation, that they are worthy of it, that there may be works and faith agreeable to the holy scriptures—walking in holiness before the Lord. (D&C 20:69)

Since keeping all of the commandments is so intertwined with every formula of success, I will omit listing the hundreds of scriptural references dealing with that topic and use them where it seems appropriate in each of the chapters.

4

A HAPPY, SUCCESSFUL MARRIAGE

Although the world attempts to change God's definition of marriage through legislation or discard marriage as an old-fashioned concept, the Great God of Heaven has established marriage as the ultimate and final test to become like Him. However, as outlined in the chapter on the pathway to exaltation, it is a long and sometimes challenging road from the beginning to the end.

The fact that "going through the motions" without real intent is not acceptable to God comes clearly from a letter Mormon wrote to his son, Moroni:

> For I remember the word of God which saith by their works ye shall know them; for if their works be good, then they are good also.
>
> For behold, God hath said a man being evil cannot do that which is good; for if he offereth a gift, or prayeth unto God, **except he shall do it with real intent** it profiteth him nothing.
>
> For behold, it is not counted unto him for righteousness.
>
> For behold, if a man being evil giveth a gift, he doeth it grudgingly; wherefore it is counted unto him the same as if he had retained the gift; wherefore he is counted evil before God.
>
> And likewise also is it counted evil unto a man, if he shall pray and not with real intent of heart; yea, and it profiteth him nothing, for God receiveth none such.

> Wherefore, a man being evil cannot do that which is good; neither will he give a good gift. (Moroni 7:5–10)

Once pointed out, it is easy to see that baptism without faith or repentance is not going to bring the promised blessings. Attending church meetings without physically and spiritually engaging is just a nice way of spending two hours on Sunday. The same is true of every activity designed by the Lord to prepare us for exaltation.

The Lord revealed the prerequisites for making any covenant eternal:

> And verily I say unto you, that the conditions of this law are these: **All covenants**, contracts, bonds, obligations, oaths, vows, performances, connections, associations, or expectations, **(1) that are not made and (2) entered into and (3) sealed by the Holy Spirit of promise**, of him who is anointed, both as well for time and for all eternity, and that too most holy, by revelation and commandment through the medium of mine anointed, whom I have appointed on the earth to hold this power (and I have appointed unto my servant Joseph to hold this power in the last days, and there is never but one on the earth at a time on whom this power and the keys of this priesthood are conferred), **are of no efficacy, virtue, or force in and after the resurrection from the dead**; for all contracts that are not made unto this end have an end when men are dead. (D&C 132:7; numbers and emphasis added)

"Making" a covenant is simple. We stand in the water, a few words are pronounced, we are immersed in the water, we come out of the water, and we are baptized. The same is true of eternal marriage. We kneel at an altar in a temple, one having authority says a few words, we respond in the affirmative, we embrace over the altar, and we're married—as far as the ordinance can seal us, we are eternally married.

However, now comes the challenge for all ordinances and covenants we make. We must "enter into" the covenant. Using baptism as an example, we must be "willing to bear one another's burdens, that they may be light; Yea, and are willing to mourn with those that mourn; yea, and comfort those that stand in need of comfort, and to stand as witnesses of God at all times and in all things, and in all places that ye may be in, even until death" (Mosiah 18:8–9).

You may question why I am referring to baptism when the chapter is devoted to eternal marriage. Baptism is the key to open the door to the celestial kingdom. Eternal marriage is the key to open the door to the highest degree of the celestial kingdom. There is no need to examine the prerequisites to get into the highest degree of the celestial kingdom unless we qualify to enter the celestial kingdom itself.

Joseph Smith gives the following instruction: "In the celestial glory there are three heavens or degrees; And in order to obtain the highest, a man must enter into this order of the priesthood [meaning the new and everlasting covenant of marriage]; And if he does not, he cannot obtain it. He may enter into the other, but that is the end of his kingdom; he cannot have an increase" (D&C 131:1–4).

That is a very conclusive and exclusive definition of who can or will attain the highest degree of the celestial kingdom and who will not. A serious consideration of those four verses should cement in the mind of any faithful Latter-day Saint the necessity of marriage between a man and a woman (as we will consider when we analyze D&C 132:19).

There has been much talk about the Church altering its stance on same-sex marriage. While compassion and understanding are enjoined, one can see that in order to allow two people of the same gender to marry, the Church would have to abdicate its God-assigned role as the sole facilitator charged to get couples into the highest degree of the celestial kingdom. That isn't going to happen.

If the Church was a manmade organization with the prerogative of making and changing rules left up to its leaders, then that change could be made. However, since this is the Lord's Church, only He can make the rules. Our leaders are in place to implement those rules and commandments—not make them.

Over nearly four decades of teaching, I have heard numerous times couples who have chosen to marry outside the temple say, "Oh, we believe God will understand. We don't think He will keep us apart eternally just because we didn't marry in the temple!" They were always surprised when I agreed with them. However, my next statement puts the consequences directly on the couple when I said: "No, God will not keep you apart eternally because of the decision you are making to marry outside the temple—YOU WILL!"

The Lord gives us the key to the lock which opens the door to the celestial kingdom—it is baptism. If a person refuses to use the key, one can hardly blame the Lord for excluding them from that kingdom. The same is true of eternal marriage. If a couple refuses to accept and use the key to the lock on the door of the highest degree of the celestial kingdom when it is offered to them, they can hardly accuse God of barring their entrance.

The Lord clearly points this out in D&C 132:9–14:

> Will I accept of an offering, saith the Lord, that is not made in my name?
>
> Or will I receive at your hands that which I have not appointed?
>
> And will I appoint unto you, saith the Lord, except it be by law, even as I and my Father ordained unto you, before the world was?
>
> I am the Lord thy God; and I give unto you this commandment—that no man shall come unto the Father but by me or by my word, which is my law, saith the Lord.
>
> And everything that is in the world, whether it be ordained of men, by thrones, or principalities, or powers, or things of name, whatsoever they may be, that are not by me or by my word, saith the Lord, shall be thrown down, and shall not remain after men are dead, neither in nor after the resurrection, saith the Lord your God.
>
> For whatsoever things remain are by me; and whatsoever things are not by me shall be shaken and destroyed.

Now follows two scenarios explaining in detail the result of choosing to marry outside the temple. The first example I have labeled as "a Las Vegas marriage," or a civil marriage. Read carefully what the Lord has revealed:

> Therefore, if a man marry him a wife in the world, and he marry her not by me nor by my word, and **he covenant with her so long as he is in the world and she with him,** their covenant and marriage are not of force when they are dead, and when they are out of the world; therefore, they are not bound by any law when they are out of the world.
>
> Therefore, when they are out of the world they neither marry nor are given in marriage; but are appointed angels in heaven, which angels are ministering servants, to minister for those who are worthy of a far more, and an exceeding, and an eternal weight of glory.
>
> For these angels did not abide my law; therefore, they cannot be enlarged, but remain separately and singly, without exaltation, in their saved condition, to all eternity; and from henceforth are not gods, but are angels of God forever and ever. (D&C 132:15–17)

It is sobering but true that there is an invisible bill of divorcement under each civil marriage certificate. Both parties agree that they are only married "so long as we both shall live" or "until death do us part." They lay no claim on having their relationship last into the eternal worlds. So, with the same signature that they become married, they also agree to terminate that marriage.

The result of that civil marriage is that they will not earn the status of gods, but will be relegated to the status of angels who are labeled as "ministering servants" to those who do qualify for exaltation. That condition, according to these verses, is not a temporary restraint but will last "forever and ever." Certainly something to consider. Some believe that the very God who Enos recognized as not being able to lie (see Enos 1:6) somehow really doesn't mean what He says about consigning the civilly married couple to live "separately and singly, without exaltation, in their saved condition, to all eternity" (D&C 132:17). Personally, I would not care to test whether God is "only kidding" when He made that pronouncement.

Two other groups who either marry outside the temple or marry in the temple but are not faithful are those mentioned in Doctrine and Covenants 132:18. I call these the "counterfeit eternal marriage" groups.

> And again, verily I say unto you, if a man marry a wife, and make a covenant with her for time and for all eternity, **if that covenant is not by me or by my word, which is my law, and is not sealed by the Holy Spirit of promise**, through him whom I have anointed and appointed unto this power, **then it is not valid neither of force when they are out of the world,** because they are not joined by me, saith the Lord, neither by my word; when they are out of the world it cannot be received there, **because the angels and the gods are appointed there, by whom they cannot pass;** they cannot, therefore, inherit my glory; for my house is a house of order, saith the Lord God.

There seems to be two separate groups represented in this verse: (1) those who ask the person performing the marriage ceremony to pronounce the words, "I marry you for time and for all eternity," but that person has no authority so the words are hollow and meaningless; (2) the second group seems to be those who marry in the temple by one having the authority but they do not fully "enter into" the covenant by living as they covenanted they would, and therefore the seal of the Holy Spirit of Promise (which we will discuss later) is not on their marriage.

What is to prevent them from entering into the highest degree of the celestial kingdom? There are "angels and gods" that require certain key words (see D&C 130:11—a subject not to be discussed in this book) that they do not know. However, given how "smart" some people are, why couldn't they just log onto the internet, to some anti-Mormon site, and learn the words from that source? The thing that would prevent them from passing the angels even though they can mouth the correct words is the absence of the seal of the Holy Spirit of Promise. No one is going to "sneak" by and gain entrance into the highest degree of the celestial kingdom if they have not properly made the covenant of eternal marriage, entered into the covenant, and lived well enough to have the Holy Spirit acting in His office as a promisor and seal them up to eternal life.

What does it mean to "enter into" the covenant of marriage? It means that we follow the command: "Thou shalt love thy wife with all thy heart, and shalt cleave unto her and none else" (D&C 42:22). If we would do that one simple thing—stop looking and shopping after we are married—divorce would all but disappear from temple marriages.

When we ignore that command, consequences follow and deal a death blow to our eternal marriage: "And verily I say unto you, as I have said before, he that looketh on a woman to lust after her, or if any shall commit adultery in their hearts, they (1) **shall not have the Spirit, but (2) shall deny the faith and (3) shall fear"** (D&C 63:16, numbers and emphasis added).

The very first consequence of "looking and lusting" is the loss of the Spirit. Remember, in order to have an ordinance continue into the eternal worlds it must be "sealed by the Holy Spirit of Promise." The withdrawal of the Spirit is the Lord's way of indicating that the path we are pursuing will not lead us back to His presence. The presence of the Spirit is the Lord signaling that we are heading in the right direction and doing what is necessary to eventually receive our exaltation (see D&C 111:8). Obviously, we are not perfect, but we are living as well as the Lord expects us to, given the light and knowledge He has blessed us with.

You may recall that 1 John 4:16 defines God as "Love."

> And we have known and believed the love that God hath to us. **God is love**; and he that dwelleth in love dwelleth in God, and God in him.
>
> Herein is our love made perfect, that we may have boldness in the day of judgment: because as he is, so are we in this world.
>
> There is no fear in love; but perfect love casteth out fear: because fear hath torment. He that feareth is not made perfect in love. (1 John 4:16–18)

Lest we overlook a very significant part of keeping the love alive in marriage, we must note that God manifests His presence in our marriages by leaving His Spirit there. When one or both parties offend the Spirit and causes it to withdraw, God withdraws. Hence, love drains out of our relationship.

The second consequence for looking and lusting after marriage is "they shall deny the faith." Unless one responds to the wake-up-call of the withdrawal of the Spirit, repents, and gets his life in order, he will eventually begin to rationalize the keeping of other commandments. Then he will begin to dispute the counsel of Church leaders. Eventually he will claim he no longer believes in the Church and its doctrine. Although I have written this in the masculine, there is an increasing number of women who fall into this trap.

What about the third consequence, "they shall fear?" Sometimes that happens when a Church disciplinary council tells them that they have been excommunicated from the Church. Some, at that point, realize that they have lost their spouse, their family, their ties to their ancestors, the right to the Spirit, the priesthood, many times their friends, sometimes their employment, and so on. Having participated in many such councils, I have been eyewitness to the fear that overwhelms many newly excommunicated men.

For others whose pride will not permit them to admit their mistake, fear may be postponed until the spirit world. Alma described this state to his errant son, Corianton:

> And then shall it come to pass, that the spirits of the wicked, yea, who are evil—for behold, **they have no part nor portion of the Spirit of the Lord; for behold, they chose evil works rather than good**; therefore the spirit of the devil did enter into them, and take possession of their house—and these shall be cast out into outer darkness; there shall be weeping, and wailing, and gnashing of teeth, and this because of their own iniquity, being led captive by the will of the devil.
>
> Now this is the state of the souls of the wicked, yea, in darkness, and **a state of awful, fearful looking for the fiery indignation of the wrath of God upon them**; thus they remain in this state, as well as the righteous in paradise, until the time of their resurrection. Alma 40:13–14

Besides cleaving to your mate, how can a couple "enter into" the covenant of marriage? Paul gave some timely advice two thousand years ago: "Husbands, love your wives, even as Christ also loved the church, and gave himself for it. . . . So ought men to love their wives as their own bodies. He that loveth his wife loveth himself. . . . Nevertheless let every one of you in particular so love his wife even as himself; and the wife *see* that she reverence *her* husband" (Ephesians 5:25, 28, 33).

As the Saints were preparing to travel west, the Lord said, "Cease to contend one with another; cease to speak evil one of another" (D&C 136:23). Earlier in His "message of peace" the Lord revealed: "See that ye love one another; cease to be covetous. . . . Cease to be idle; cease to be unclean; cease to find fault one with another. . . . And above all things, clothe yourselves with the bond of charity, as with a mantle, which is the bond of perfectness and peace" (D&C 88:123–125).

Although much could be written elaborating on the above instructions, perhaps saying a word about what the Lord designated as "above all things" is sufficient. If, in our interactions with each other, we would stand back long enough to honestly ask two questions, we could eliminate almost all of the inroads Satan is making into our marriages. (1) If I do, say, or act in what I am planning, will it honestly help perfect my marriage or the family? And (2) If I do, say, or act in what I am planning, will it bring peace to my relationship with my spouse and the family or situation? If the answer is "no" to either or both of those questions, then you are not acting charitably—don't do it!

In one verse the Lord unmistakably punctuates the necessity of being unified in marriage. In D&C 38:27 He revealed: "Behold, this I have given unto you as a parable, and it is even as I am. I say unto you, be one; and **if ye are not one ye are not mine**." Although it is a constant struggle, and requires daily vigilance because of satanic opposition, it certainly is possible to "live together in love" (see D&C 42:45). Couples who constantly strive for peace and unity in their marriage enjoy the promised reward of peace in this life and hope of eternal life in the world to come or in the Lord's own words: "That ye might be sanctified from all sin, and enjoy the words of eternal life in this world, and eternal life in the world to come, even immortal glory" (Moses 6:59).

As we consider the covenants necessary to gain exaltation, we discover that every covenant—except one—is made between the individual and the Lord. Only the covenant of eternal marriage is made between the Lord, the individual, and one other person. Why would the Lord enter into the marriage covenant? Perhaps one answer might be that He realizes how difficult it can be to live a celestial life in a telestial world. Add to that the complexity of living with another person and then adding children to the equation, and without His divine intervention the difficult becomes nearly impossible.

Sadly, the Lord describes what happens when one of the parties ceases to keep the covenant made: "And as the covenant which they made unto me has been broken, even so it has become void and of none effect. And wo to him by whom this offense cometh, for it had been better for him that he had been drowned in the depth of the sea. But blessed are they who have kept the covenant and observed the commandment, for they shall obtain mercy" (D&C 54:4–6).

Verse 5 punctuates the seriousness of breaking a covenant. Being "drowned in the depth of the sea" hardly sounds like exaltation. However, verse 6 gives hope to the one who has faithfully tried to honor the covenant. The "mercy" they will receive is that no eternal blessing will be denied them because of the unrighteousness of another person. The Lord said: "That every man may act in doctrine and principle pertaining to futurity, according to the moral agency which I have given unto him, **that every man may be accountable for his own sins in the day of judgment**" (D&C 101:78).

Given that the devil is the enemy to ALL righteousness and that there isn't anything more righteous than a husband and wife who are making and striving to keep sacred covenants, the promise that the Lord will "lead us along" (see D&C 78:18) gives us courage to fight the battle and receive the promised reward. What are those promises if we are faithful? The Lord outlined them in Doctrine and Covenants 132:19–24:

> And again, verily I say unto you, if **a man marry a wife** by my word, which is my law, and by the new and everlasting covenant, and **it is sealed unto them by the Holy Spirit of promise**, by him who is anointed, unto whom I have appointed this power and the keys of this priesthood; and it shall be said unto them—(1) Ye shall come forth in the first resurrection; and if it be after the first resurrection, in the next resurrection; and (2) shall inherit thrones, kingdoms, principalities, and powers, dominions, all heights and depths—then shall it be (3) written in the Lamb's Book of Life, that he shall commit no murder whereby to shed innocent blood, and if ye abide in my covenant, and commit no murder whereby to shed innocent blood, it shall be done unto them in all things whatsoever my servant hath put upon them, in time, and through all eternity; and shall be of full force when they are out of the world; and (4) they shall pass by the angels, and the gods, which are set there, to their exaltation and glory in all things, as hath been sealed upon their heads, which (5) glory shall be a fulness and (6) a continuation of the seeds forever and ever.
>
> (7) Then shall they be gods, because (8) they have no end; therefore (9) shall they be from everlasting to everlasting, because they continue; (10) then shall they be above all, because all things are subject unto them. Then shall they be gods, because (11) they have all power, and the angels are subject unto them.
>
> Verily, verily, I say unto you, except ye abide my law ye cannot attain to this glory.

> For strait is the gate, and narrow the way that leadeth unto the exaltation and continuation of the lives, and few there be that find it, because ye receive me not in the world neither do ye know me.
>
> But if ye receive me in the world, then shall ye know me, and shall receive your exaltation; that where I am ye shall be also.
>
> This is eternal lives—to know the only wise and true God, and Jesus Christ, whom he hath sent. I am he. Receive ye, therefore, my law." (Numbers and emphasis added)

Because some trouble us and have departed from the faith, it is instructive to note that in the beginning of verse 19 the Lord states, "If *a* man marry *a* woman" and then describes exaltation. Two points of interest: (1) Although plural marriage was practiced for a time in the Church under the direction of the Lord (see Jacob 2:27–30), and there will be men in the celestial kingdom who have more than one wife, having more than one wife is not a prerequisite of exaltation. (2) The Lord definitely states that marriage is between a man and a woman. In spite of modern efforts to change the definition of marriage, the unchangeable God has not changed His commandment. All of the legislation in the world, all of the demonstrations, all of the condemning diatribes against heterosexual marriage will not change the revealed commandment. We may break ourselves against the commandment, but we cannot change the commandment.

Scripturally explaining the meaning of all eleven of the promises listed above would go beyond the scope of this work. However, for an enlightening and edifying experience, that study would be well worth your time and effort.

One further punctuation mark by the Apostle Paul: "Nevertheless neither is the man without the woman, neither the woman without the man, in the Lord" (1 Corinthians 11:11). If we want to go where the Lord is and dwell there eternally, we will go as couples. Now is a great time to reassess the state of our relationship and make the modifications necessary to be in total alignment with the counsel from the Lord and His leaders.

POINTS FOR FURTHER CONSIDERATION

Cleave unto thy wife

Genesis 2:24 (see also Matthew 19:5; Mark 10:7; Ephesians 5:31; Moses 3:24; Abraham 5:18)

Do no covet thy neighbor's wife

Exodus 20:17 (see also Mosiah 13:24; D&C 19:25)

Proverbs 18:22

Whoso findeth a wife findeth a good thing.

Proverbs 19:14

House and riches are the inheritance of fathers: and a prudent wife is from the Lord.

Ecclesiastes 9:9

Live joyfully with the wife whom thou lovest all the days of the life of thy vanity, which he hath given thee under the sun, all the days of thy vanity: for that *is* thy portion in *this* life, and in thy labour which thou takest under the sun.

1 Corinthians 7:3

Let the husband render unto the wife due benevolence: and likewise also the wife unto the husband.

3 Nephi 18:21

Pray in your families unto the Father, always in my name, that your wives and your children may be blessed.

Doctrine and Covenants 25:5

And the office of thy calling shall be for a comfort unto my servant, Joseph Smith, Jun., thy husband, in his afflictions, with consoling words, in the spirit of meekness.

Doctrine and Covenants 42:45

Thou shalt live together in love.

5

SUCCESSFULLY RAISING CHILDREN AND SURVIVING PARENTING

Multiple books have been written about how to raise children. Some have determined, after damaging an entire generation, that their ideas did not bring the positive results they had promised. In this chapter, principles the Lord has revealed and principles we can draw from the story of God's children on earth will at least point us in the right direction.

Let it be clearly stated at the beginning that your success as a parent is not determined solely on the behavior of your children. That would deny the very doctrine upon which the war in heaven was fought—agency. Every person must choose for himself how he will act and the course in life he will pursue. While it is true that parents can and do have a great influence on their children, to base the success rate of the parent solely upon choices their children make would be a serious mistake.

Perfect Parents, the kind we were born to as spirit children, not only had remarkable success in influencing Their spirit children, but also, when gifting them their agency, sadly watched as "one third part" (see D&C 29:36) chose a course that would eternally deny them access to their heavenly home.

First it is no secret that being the spirit children of God has been known and taught for a very long time. The Savior in teaching us to pray said:

"Our Father who art in Heaven" (Matthew 6:9; 3 Nephi 13:9). Repeatedly throughout His mortal ministry, the Lord referred to "our Father," "my Father," "your Father," and so on.

Paul wrote: "Furthermore we have had fathers of our flesh which corrected *us*, and we gave *them* reverence: shall we not much rather be in subjection unto the Father of spirits, and live?" (Hebrews 12:9).

Earlier he had taught the Athenians:

> And hath made of one blood all nations of men for to dwell on all the face of the earth, and hath determined the times before appointed, and the bounds of their habitation;
>
> That they should seek the Lord, if haply they might feel after him, and find him, though he be not far from every one of us:
>
> For in him we live, and move, and have our being; as certain also of your own poets have said, For **we are also his offspring.**
>
> Forasmuch then as **we are the offspring of God**, we ought not to think that the Godhead is like unto gold, or silver, or stone, graven by art and man's device. (Acts 17:26–29)

In Doctrine and Covenants 29:36–37 the Lord revealed: "And it came to pass that Adam, being tempted of the devil—for, behold, the devil was before Adam, for he rebelled against me, saying, Give me thine honor, which is my power; and also a third part of the hosts of heaven turned he away from me because of their agency; And they were thrust down, and thus came the devil and his angels."

It is disappointing to note that all of the evil, murder, adultery, sin, and corruption in the world today, and all of the satanic opposition we are experiencing in our marriages and families, is caused by the evil influence of our spirit siblings!

When Lucifer ("the dragon") was cast out of heaven into the earth with all of his followers, we not only knew them but loved them. "And the great dragon was cast out, that old serpent, called the Devil, and Satan, which deceiveth the whole world: he was cast out into the earth, and his angels were cast out with him" (Revelation 12:9).

One of six glorious visions recorded in Doctrine and Covenants 76 notes the following that applies to what we must now look to as our lot in life:

> And this we saw also, and bear record, that an angel of God who was in authority in the presence of God, who rebelled against the Only Begotten Son whom the Father loved and who was in the bosom of the Father, was thrust down from the presence of God and the Son,

> And was called Perdition, for **the heavens wept over him**—he was Lucifer, a son of the morning.
>
> And we beheld, and lo, he is fallen! is fallen, even a son of the morning!
>
> And while we were yet in the Spirit, the Lord commanded us that we should write the vision; for we beheld Satan, that old serpent, even the devil, who rebelled against God, and sought to take the kingdom of our God and his Christ—
>
> Wherefore, **he maketh war with the saints of God, and encompasseth them round about.** (D&C 76:25–29)

First, note that "the heavens" wept over Lucifer and his followers. Who was "the heavens" referring to? All of the spirit sons and daughters of God who accepted the Father's plan as championed by the Savior. Next, note that Satan and his followers "tempt the children of men" (see D&C 29:39) but he "maketh war with the saints of God" and doesn't just "tempt" us but "encompasseth us round about." Can you see the intensity difference between what Satan and his followers do to "the children of men" (non-members) and what they do to the saints of God? Keeping that in mind, let's look to what the Lord has said about raising children.

Adam and Eve began the assigned task of peopling the earth—which, according to the Lord, is the very purpose for which the earth was created. "Wherefore, it is lawful that he should have one wife, and they twain shall be one flesh, and all this that the earth might answer the end of its creation; And that it might be filled with the measure of man, according to his creation before the world was made" (D&C 49:16–17).

However, Adam and Eve's initial efforts at holding "family home evening" with their children did not prove successful: "And Adam and Eve blessed the name of God, and they made all things known unto their sons and their daughters. And Satan came among them, saying: I am also a son of God; and he commanded them, saying: Believe it not; and they believed it not, and they loved Satan more than God. And men began from that time forth to be carnal, sensual, and devilish" (Moses 5:12–13).

Following the first recorded murder (Cain killing Abel), Moses recorded the following: "And Adam and his wife mourned before the Lord, because of Cain and his brethren" (Moses 5:27).

Although some of our greatest joys will be experienced as we raise our children, some of the most bitter, heart-wrenching times will also be experienced as our children exercise their agency in direct opposition to God's revealed truths and give way to the unseen, but very real, temptations and influences of our spirit brothers and sisters who followed Satan.

It seems that many of the principles of successful parenting are gleaned from negative examples. Eli, an ancient priest in Israel, had two sons who were not faithful commandment keepers. They were immoral with the women who came to offer sacrifices, they glutted themselves on the sacrifices of the people, and were basically headed in the wrong direction. The Lord commanded Eli to restrain his sons and get them back on the strait and narrow path. The scriptures record Eli's efforts and its results: "Nay, my sons; for it is no good report that I hear: ye make the Lord's people to transgress. If one man sin against another, the judge shall judge him: but if a man sin against the Lord, who shall entreat for him? **Notwithstanding they hearkened not unto the voice of their father**, because the Lord would slay them" (1 Samuel 2:24–25).

Evidently Eli's attempts to get the sons to repent was not sufficient. In verse 29 the man of God who confronts Eli said, "Thou honourest thy sons above me." This is a powerful lesson. When the behavior of the children is contrary to the commandments of God, parents don't side with the children. In the Church today, there are examples of parents siding with their children's decision for an alternate lifestyle in choosing homosexuality over the God-revealed standard of marriage. What a tragic mistake. Paul emphasized this point many years after the above examples: "Be ye therefore followers of God, as dear children" (Ephesians 5:1).

Paul continues his counsel: "Children, obey your parents in the Lord: for this is right. Honour thy father and mother (which is the first commandment with promise); That it may be well with thee, and thou mayest live long on the earth. And, ye fathers, **provoke not your children to wrath**: but bring them up in the nurture and admonition of the Lord" (Ephesians 6:1–4).

It appears that we are to teach our children to obey their parents and to honor them. Although many children in today's world opt not to honor or obey parents, it does not negate the fact we are to teach them.

With the withdrawing of the Spirit of the Lord (Light of Christ) from the world because of wickedness (D&C 63:32: "I, the Lord, am angry with the wicked; I am holding my Spirit from the inhabitants of the earth"), we will continue to see the inhumanity of man to man escalate to unbelievable levels. This adds even more emphasis to the charge to teach our children.

King Benjamin in his farewell address to his people addressed their responsibility to their children.

> And (1) ye will not have a mind to injure one another, but (2) to live peaceably, and (3) to render to every man according to that which is his due.
>
> And (4) ye will not suffer your children that they go hungry, or naked; (5) neither will ye suffer that they transgress the laws of God, and (6) fight and quarrel one with another, and (7) serve the devil, who is the master of sin, or who is the evil spirit which hath been spoken of by our fathers, he being an enemy to all righteousness.
>
> But (8) ye will teach them to walk in the ways of truth and soberness; (9) ye will teach them to love one another, and (10) to serve one another. (Mosiah 4:13–15, numbers added)

That list provides a great curriculum for family home evening lessons.

However, if we confine ourselves to "once a week" teaching, we are missing a vital lesson the Lord taught to Moses anciently:

> Hear, O Israel: The Lord our God *is* one Lord:
>
> And thou shalt love the Lord thy God with all thine heart, and with all thy soul, and with all thy might.
>
> And these words, which I command thee this day, shall be in thine heart:
>
> And **thou shalt teach them diligently unto thy children, and shalt talk of them when thou sittest in thine house, and when thou walkest by the way, and when thou liest down, and when thou risest up.**
>
> And thou shalt bind them for a sign upon thine hand, and they shall be as frontlets between thine eyes.
>
> And thou shalt **write them upon the posts of thy house**, and on thy gates.
>
> And it shall be, when the Lord thy God shall have brought thee into the land which he sware unto thy fathers, to Abraham, to Isaac, and to Jacob, to give thee great and goodly cities, which thou buildedst not,
>
> And houses full of all good *things*, which thou filledst not, and wells digged, which thou diggedst not, vineyards and olive trees, which thou plantedst not; when thou shalt have eaten and be full;
>
> ***Then* beware lest thou forget the Lord**, which brought thee forth out of the land of Egypt, from the house of bondage. (Deuteronomy 6:4–12)

With a little effort and planning, almost everything in life can be tied to gospel principles. Thinking "eternally" can become natural to our children who seem to be so caught up in the "me, here, and now" rather than considering the long-term impact of some of their childish decisions. Too many of our youth (and older people too!) become addicted to any of a hundred things before they realize they have lost their agency and put in jeopardy eternal life for some temporary, fleeting pleasure or activity.

So important is the role of parents in teaching their children that the Lord outlines another list of "things to teach to your children" in our dispensation.

> And again, **inasmuch as parents have children in Zion,** or in any of her stakes which are organized, that teach them not to (1) understand the doctrine of repentance, (2) faith in Christ the Son of the living God, and of (3) baptism and (4) the gift of the Holy Ghost by the laying on of the hands, when eight years old, the sin be upon the heads of the parents.
>
> For this shall be a law unto the inhabitants of Zion, or in any of her stakes which are organized.
>
> And their children shall be baptized for the remission of their sins when eight years old, and receive the laying on of the hands.
>
> And they shall (5) also teach their children to pray, and (6) to walk uprightly before the Lord.
>
> And the inhabitants of Zion shall (7) also observe the Sabbath day to keep it holy.
>
> And the inhabitants of Zion (8) also shall remember their labors, inasmuch as they are appointed to labor, in all faithfulness; (9) for the idler shall be had in remembrance before the Lord.
>
> Now, I, the Lord, am not well pleased with the inhabitants of Zion, for there are idlers among them; and (10) their children are also growing up in wickedness; they (11) also seek not earnestly the riches of eternity, but (12) their eyes are full of greediness.
>
> **These things ought not to be, and must be done away from among them**; wherefore, let my servant Oliver Cowdery carry these sayings unto the land of Zion.
>
> And a commandment I give unto them—that (13) he that observeth not his prayers before the Lord in the season thereof, let him be had in remembrance before the judge of my people.
>
> **These sayings are true and faithful; wherefore, transgress them not, neither take therefrom.** (D&C 68:25–34, numbers and emphasis added)

While the greatest sorrow comes to parents as children choose evil over good, John the Beloved made this observation: "*I have no greater joy than to hear that my* **children walk in truth**" (3 John 1:4).

Lehi, in his final address to the sons and daughters of his wayward sons, said: "But behold, my sons and my daughters, I cannot go down to my grave save I should leave a blessing upon you; for behold, I know that **if ye are brought up in the way ye should go ye will not depart from it"** (2 Nephi 4:5).

Perhaps wise King Solomon put our mortal experience with some of our challenging children best when he taught: "Train up a child in the way he should go: and **when he is old,** he will not depart from it" (Proverbs 22:6). He didn't say they would "never depart" but that when "he is old, he will not depart from it." There seems to be that time of varying length when many people want to "try their wings" in engaging in activities contrary to what they have been taught. Although sorrowful and hurtful to parents, many of those children return to their roots later in life.

For those who depart earth life still embracing the wrong, the Lord has made provisions for them. In a mind-expanding vision of the postmortal spirit world, Joseph F. Smith records:

> Thus was the gospel preached to those who had died in their sins, without a knowledge of the truth, **or in transgression, having rejected the prophets.**
>
> These were taught faith in God, repentance from sin, vicarious baptism for the remission of sins, the gift of the Holy Ghost by the laying on of hands,
>
> And all other principles of the gospel that were necessary for them to know in order to qualify themselves that they might be judged according to men in the flesh, but live according to God in the spirit. (D&C 138:32–34)

We all recognize that a true and loving Father would give an opportunity to every spirit son or daughter to accept or reject the gospel either during their mortal stay or in the postmortal, pre-resurrection life. However, we often skip the fact that even those who died in transgression who rejected the prophets will get a full opportunity. We are not privy to what constitutes a full opportunity. Just being born and raised in a good LDS home with faithful parents who taught diligently may or may not qualify as the errant child's full opportunity to accept and live the gospel.

You will note from the above passage that they were taught those principles and ordinances which are prerequisite for the celestial kingdom but are not required for the other kingdoms of glory. Why worry about joining the Church and living righteously here in mortality? Why not just wait until the next life to fully embrace the gospel? Later in the same vision, President Smith recorded: "The **dead who repent** will be redeemed, through obedience to the ordinances of the house of God, And **after they have paid the penalty of their transgressions**, and are washed clean, shall receive a reward according to their works, for they are heirs of salvation" (D&C 138:58–59).

With the number of times the scriptures describe the punishments of God as a place of "weeping, wailing, and gnashing of teeth" (see Alma 40:13 as an example) it seems that only a fool would choose that course over repenting, living according to God's commandments, and thus avoid the punishment. Paul wrote to the Hebrew saints: "For we know him that hath said, Vengeance belongeth unto me, I will recompense, saith the Lord. And again, The Lord shall judge his people. *It is* a fearful thing to fall into the hands of the living God" (Hebrews 10:30–31).

It wouldn't be unusual for parents to lament over having children during those dark times when children have turned away from the strait and narrow pathway leading to the presence of God. However, the Psalmist wrote: "Weeping may endure for a night, but joy cometh in the morning" (Psalm 30:5).

Even though that joy may be postponed until the morning of the first resurrection, it will inescapably come because everything the Lord promised will come to pass. Perhaps our emphasis has been placed too much on the behavior of the children to determine our success as parents. Since they have their agency and we cannot control that, one would ask, "How can God have any happiness when His spirit children are acting like so many here on earth—like devils?" Perhaps as least a partial answer would be: "Because He knows that He has given them every opportunity, every resource, and all of the time necessary to be successful short of His overriding their agency—which He will not do." If that be the case, is that also a key for parents with challenging children—glory in the fact that you have provided the environment, the opportunities, and the resources necessary for their happiness? You may not be perfect—none of us are! But I suspect if you had known how to be better parents while going through those trials, you would have done it. Then why beat yourself up for not doing that which you did not know how to do?

In the final analysis this Old Testament statement may be applicable today: "But he slew not their children, but *did* as *it is* written in the law in the book of Moses, where the Lord commanded, saying, **The fathers shall**

not die for the children, neither shall the children die for the fathers, **but every man shall die for his own sin**" (2 Chronicles 25:4).

POINTS FOR FURTHER CONSIDERATION

Children destroyed in flesh because of unbelief will be reclaimed (2 Nephi 10:2)

For behold, the promises which we have obtained are promises unto us according to the flesh; wherefore, as it has been shown unto me that **many of our children shall perish in the flesh because of unbelief,** *nevertheless, God will be merciful unto many; and our children shall be restored,* that they may come to that which will give them the true knowledge of their Redeemer.

Little children are sanctified through the Atonement of Christ (D&C 74:7)

But **little children** *are holy, being sanctified through the atonement of Jesus Christ;* and this is what the scriptures mean.

Little children's sins are paid by the Atonement (Mosiah 3:16)

And even if it were possible that *little children* could sin they could not be saved; but I say unto you they are blessed; for behold, as in Adam, or by nature, they fall, even so **the blood of Christ atoneth for their sins.**

Children are not to save up for parents, but vice versa (2 Corinthians 12:14)

Behold, the third time I am ready to come to you; and I will not be burdensome to you: for I seek not yours, but you: for the *children ought not to lay up for the parents,* but **the parents for the children.**

Children obey parents (Colossians 3:20; see also Ephesians 6:1–2)

Children, *obey your parents in all things:* for this is well pleasing unto the Lord.

When dealing with our errant children we may be inclined to say: "The rebellious 'third part' never got bodies. We are dealing with the 'two-third parts' who were faithful." However, there must have been a great variety among those who got bodies in their devotion and faithfulness to the gospel of Jesus Christ. Remember, in the great vision given to Joseph

Smith and Sidney Rigdon (see D&C 76), the following was revealed about the inhabitants of the telestial kingdom: "But behold, and lo, we saw the glory and the inhabitants of the telestial world, that **they were as innumerable as the stars in the firmament of heaven, or as the sand upon the seashore.**"

6

PHYSICAL AND MENTAL HEALTH

One may be tempted to assume that Doctrine and Covenants 89—the Word of Wisdom—contains all that the Lord has revealed concerning health. While many worthwhile principles are found in that section, there is much more that the Lord has revealed. Given past experience with many peoples' take on the Word of Wisdom, a word of caution seems appropriate: Don't let the Word of Wisdom become your entire religion.

In Romans 14:17 Paul warned against making "meat and drink" our total religion: "For the kingdom of God is not meat and drink; but righteousness, and peace, and joy in the Holy Ghost."

The entire chapter of Romans 14 deserves a careful reading, but we will confine ourselves to one principle here and another later on:

> Him that is weak in the faith receive ye, *but* not to doubtful disputations.
>
> For one believeth that he may eat all things: another, who is weak, eateth herbs.
>
> Let not him that eateth despise him that eateth not; and let not him which eateth not judge him that eateth: for God hath received him. (Romans 14:1–3)

If we can get past accusing and arguing over what we can and cannot eat, based on our interpretation of the Word of Wisdom, we can learn some very important lessons. Perhaps we should address at the very beginning the oft quoted verse about eating meat: "Yea, flesh also of beasts and of the fowls of the air, I, the Lord, have ordained for the use of man with thanksgiving; nevertheless they are to be used sparingly; And it is pleasing unto me that they should not be used, only in times of winter, or of cold, or famine" (D&C 89:12–13).

Those who favor vegetarianism quote these verses frequently but totally ignore what the Lord revealed earlier: "And whoso forbiddeth to abstain from meats, that man should not eat the same, is not ordained of God; For, behold, the beasts of the field and the fowls of the air, and that which cometh of the earth, is ordained for the use of man for food and for raiment, and **that he might have in abundance**" (D&C 49:18–19).

How much meat to eat and when to eat it is not the subject of this chapter. If a person can eat meat and keep the Spirit with him, then he is just or justified in the eyes of God. Thanks be to God, He is willing to reveal to each individual what is good for him personally and what is not. If God approves, who are we to condemn?

To the spiritually juvenile children of Israel who had been in captivity for hundreds of years, God gave a very detailed word of wisdom (see Leviticus 11). Much of what was revealed to Moses was done away at the time of Christ due to the advance in understanding of what is wrong with those things forbidden under the law of Moses.

Paul was at a very difficult crossroad between the law of Moses and the New Testament law of Christ. To the Roman Saints he said:

> Let us not therefore judge one another any more: but judge this rather, that no man put a stumblingblock or an occasion to fall in *his* brother's way.
>
> **I know, and am persuaded by the Lord Jesus, that *there is* nothing unclean of itself: but to him that esteemeth any thing to be unclean, to him *it is* unclean.**
>
> But if thy brother be grieved with *thy* meat, now walkest thou not charitably. **Destroy not him with thy meat, for whom Christ died.** (Romans 14:13–15)

To the Saints in Corinth he wrote:

> All things are lawful for me, but all things are not expedient: all things are lawful for me, but all things edify not.
>
> Let no man seek his own, but every man another's *wealth*.
>
> Whatsoever is sold in the shambles [markets], *that* eat, asking no question for conscience sake:
>
> For the earth *is* the Lord's, and the fulness thereof.
>
> If any of them that believe not bid you *to a feast*, and ye be disposed to go; whatsoever is set before you, eat, asking no question for conscience sake. (1 Corinthians 10:23–27, definition added)

Anyone who has served a mission or travelled extensively in foreign countries can readily identify with what Paul is saying. As a young missionary in Samoa many years ago, I found many of the local people's staples repulsive. Thankfully, even then, I learned to eat without causing offense.

It is instructive to see the purpose behind the Lord's revelation on the Word of Wisdom: "Behold, verily, thus saith the Lord unto you: In consequence of evils and designs which do and will exist in the hearts of conspiring men in the last days, I have warned you, and forewarn you, by giving unto you this word of wisdom by revelation" (D&C 89:4).

Some members of the Church want to arm wrestle (figuratively speaking) with the Lord, saying that the Word of Wisdom wasn't given as a commandment but more as a suggestion. That is like playing Russian roulette with no blanks in the gun. Anyone who has lived in a home where alcohol has destroyed family life can readily attest to what the Lord revealed: "Inasmuch as any man drinketh wine or strong drink among you, behold it is not good, neither meet in the sight of your Father " (D&C 89:5).

Caution against drunkenness is mentioned 110 times in the scriptures. Solomon warned: "Wine is a mocker, strong drink *is* raging: and whosoever is deceived thereby is not wise" (Proverbs 20:1).

Isaiah continued the warning: "Woe unto them that rise up early in the morning, *that* they may follow strong drink; that continue until night, till wine inflame them!" (Isaiah 5:11).

Almost 150 years after the Lord revealed that "tobacco is not for the body, neither for the belly, and is not good for man" (D&C 89:8), modern science finally admitted it. Once again any person who has watched a family, friend, or loved one destroyed by cancer caused from smoking needs no convincing that the Lord had it right. To watch those so addicted struggle to gain control over the addiction is painful, especially when frequent relapses occur.

The next principle, hot drinks, comes with this warning: "And again, hot drinks are not for the body or belly" (D&C 89:9). Although many negative side effects have been identified, drinking hot drinks may have consequences modern science hasn't yet discovered. The Lord has never elaborated upon this phrase other than to identify tea and coffee.

Moving to the positive directives of Doctrine and Covenants 89, the Lord revealed: "And again, verily I say unto you, all wholesome herbs God hath ordained for the constitution, nature, and use of man—Every herb in the season thereof, and every fruit in the season thereof; all these to be used with prudence and thanksgiving . . . . All grain is ordained for the use of man and of beasts, to be the staff of life" (D&C 89:10–11, 14).

In addition to food and substances we take into our bodies, the Lord gives the following admonitions for our physical and mental health:

> See that ye love one another; cease to be covetous; learn to impart one to another as the gospel requires.
>
> Cease to be idle; cease to be unclean; cease to find fault one with another; **cease to sleep longer than is needful; retire to thy bed early, that ye may not be weary; arise early, that your bodies and your minds may be invigorated.**
>
> And above all things, clothe yourselves with the bond of charity, as with a mantle, which is the bond of perfectness and peace.
>
> Pray always, that ye may not faint, until I come. Behold, and lo, I will come quickly, and receive you unto myself. (D&C 88:123–126)

Taking some commentated liberty, the Lord says to "retire early," the purpose for which is "that ye be not weary"—perhaps "grouchy" is another word to help us understand. Think of when the most harsh and hurtful words are spoken. Likely it is not in the morning, but when one is tired. The Lord's solution to saying something that will have long-term negative results is to go to bed. So when is "early"? Just before you get grouchy!

Considering that these verses are part of the Lord's Word of Wisdom, how can we apply what He has revealed and maintain or regain our mental health? First, learn to live together in love. Since the scriptures describe God as "Love" (see 1 John 4:16), if we live as God has empowered us to live, we will learn to love even those who do not reciprocate that love. When our mental attitude is not totally dependent on what others think of us or act toward us, we can enjoy peace with hatred, turmoil, and contention all around us. The Savior was the Master at not allowing others to determine His attitude.

Next, be satisfied with what you have. Covetousness is never satisfied. Or, as Isaiah put it, "Yea, they are greedy dogs which can never have enough" (Isaiah 56:11). If we are willing to work for what we want, the reward is not only getting what we want but in expending the energy and resources to make it really our own.

Next is to learn to be unselfish. Learn to give without expecting a return, give without demanding that we get, serve without expecting to be served. Paul wrote: "Let no man seek his own, but every man another's wealth" (1 Corinthians 10:24). In our dispensation the Lord revealed: "Every man seeking the interest of his neighbor, and doing all things with an eye single to the glory of God" (D&C 82:19).

Next is "cease to be idle." In the "Law of the Lord to the Church" the Lord reveals: "Thou shalt not be idle; for he that is idle shall not eat the bread nor wear the garments of the laborer" D&C 42:42). Idleness has been warned against for thousands of years. Solomon said: "Slothfulness casteth into a deep sleep; and an idle soul shall suffer hunger" (Proverbs 19:15).

Not only are we commanded against idleness, but we are enjoined to develop our talents. "Thou shalt not idle away thy time, neither shalt thou bury thy talent that it may not be known" (D&C 60:13).

Next is "cease to be unclean." Although "uncleanness" refers often to conditions under the law of Moses, it also refers to sins made against the body.

> But fornication, and all **uncleanness**, or covetousness, let it not be once named among you, as becometh saints;
>
> Neither filthiness, nor foolish talking, nor jesting, which are not convenient: but rather giving of thanks.
>
> For this ye know, that no whoremonger, nor unclean person, nor covetous man, who is an idolater, hath any inheritance in the kingdom of Christ and of God. (Ephesians 5:3–5)

> Be wise in the days of your probation; strip yourselves of all uncleanness; ask not, that ye may consume it on your lusts, but ask with a firmness unshaken, that ye will yield to no temptation, but that ye will serve the true and living God. (Mormon 9:28)

Finally, in Doctrine and Covenants 90:17–18 the Lord says: "Be not ashamed, neither confounded; but be admonished in all your high–mindedness and pride, for it bringeth a snare upon your souls. Set in order your houses; keep slothfulness and uncleanness far from you."

The next admonition promoting good mental health is "cease to find fault one with another." The Psalmist wrote: "Whoso privily slandereth his neighbour, him will I cut off: him that hath an high look and a proud heart will not I suffer" (Psalm 101:5).

Paul understood the problem with speaking evil of another. "Let all bitterness, and wrath, and anger, and clamour, and evil speaking, be put away from you, with all malice: And be ye kind one to another, tender-hearted, forgiving one another, even as God for Christ's sake hath forgiven you" (Ephesians 4:31–32). As the Jewish leaders found sin in the Sinless One, because that is what they were looking for, so an aspiring Saint slows his spiritual progress by looking for faults in others.

James, the Lord's half-brother, wrote: "Grudge not one against another, brethren, lest ye be condemned: behold, the judge standeth before the door" (James 5:9).

As part of the instructions preparing the fleeing Saints for their trek to the Rocky Mountains, the Lord said: "Cease to contend one with another; cease to speak evil one of another" (D&C 136:23). Since we are admonished to "leave judgment alone with me [the Lord]" (see D&C 82:23), part of lifting the mental burdens of mortality is to insure that we not try to magnify the Lord's office as Judge.

The next admonition deals with both physical and mental health. "Cease to sleep longer than is needful; retire to thy bed early, that ye may not be weary; arise early, that your bodies and your minds may be invigorated" (D&C 88:124). King Solomon seems to have counsel for everything. He said: "Love not sleep, lest thou come to poverty; open thine eyes, and thou shalt be satisfied with bread" (Proverbs 20:13). Too often mean and hurtful words are uttered by one who is weary and worn down by the pressures of the day. The Lord's remedy for eliminating the mental anguish that comes when unkind words have been exchanged is to retire to thy bed early. For those of us who live in a world that does not require strenuous exercise, the Lord provides a time for bodily exercise: "Arise early that your bodies . . . may be invigorated." For those who claim there is no time to read the scriptures or good books, the Lord again provides the time: "Arise early that . . . your minds may be invigorated."

Finally, above everything the Lord has provided for our mental and physical health, He says: "And above all things, clothe yourselves with the bond of charity, as with a mantle, which is the bond of perfectness and peace." Although the definition most often attached to charity is "the pure love of Christ" which certainly is an accurate definition (see Moroni 7:47), Peter explains what charity will do for us: "And above all things have fervent charity among yourselves; for **charity** *preventeth a multitude of sins*" (JST, 1 Peter 4:8). When Christ becomes the focal point of our thoughts, the inclination to succumb to temptations is lessened.

James wrote:

> Blessed is the man that endureth temptation: for when he is tried, he shall receive the crown of life, which the Lord hath promised to them that love him.
>
> Let no man say when he is tempted, I am tempted of God: for God cannot be tempted with evil, neither tempteth he any man:
>
> But every man is tempted, when he is drawn away of his own lust, and enticed.
>
> Then when lust hath conceived, it bringeth forth sin: and sin, when it is finished, bringeth forth death. (James 1:12–15)

Although it is a lifelong quest, charity is the key to mental stability in these difficult times.

> And charity suffereth long, and is kind, and envieth not, and is not puffed up, seeketh not her own, is not easily provoked, thinketh no evil, and rejoiceth not in iniquity but rejoiceth in the truth, beareth all things, believeth all things, hopeth all things, endureth all things.
>
> Wherefore, my beloved brethren, if ye have not charity, ye are nothing, for charity never faileth. Wherefore, cleave unto charity, which is the greatest of all, for all things must fail —
>
> But charity is the pure love of Christ, and it endureth forever; and whoso is found possessed of it at the last day, it shall be well with him.
>
> Wherefore, my beloved brethren, **pray unto the Father with all the energy of heart, that ye may be filled with this love,** which he hath bestowed upon all who are true followers of his Son, Jesus Christ; that ye may become the sons of God; that when he shall appear we shall be like him, for we shall see him as he is; that we may have this hope; that we may be purified even as he is pure. (Moroni 7:45–48)

As you mentally review each of the outlined attributes of charity, make whatever corrections are necessary to align yourself with the descriptors. Then pray to the Father with all the energy of your soul for the gift. The promise is, "For if these things be in you, and abound, they make *you that ye shall* neither *be* barren nor unfruitful in the knowledge of our Lord Jesus Christ" (2 Peter 1:8). "And be not conformed to this world: **but be**

ye transformed by the renewing of your mind, that ye may prove what is that good, and acceptable, and perfect, will of God" (Romans 12:2).

You may question my associating keeping the commandments with good mental health. However, the Lord told Martin Harris: "Wherefore, I command you again to repent, lest I humble you with my almighty power; and that you confess your sins, lest you suffer these punishments of which I have spoken, of which in the smallest, yea, even in the least degree you have tasted at the time I withdrew my Spirit" (D&C 19:20). And to Joseph Smith after allowing the 116 manuscript pages to go out of his hands, the Lord said: "And you also lost your gift at the same time, and your mind became darkened" (D&C 10:2).

Because the Lord's chosen method of "signalizing" His approval is the presence of His Spirit and peace (see D&C 111:8), it would be contrary for Him to approve of a course of action that would not eventually bring His spirit children back into His presence.

The great challenge is to live all of His commandments to the degree that the Lord's Spirit is undeniably present in your life. Then note carefully what your mental health is like. You may have physical problems and still have emotional turmoil, but your mental health will be at peace and you can and will look at the challenges of mortality as tests to be passed rather than experiences to endure.

7

SEEING GOD

Once a person has established a relationship with God through prayer, it seems like a natural desire to deepen that relationship by vision or visitation. While caution is needed (because too many people want to force that kind of an experience), the scriptures are filled with invitations, promises, and prerequisites for seeing God.

The Psalmist said: "When thou saidst, Seek ye my face; my heart said unto thee, Thy face, Lord, will I seek" (Psalm 27:8). Was that an idle invitation by the Lord or an impossible search by man?

Following Abraham's deliverance by "the angel of his presence" (Christ, see D&C 133:53, Isaiah 63:9), he said: "Now, after the Lord had withdrawn from speaking to me, and withdrawn his face from me, I said in my heart: Thy servant has sought thee earnestly; now I have found thee" (Abraham 2:12).

There is a preparation necessary to enjoy such an epiphany. Urging the early brethren of this dispensation to recognize and overcome impediments preventing them from enjoying great spiritual experiences, the Lord said:

> And again, verily I say unto you that it is **your privilege, and a promise** I give unto you that have been ordained unto this ministry, that inasmuch as you **strip yourselves from jealousies and fears, and**

> **humble yourselves before me,** for ye are not sufficiently humble, **the veil shall be rent and you shall see me and know that I am**—not with the carnal neither natural mind, but with the spiritual.
>
> For no man has seen God at any time in the flesh, except **quickened by the Spirit of God.**
>
> Neither can any natural man abide the presence of God, neither after the carnal mind.
>
> Ye are not able to abide the presence of God now, neither the ministering of angels; wherefore, **continue in patience until ye are perfected.**
>
> **Let not your minds turn back; and when ye are worthy, *in mine own due time,* ye shall see and know** that which was conferred upon you by the hands of my servant Joseph Smith, Jun. (D&C 67:10–14)

Start your quest by getting rid of jealousies and fears. Make humility an ongoing effort. Work endlessly on developing godly patience. As you free yourself from worldliness, don't let your mind turn back—like Lot's wife—to the enticements of a carnal world. Then, as you continue to perfect yourself (with the help of the Lord), let Him decide when you are prepared to enjoy His presence and the ministering of angels.

The Lord seems anxious to reveal Himself to His people. He said: "Therefore, **sanctify yourselves that your minds become single to God,** and the days will come that you shall see him; for he will unveil his face unto you, and it shall be in his own time, and in his own way, and according to his own will. Remember the great and last promise which I have made unto you; **cast away your idle thoughts and your excess of laughter far from you**" (D&C 88:68–69).

How is the sanctifying process to proceed? In Helaman 3:35 more instructions are given, helping us understand how we are to become sanctified: "Nevertheless they did fast and pray oft, and did wax stronger and stronger in their humility, and firmer and firmer in the faith of Christ, unto the filling their souls with joy and consolation, yea, even to the purifying and the sanctification of their hearts, which sanctification cometh because of their yielding their hearts unto God."

Once again fasting and prayer, stronger efforts in developing humility, and constantly strengthening our faith in Christ leads us to a state where we gladly "yield our hearts unto God" or do whatever He asks us to do—and do it willingly. It is interesting to note that we hold the key to how quickly we are sanctified by how willing we are to yield our hearts unto God and do whatever He requires of us.

In what is probably the deepest doctrinal section of the Doctrine and Covenants (section 93), the Lord begins by outlining five things a person must do to see His face: "Verily, thus saith the Lord: It shall come to pass that **every soul** who (1) forsaketh his sins and (2) cometh unto me, and (3) calleth on my name, and (4) obeyeth my voice, and (5) keepeth my commandments, **shall see my face and know that I am"** (numbers added).

Before analyzing those five prerequisites, it should be noted and emphasized that this is a promise to "every soul"—not just prophets and apostles. As we discuss each of the five elements, it will become readily apparent that none is outside the reach of a true seeker.

First, we must forsake our sins. Sin is a "willful transgression of the law." In the Book of Mormon we read, "Now they did not sin ignorantly, for they knew the will of God concerning them, for it had been taught unto them; therefore they did wilfully rebel against God" (3 Nephi 6:18). It is an interesting study in the law of Moses to see the difference between those who sinned ignorantly and those who knowingly sinned.

Start where you are. In times of sober reflection, it becomes apparent where you need to improve. If you are honestly at the point where you don't know where you need to improve, then the Lord has promised that He will show you: "Let us therefore, as many as be perfect, be thus minded: and if in any thing ye be otherwise minded, God shall reveal even this unto you" (Philippians 3:15; see also D&C 66:3).

Don't be overwhelmed. Take your weaknesses one at a time, and allow the Lord to make your weaknesses become strengths to you. The Lord promised, "And if men come unto me I will show unto them their weakness. I give unto men weakness that they may be humble; and my grace is sufficient for all men that humble themselves before me; for if they humble themselves before me, and have faith in me, **then will I make weak things become strong unto them**" (Ether 12:27).

Second, the Savior invites us to "come unto me." We know He resides in the celestial kingdom, which, because of its descriptive fiery nature ("But they reside in the presence of God, on a globe like a sea of glass and fire" [D&C 130:7]), our present condition would not allow us to be there. So where else could we go to Him? How about in one of His designated houses—the temple? As we strive to be worthy of our temple recommends and then attend the temple as often as possible, we increase the likelihood that we will see God.

Note the promise given in Doctrine and Covenants 97:15–17:

> And inasmuch as my people build a house unto me in the name of the Lord, and do not suffer any unclean thing to come into it, that it be not defiled, **my glory** shall rest upon it;
>
> Yea, and **my presence** shall be there, for I will come into it, and **all the pure in heart that shall come into it shall see God.**
>
> But if it be defiled I will not come into it, and my glory shall not be there; for I will not come into unholy temples.

While it is impossible to control everyone who enters the temples, it is very doable that we not be the ones who prevent such a transcendent spiritual experience for ourselves and others. Remember Doctrine and Covenants 67:10–14—it is a growing process to be prepared to see God, even in His temple.

Third, "call on His name." In today's rush-about world, it is too easy to neglect our prayers. Perhaps that has always been the case. The brother of Jared, whose faith enabled him to break through the veil and see the premortal Christ—first His finger and then His whole being—had neglected his prayers for an unspecified part of four years: "And it came to pass at the end of four years that the Lord came again unto the brother of Jared, and stood in a cloud and talked with him. And for the space of three hours did the Lord talk with the brother of Jared, and chastened him because he remembered not to call upon the name of the Lord" (Ether 2:14).

Failing to be diligent in establishing a prayer relationship with God is not just an oversight. It is a manifestation that we are being influenced by the devil.

> And now, my beloved brethren, I perceive that ye ponder still in your hearts; and it grieveth me that I must speak concerning this thing. For if ye would hearken unto the Spirit which teacheth a man to pray ye would know that ye must pray; for the evil spirit teacheth not a man to pray, but teacheth him that he must not pray.
>
> But behold, I say unto you that ye must pray always, and not faint; that ye must not perform any thing unto the Lord save in the first place ye shall pray unto the Father in the name of Christ, that he will consecrate thy performance unto thee, that thy performance may be for the welfare of thy soul. (2 Nephi 32:8–9)

Taking stock of our prayer habits could improve the spiritual quality of our lives and help us move closer to realizing the promise of the Lord to show Himself to us.

Fourth, "obey my voice." Perhaps you might say, "If I heard His voice, I would definitely obey." Ponder this verse: "Behold, that which you hear is as the voice of one crying in the wilderness—in the wilderness, because you cannot see him—my voice, because **my voice is Spirit**; my Spirit is truth; truth abideth and hath no end; and if it be in you it shall abound" (D&C 88:66).

Learning to listen more closely to the promptings of the Spirit is a lifelong quest. In today's troubled world it is difficult to turn off all media interruptions, disengage from all social interaction, and be still. However, that is exactly how the Lord said we would come to know Him: "Therefore, let your hearts be comforted concerning Zion; for all flesh is in mine hands; be still and know that I am God" (D&C 101:16).

In the Lord's preface to the Doctrine and Covenants He commands: "Search these commandments, for they are true and faithful, and the prophecies and promises which are in them shall all be fulfilled. What I the Lord have spoken, I have spoken, and I excuse not myself; and though the heavens and the earth pass away, my word shall not pass away, but shall all be fulfilled, **whether by mine own voice or by the voice of my servants, it is the same**" (D&C 1:37–38).

If I asked a Primary child how we hear God's voice, they would likely respond, "Scriptures, prayer, and prophets." We have addressed prophets and prayers, but note how reading the scriptures under the influence of the Spirit is God's way of introducing us to His voice:

> These words are not of men nor of man, but of me; wherefore, you shall testify they are of me and not of man;
>
> For **it is my voice which speaketh them unto you**; for they are given by my Spirit unto you, and by my power you can read them one to another; and save it were by my power you could not have them;
>
> Wherefore, you can testify that you have heard my voice, and know my words. (D&C 18:34–36)

Learning to differentiate between your own voice as you speak silently to yourself in your mind and the very distinctive voice that you hear while silently reading the scriptures seems more difficult for men than for women. I assume men hear a masculine voice as they think or speak with themselves mentally. Women, however, have often reported that it is man's voice that they hear while reading the scriptures silently to themselves. Several of the General Authorities have addressed this point. With practice everyone can "hear His voice" as He reads the scriptures to you.

Fifth, "keep His commandments." You cannot keep all of His commandments unless you know them. Without a regular scripture study program and a diligent study of the addresses of living apostles and prophets, it is impossible to remember all that God has commanded.

King Benjamin emphasized the importance of having the scriptures:

> And he also taught them concerning the records which were engraven on the plates of brass, saying: My sons, I would that ye should remember that were it not for these plates, which contain these records and these commandments, we must have suffered in ignorance, even at this present time, not knowing the mysteries of God.
>
> For it were not possible that our father, Lehi, could have remembered all these things, to have taught them to his children, **except it were for the help of these plates**; for he having been taught in the language of the Egyptians therefore he could read these engravings, and teach them to his children, that thereby they could teach them to their children, and so fulfilling the commandments of God, even down to this present time.
>
> I say unto you, my sons, were it not for these things, which have been kept and preserved by the hand of God, that we might read and understand of his mysteries, and have his commandments always before our eyes, that **even our fathers would have dwindled in unbelief, and we should have been like unto our brethren, the Lamanites**, who know nothing concerning these things, or even do not believe them when they are taught them, because of the traditions of their fathers, which are not correct. (Mosiah 1:3–5)

All of the written scriptures in the world will do no good unless we read, search, ponder, pray, and apply their teachings.

It is a true statement that we see what we look for. Korihor, one of the anti-Christ's of the Book of Mormon, deceived the people by saying: "Behold, ye cannot know of things which ye do not see; therefore ye cannot know that there shall be a Christ" (Alma 30:15).

Countering his argument Alma said:

> And now what evidence have ye that there is no God, or that Christ cometh not? I say unto you that ye have none, save it be your word only.
>
> But, behold, I have all things as a testimony that these things are true; and ye also have all things as a testimony unto you that they are true; and will ye deny them? Believest thou that these things are true? (Alma 30:40–41)

After Korihor arrogantly demanded another sign as proof that there is a God, Alma said: "Thou hast had signs enough; will ye tempt your God? Will ye say, Show unto me a sign, when ye have the testimony of all these thy brethren, and also all the holy prophets? The scriptures are laid before thee, yea, and **all things denote there is a God**; yea, even the earth, and all things that are upon the face of it, yea, and its motion, yea, and also all the planets which move in their regular form do witness that there is a Supreme Creator" (Alma 30:44).

Even from the very beginning God revealed to Adam: "And behold, all things have their likeness, and all things are created and made to bear record of me, both things which are temporal, and things which are spiritual; things which are in the heavens above, and things which are on the earth, and things which are in the earth, and things which are under the earth, both above and beneath: all things bear record of me" (Moses 6:63).

When we tune our spiritual eyes to look for evidences of God, virtually everything around us bears testimony of Him. After teaching a rather Spirit-filled seminary class many years ago, a student asked a question which is not totally appropriate: "Brother Bott, have you ever seen God?" My first inclination was to explain that such an experience would be far too sacred to share without divine permission. However, I shocked him, and myself, by saying, "Why yes, and so have you!" There was a noted silence as the class waited for me to explain my answer. I turned to Doctrine and Covenants 88:47–50:

> Behold, all these are kingdoms, and **any man who hath seen any or the least of these hath seen God moving in his majesty and power.**
>
> **I say unto you, he hath seen him**; nevertheless, he who came unto his own was not comprehended.
>
> The light shineth in darkness, and the darkness comprehendeth it not; nevertheless, the day shall come when you shall comprehend even God, being quickened in him and by him.
>
> Then shall ye know that ye have seen me, that I am, and that I am the true light that is in you, and that you are in me; otherwise ye could not abound.

I recounted experiences from my youth when jet airplanes were just starting to be used for commercial travel. When we would hear the sound of a plane overhead, we would lay on the grass and try to see it. Often, we could locate the vapor trail but didn't immediately see the plane. Because of the speed of the plane and the speed at which sound travels, the plane was often ahead of the vapor trail by a short distance. I explained that it would have been difficult, if not impossible, to locate the plane if it hadn't left a vapor trail.

That is also the way we learn to prepare ourselves to see God—by following the vapor trail of landmarks that He has left for us in virtually everything around us. If we are blind (as Korihor was) to those signs, then the same signs that prove to each honest seeker which leads them to God are misinterpreted and argued over (by scientists and others) as they try to explain the existence of all things without ascribing the wonders of eternity to an all-powerful Creator.

In closing this chapter, it is instructive to quote the Savior Himself as He prepared to leave His disciples:

> Yet a little while, and the world seeth me no more; but ye see me: because I live, ye shall live also.
>
> At that day ye shall know that I *am* in my Father, and ye in me, and I in you.
>
> **He that hath my commandments**, and keepeth them, he it is that loveth me: and he that loveth me shall be loved of my Father, and **I will love him, and will manifest myself to him.**
>
> Judas saith unto him, not Iscariot, Lord, how is it that thou wilt manifest thyself unto us, and not unto the world?
>
> Jesus answered and said unto him, **If a man love me, he will keep my words: and my Father will love him, and we will come unto him, and make our abode with him.** (John 14:19–23)

Let that be a goal that we work toward, not in a fanatical way, but in a daily, ever sanctifying way. Then when that day comes, we will know for sure that His promises are fulfilled.

POINTS FOR FURTHER CONSIDERATION

To see God, you must be sanctified (D&C 84:23)

> Now this Moses plainly taught to the children of Israel in the wilderness, and sought diligently to **sanctify his people** *that they might behold the face of God.*

To see God, you must have oridnances performed and power of the priesthood (D&C 84:20–22)

> Therefore, in the **ordinances** thereof [greater priesthood see verse 19], the *power of godliness is manifest.* And **without the ordinances**

thereof, **and the authority of the priesthood**, the *power of godliness is not manifest unto men in the flesh;* For **without this no man can see the face of God, even the Father, and live.**

Who shall see God? (3 Nephi 12:8; see also Matthew 5:8)

And blessed are all the *pure in heart*, for they shall **see God.**

Five hundred see the resurrected Christ (1 Corinthaisn 15:4–8)

And that he was buried, and that he rose again the third day according to the scriptures:

And that he was seen of Cephas, then of the twelve:

After that, **he was seen of above five hundred brethren at once**; of whom the greater part remain unto this present, but some are fallen asleep.

After that, he was seen of James; then of all the apostles.

And last of all he was seen of me also, as of one born out of due time.

Moses and seventy elders see God (Exodus 24:9–11)

Then went up Moses, and Aaron, Nadab, and Abihu, and seventy of the elders of Israel:

And they saw the God of Israel: and *there was* under his feet as it were a paved work of a sapphire stone, and as it were the body of heaven in *his* clearness.

And upon the nobles of the children of Israel he laid not his hand: also they saw God, and did eat and drink.

Isaiah sees the Lord (Isaiah 6:1, 5)

In the year that king Uzziah died I saw also the Lord sitting upon a throne, high and lifted up, and his train filled the temple." "Then said I, Woe *is* me! for I am undone; because I *am* a man of unclean lips, and I dwell in the midst of a people of unclean lips: for mine eyes have seen the King, the Lord of hosts.

Nephi and Jacob have seen the Lord (2 Nephi 11:2–3)

And now I, Nephi, write more of the words of Isaiah, for my soul delighteth in his words. For I will liken his words unto my people, and I will send them forth unto all my children, for he verily saw my Redeemer, even as I have seen him.

And my brother, Jacob, also has seen him as I have seen him; wherefore, I will send their words forth unto my children to prove unto them that my words are true.

King Lamoni sees Christ (Alma 19:13)

For as sure as thou livest, behold, I have seen my Redeemer; and he shall come forth, and be born of a woman, and he shall redeem all mankind who believe on his name.

Joseph Smith and Oliver Cowdery see Christ in Kirtland Temple (D&C 110:1–4)

The veil was taken from our minds, and the eyes of our understanding were opened.

We saw the Lord standing upon the breastwork of the pulpit, before us; and under his feet was a paved work of pure gold, in color like amber.

His eyes were as a flame of fire; the hair of his head was white like the pure snow; his countenance shone above the brightness of the sun; and his voice was as the sound of the rushing of great waters, even the voice of Jehovah, saying:

I am the first and the last; I am he who liveth, I am he who was slain; I am your advocate with the Father.

Joseph Smith and Sidney Rigdon see God and Christ (D&C 76:14, 20–24)

Of whom we bear record; and the record which we bear is the fulness of the gospel of Jesus Christ, who is the Son, whom we saw and with whom we conversed in the heavenly vision." "And we beheld the glory of the Son, on the right hand of the Father, and received of his fulness;

And saw the holy angels, and them who are sanctified before his throne, worshiping God, and the Lamb, who worship him forever and ever.

And now, after the many testimonies which have been given of him, this is the testimony, last of all, which we give of him: That he lives!

For we saw him, even on the right hand of God; and we heard the voice bearing record that he is the Only Begotten of the Father—

That by him, and through him, and of him, the worlds are and were created, and the inhabitants thereof are begotten sons and daughters unto God.

Many more examples are recorded in the scriptures but this is sufficient to demonstrate that God is willing to reveal Himself to mortals who apply His revealed formula.

8

ACHIEVING AND MAINTAINING PEACE

It may seem strange to start a chapter concerning peace by discussing how peace has been taken from the earth. However, a careful analysis for the reasons it has been taken away may also reveal elements of the formula for achieving and maintaining peace in our lives.

In the first section of the Doctrine and Covenants (which the Lord designates as "My Preface" [verse 6]), He reveals: "And again, verily I say unto you, O inhabitants of the earth: I the Lord am willing to make these things known unto all flesh; For I am no respecter of persons, and will that all men shall know that the day speedily cometh; the hour is not yet, but is nigh at hand, when peace shall be taken from the earth, and the devil shall have power over his own dominion" (D&C 1:34–35).

If the various media sources can be relied upon to tell things as they really are, peace has become an almost unheard-of commodity. But why has it been taken away? The Lord revealed: "I, the Lord, am angry with the wicked; I am holding my Spirit from the inhabitants of the earth. I have sworn in my wrath, and decreed wars upon the face of the earth, and the wicked shall slay the wicked, and fear shall come upon every man" (D&C 63:32–33).

While still walking the dusty roads of Palestine, the Savior said: "These things I have spoken unto you, that in me ye might have peace. In the world ye shall have tribulation: but be of good cheer; I have overcome the world" (John 16:33).

Just before this declaration, the Savior said: "Peace I leave with you, my peace I give unto you: not as the world giveth, give I unto you. Let not your heart be troubled, neither let it be afraid" (John 14:27).

In the Savior's mind there is a distinction between the peace the world gives and that which comes from Him. Merriam Webster defines peace as: "1: a state of tranquility or quiet: as a: freedom from civil disturbance. b: a state of security or order within a community provided for by law or custom." The Savior prophesied that the dictionary definition of peace would not exist before His Second Coming.

From the brief recital above, we can discern that the influence of the devil certainly is a destroyer of peace. A second point revealed from Doctrine and Covenants 63:32–33 is the withholding of the Lord's Spirit. That must be referring to the Light of Christ, for the world never has enjoyed the presence of the Holy Ghost.

Among many other things, the Light of Christ is "the light which shineth, which giveth you light, is through him who enlighteneth your eyes, which is the same light that quickeneth your understandings" (D&C 88:11) and is "the light which is in all things, which giveth life to all things, **which is the law by which all things are governed"** (D&C 88:13).

From those two verses in D&C 88 it seems apparent that the more we do that offends the Spirit or the Light of Christ, the more confused we become and the less we understand the things of God. Alma gave this sobering sequence of what happens when the Spirit withdraws:

> It is given unto many to know the mysteries of God; nevertheless they are laid under a strict command that they shall not impart only according to the portion of his word which he doth grant unto the children of men, according to the heed and diligence which they give unto him.
>
> **And therefore, he that will harden his heart, the same receiveth the lesser portion of the word**; and he that will not harden his heart, to him is given the greater portion of the word, until it is given unto him to know the mysteries of God until he know them in full.
>
> **And they that will harden their hearts, to them is given the lesser portion of the word until they know nothing concerning his mysteries; and then they are taken captive by the devil, and led by his will down to destruction. Now this is what is meant by the chains of hell.** (Alma 12:9–11)

With the prophesied peace being taken from the world, how do Christians, and particularly Latter-day Saints, keep that Spirit of peace with them? There is an inner peace that the ancient Apostle Paul pointed the way to obtaining:

> Rejoice in the Lord alway: and again I say, Rejoice.
>
> Let your moderation be known unto all men. The Lord *is* at hand.
>
> Be careful for nothing; but in every thing by prayer and supplication with thanksgiving let your requests be made known unto God.
>
> And the peace of God, which passeth all understanding, shall keep your hearts and minds through Christ Jesus.
>
> Finally, brethren, whatsoever things are true, whatsoever things *are* honest, whatsoever things *are* just, whatsoever things *are* pure, whatsoever things *are* lovely, whatsoever things *are* of good report; if *there be* any virtue, and if *there be* any praise, think on these things. (Philippians 4:4–8)

We would be wise to list what Paul taught:

1. Keep your focus on the Lord and look for the good, for the lessons from the wisdom you receive through the tribulations and trials you are enduring. Then rejoice in those very elements that move you closer to your goal of exaltation and give thanks in everything, even the bad things (see D&C 78:17–19; 98:1–3; 122:7–9).
2. Be moderate or temperate in all things. "And every man that striveth for the mastery is temperate in all things. Now they *do it* to obtain a corruptible crown; but we an incorruptible" (1 Corinthians 9:25).
3. "Be careful for nothing" is a biblical way of saying "don't be overly concerned about anything" but make your desires and requests to God.
4. Hold tight to those things which are true.
5. Be totally honest in your dealings.
6. Deal justly one with another.
7. Strive for things which are pure and undefiled.
8. Stay away from the gross and focus on what is lovely.
9. Good people still report good things. Stay with those things that are reported to be good.
10. Virtue is the very best of everything. Focus on only the best of activities.
11. Give and receive praise as it is justified. Look for the good and acknowledge it.

The more we know and understand about the Father's plan for us, the greater peace we can enjoy during the difficult times of worldly turmoil. Peter must have seen our day when he wrote: "**Grace and peace be multiplied unto you** *through the knowledge of God, and of Jesus our Lord*" (2 Peter 1:2; emphasis added). "Grace" is defined as "divine enabling power." If the knowledge of God and Christ and the knowledge that comes through Them gives us the power to not only survive but thrive through these deteriorating days preceding the Second Coming, then it seems logical that we take whatever time is necessary to dig deeper into our understanding of the plan of salvation and its authors.

Another key element bringing not only peace but prosperity is recorded in Alma 49:30: "Yea, and there was *continual peace among them, and exceedingly great prosperity* in the church **because of their heed and diligence which they gave unto the word of God**, which was declared unto them." Alma is teaching that not only listening to the word of God but giving consistent diligence to living according to the teachings brought the "continual peace . . . and exceedingly great prosperity" to the Nephites. Since God is an unchangeable being, if we follow their pattern, we can expect the same results.

The more one studies scriptural declarations about peace, the more it becomes evident that there is no other source of peace than in God and Christ. Even before the Church was restored, the Lord revealed: "*Learn of me, and listen to my words; walk in the meekness of my Spirit,* and you shall have **peace** in me" (D&C 19:23).

Isaiah, who spent much of his prophetic life viewing our day, recorded: "There is **no peace**, saith the Lord, *unto the wicked*" (Isaiah 48:22, see also Isaiah 57:21; 1 Nephi 20:22).

While struggling to have a sure testimony that Joseph Smith had the gold plates and that the translation was being done under divine supervision, Oliver Cowdery asked for some way of knowing that everything was legitimate. The Lord revealed: "Verily, verily, I say unto you, if you desire a further witness, cast your mind upon the night that you cried unto me in your heart, that you might know concerning the truth of these things. Did I not **speak peace to your mind** concerning the matter? What greater witness can you have than from God" (D&C 6:22–23)?

So many voices are vying for our attention. There are so many detractions keeping us on a continual detour—all of which end up at a dead end, that it is difficult to know when we are doing all we should be doing and heading in a direction that has divine approval. In one short verse the

Lord gives us the key to eliminate all confusion. In Doctrine and Covenants 111:8 He revealed: "And the place where it is my will that you should tarry, for the main, shall be signalized unto you by the **peace** and power of my Spirit, that shall flow unto you."

It seems like a contradiction that all "hell" can be swirling around us and yet we can enjoy that inner peace that passeth all understanding that Paul described. The adversary will always be there whispering in your ear that you are not living well enough to qualify for the celestial kingdom. Perhaps that is one reason he is called "the liar from the beginning" (see D&C 93:25). If we could only learn to trust the Lord, who knows us infinitely well, to manifest His approval or disapproval of us, we could divest Satan of that evil tool in destroying our peace and enjoyment of life.

There is no need to be in a constant state of agitation. The Lord said: "But learn that he **who doeth the works of righteousness shall receive his reward, even peace in this world** and eternal life in the world to come" (D&C 59:23). What are the works of righteousness? Attend to your church meetings, pay an honest tithe, keep the Word of Wisdom, attend the temple when possible, read the scriptures and talks from latter-day prophets and apostles, hold family home evening, pray always, and devote as much time as reasonable to serving others—none of which require super human strength.

As we identify evil, which the Lord told us He would help us do, and strive to eliminate it, He will "signal" His acceptance of our efforts, although we are still far from perfect, by the presence of His Spirit which speaks peace to our souls.

Where do you start on your quest to enjoy this peace? Right where you are. There is no value in wishing you were further ahead on your quest for perfection. There are two scriptures that come to mind suggesting that the Lord will help us not only get a good start but continue with us throughout our quest for perfection.

In D&C 66:3–4 the Lord revealed to William E. McLellin: "Verily I say unto you, my servant William, that you are clean, but not all; repent, therefore, of those things which are not pleasing in my sight, saith the Lord, for the Lord will show them unto you. And now, verily, I, the Lord, will show unto you what I will concerning you, or what is my will concerning you."

This promise is not of modern origin. The Lord revealed through Paul: "Let us therefore, as many as be perfect, be thus minded: and if in any thing ye be otherwise minded, God shall reveal even this unto you" (Philippians 3:15).

As you allow the Lord to work with you individually and constantly, you will discover that illusive "peace" that is increasingly absent in the world is abundantly present within your heart. Today can be the very day that changes your life, your outlook on life, and your enjoyment of the journey of mortality forever.

Just one final note that is addressed in greater detail in another chapter. In Doctrine and Covenants 88:125 (noting that the Lord designated all of Doctrine and Covenants 88 as "the Lord's message of peace" to us) the Lord said: "And above all things, clothe yourselves with the bond of charity, as with a mantle, which is the bond of perfectness and peace. Pray always, that ye may not faint, until I come. Behold, and lo, I will come quickly, and receive you unto myself. Amen" (D&C 88:125–126; read Moroni 7:45 for characteristics of charity).

Have I forgotten the one-word solution to all of our problems? Certainly not! Isaiah said it best when he wrote: "For unto us a child is born, unto us a son is given: and the government shall be upon his shoulder: and his name shall be called Wonderful, Counsellor, The mighty God, The everlasting Father, **The Prince of Peace**" (Isaiah 9:6). First, last, and always, Christ is the source of peace in this world and eternal life in the world to come.

9

SUCCESSFULLY HANDLING ADVERSITY

"Why, when I am trying so hard, do bad things happen to me?" That is a frequently asked question that seems to defy a reasonable answer. However, the Savior told us that mortality would not be smooth sailing. He said: "These things I have spoken unto you, that in me ye might have peace. **In the world ye shall have tribulation:** but be of good cheer; I have overcome the world" (John 16:33).

But why are trials, tribulations, and adversities necessary as part of our mortal life? In this, as in everything else, the Savior is the role model. Paul said of the Savior:

> Seeing then that we have a great high priest, that is passed into the heavens, Jesus the Son of God, let us hold fast *our* profession.
>
> **For we have not an high priest which cannot be touched with the feeling of our infirmities; but was in all points tempted like as *we are, yet* without sin.**
>
> Let us therefore come boldly unto the throne of grace, that we may obtain mercy, and find grace to help in time of need. (Hebrews 4:14–16; emphasis added)

What benefit does the Savior's experience of being tempted have for us? He explains that Himself: "Behold, and hearken, O ye elders of my church, saith the Lord your God, even Jesus Christ, your advocate, who **knoweth the weakness of man and how to succor them who are tempted**" (D&C 62:1; emphasis added).

There is great benefit in having someone who has gone through the same trial we are going through. The Savior knows the weakness of man and how, when, and where to give assistance so that the trials do not destroy us.

Then in turn, we can, with much greater understanding and empathy, reach out to others who are going through similar trials but are not blessed with the same understanding that we have. Paul wrote to the Saints in Corinth:

> Grace *be* to you and peace from God our Father, and from the Lord Jesus Christ.
>
> Blessed be God, even the Father of our Lord Jesus Christ, the Father of mercies, and the God of all comfort;
>
> **Who comforteth us in all our tribulation, that we may be able to comfort them which are in any trouble, by the comfort wherewith we ourselves are comforted of God.**
>
> For as the sufferings of Christ abound in us, so our consolation also aboundeth by Christ.
>
> And whether we be afflicted, it is for your consolation and salvation, which is effectual in the enduring of the same sufferings which we also suffer: or whether we be comforted, it is for your consolation and salvation. (2 Corinthians 1:2–6)

Many admiring and worshiping Christians humbly admit that following the Christlike example is an overwhelming challenge at best and a near impossibility when applied to life's challenges. However, there is a human example that we can emulate en route to becoming Christlike. That is Job.

Many people believe that Job was a mythological composite of human misery and suffering. Old Testament prophet Ezekiel and New Testament Apostle James believed he was a real person. Ezekiel attributes his reference to the word of the Lord: "The word of the Lord came again to me, saying, Son of man, when the land sinneth against me by trespassing grievously, then will I stretch out mine hand upon it, and will break the staff of the bread thereof, and will send famine upon it, and will cut off man and beast from it: Though these three men, Noah, Daniel, and Job, were in it, they should deliver but their own souls by their righteousness, saith the Lord God" (Ezekiel 14:12–14).

James charges each of us to use Job and the other prophets who suffered as an example: "Take, my brethren, the prophets, who have spoken in the name of the Lord, for an example of suffering affliction, and of patience. Behold, we count them happy which endure. Ye have heard of the patience of Job, and have seen the end of the Lord; that the Lord is very pitiful, and of tender mercy" (James 5:10–11).

Job is described as "a man in the land of Uz, whose name was Job; and that man was perfect and upright, and one that feared God, and eschewed [shunned or avoided] evil" (Job 1:1).

Job was not "perfect" as the Lord challenges us to be in Matthew 5:48: "Be ye therefore perfect **even as your Father which is in heaven is perfect**" (emphasis added). "Perfect" as used referring to Job and Noah meant "whole or complete." In other words, Job lived every commandment he was given and incorporated every principle of righteousness he was aware of.

Job's sufferings were not caused by God but allowed as a means of proving that his righteousness was genuine. What can we learn from his example? When stripped of worldly wealth, devastated by the loss of his children, compromised in his health, and encouraged to curse God and die, it was written of Job: "In all this Job sinned not, nor charged God foolishly" (Job 1:22).

Even his wife turned on him: "Then said his wife unto him, Dost thou still retain thine integrity? curse God, and die" (Job 2:9).

At that point we may have been sorely tempted to just give up, quit, and admit defeat. Adding insult to injury, Job's so-called "friends" taunted him, ascribing his troubles to his unrighteousness and claiming all these maladies were punishments from God.

The depth of Job's devotion to God is demonstrated in this one verse: "Though he slay me, yet will I trust in him: but I will maintain mine own ways before him" (Job 13:15).

Job sets a standard that we can work toward as we attempt to follow his Christlike example. How did it end with Job? "So the Lord blessed the latter end of Job more than his beginning" (Job 42:12).

There must have been a lot of suffering in those early years following the Savior's crucifixion. Paul outlined the sequence and benefits of enduring tribulation: "And not only so, but we glory in tribulations also: knowing that tribulation worketh patience; And patience, experience; and experience, hope: And hope maketh not ashamed; because the love of God is shed abroad in our hearts by the Holy Ghost which is given unto us" (Romans 5:3–5).

What seems to make trials more difficult to appreciate is that seldom do we see the benefits while we are going through the trial. However, if we really trust what the Lord has said, we can be faithful in our trials, even if we don't understand the purpose behind them.

The Lord revealed:

> For verily I say unto you, **blessed is he** that keepeth my commandments, whether in life or in death; and **he that is faithful in tribulation, the reward of the same is greater in the kingdom of heaven.**
>
> Ye cannot behold with your natural eyes, for the present time, the design of your God concerning those things which shall come hereafter, and the glory which shall follow after much tribulation.
>
> For after much tribulation come the blessings. Wherefore the day cometh that ye shall be crowned with much glory; the hour is not yet, but is nigh at hand.
>
> Remember this, which I tell you before, that you may lay it to heart, and receive that which is to follow. (D&C 58:2–5)

By keeping the commandments and being faithful in tribulations the reward is "greater"—greater than what? Greater than if, during the trials we stop keeping the commandments and are not faithful. It appears that the tribulations will come one way or the other. The magnitude of our reward depends upon our faithfulness.

The promised blessings will not be permanently postponed. The Lord said: "After much tribulation come the blessings" (D&C 58:4) and then admonishes us to remember the lesson He just taught: we cannot always (maybe seldom or ever) understand with our natural eyes the purpose of the trial, but God knows and will continue to work from behind the veil to give us experiences that will lead to our exaltation.

Later He added another promise to help us through our trials:

> Verily, verily, I say unto you, ye are little children, and ye have not as yet understood how great blessings the Father hath in his own hands and prepared for you;
>
> And ye cannot bear all things now; nevertheless, be of good cheer, for I will lead you along. The kingdom is yours and the blessings thereof are yours, and the riches of eternity are yours.
>
> And he who receiveth all things with thankfulness shall be made glorious; and the things of this earth shall be added unto him, even an hundred fold, yea, more. (D&C 78:17–19)

The Lord knows that we won't pass 100 percent of the tests ("ye cannot bear all things now" [D&C 78:18]), but one element of the formula that changes how we view our trial is the Lord's command to "be of good cheer" (D&C 78:8). The "nevertheless" seems to say, "In spite of your weaknesses and stumblings, and failings you need not become depressed or discouraged." Then comes the most wonderful promise: "For I will lead you along." The devil would try to convince us that because of our shortcomings, we are cut off forever from the presence of God and that He will not be there to help us in times of trouble. Just one more reason he is called "a liar from the beginning" (see D&C 93:25).

In fact, just the opposite is true. The Lord says, "The kingdom is yours." While "the kingdom" refers frequently to the Church, it also refers to the celestial kingdom. As the Lord continues His admonition He promises the blessings of either or both the Church or the celestial kingdom and adds the "riches of eternity," which undoubtedly refers to exaltation.

Another element of the formula for successfully passing the tests of mortality is that we learn to "receive **all things** with thankfulness." The promised result of being able to "make lemonade out of lemons" is that the "things of this earth shall be added" even more than a hundred-fold. If that refers to mortality, we can expect blessings here beyond our comprehension. Remember, however, that the ultimate destiny of the earth is to become our celestial kingdom (see D&C 88:25–26).

As impossible as it may seem while in the midst of our trials, we are commanded to keep a positive attitude and thank the Lord for the trial.

> Verily I say unto you my friends, fear not, let your hearts be comforted; yea, **rejoice evermore, and in everything give thanks;**
>
> Waiting patiently on the Lord, for your prayers have entered into the ears of the Lord of Sabaoth, and are recorded with this seal and testament—the Lord hath sworn and decreed that they shall be granted.
>
> Therefore, he giveth this promise unto you, with an immutable covenant that they shall be fulfilled; and **all things wherewith you have been afflicted shall work together for your good, and to my name's glory,** saith the Lord. (D&C 98:1–3)

"All things shall work together for your good" seems to be a promise while we are still here in mortality. "And to my name's glory" suggests that everything we endure will lead to our exaltation, which, according to Moses 1:39, is the "work and the glory" of God.

The idea of trials being for our eternal benefit must have a prominent place in our Heavenly Father's mind. In the midst of some terrible conditions, having been imprisoned for months, fed on sub-human food, nearly frozen, subjected to filthy language and behavior of the guards, and deprived from almost all association of close friends, the Lord revealed to Joseph Smith in Liberty Jail:

> And if thou shouldst be cast into the pit, or into the hands of murderers, and the sentence of death passed upon thee; if thou be cast into the deep; if the billowing surge conspire against thee; if fierce winds become thine enemy; if the heavens gather blackness, and all the elements combine to hedge up the way; and above all, if the very jaws of hell shall gape open the mouth wide after thee, **know thou, my son, that all these things shall give thee experience, and shall be for thy good.**
>
> The Son of Man hath descended below them all. Art thou greater than he?
>
> Therefore, hold on thy way, and the priesthood shall remain with thee; for their bounds are set, they cannot pass. Thy days are known, and thy years shall not be numbered less; therefore, fear not what man can do, for God shall be with you forever and ever. (D&C 122:7–9)

Perhaps we (as well as Joseph Smith and his fellow prisoners) need to be reminded that "the Son of Man (Christ) has descended below them all." We all want to be exalted with the Savior, but far too many want nothing to do with our personal Gethsemanes. Following his explanation of the Savior being tempted in all things, Paul records: "Though he were a Son, yet learned he obedience by the things which he suffered" (Hebrews 5:8). The same will be true for us—we will learn obedience by being faithful during our times of suffering.

How, then, are we to cope with the seemingly senseless trials? The Lord said: "Hold on thy way." In other words, don't get discouraged, don't quit, don't think about committing suicide, don't abandon your faith, and don't turn away from the commandments or the Church. The promise: "The priesthood shall remain with thee." The priesthood is the very power of God, the power by which the worlds were made and the power by which even the very elements are controlled. With that kind of power, all things are possible. Paul said: "I can do all things through Christ which strengtheneth me" (Philippians 4:13).

I love the next part: "Their bounds are set, they cannot pass." Whether "their" refers to those who persecute us or the trials we are going through, the promise is consoling. They are limited in the intensity and the duration. They are not able to go beyond what the Lord knows we (with His help) are capable of enduring. Often, we may think we can't take another step or endure for another minute only to discover years later and miles further that the Lord knew us infinitely better than we know ourselves.

Paul again adds to our understanding: "There hath no temptation taken you but such as is common to man: but God *is* faithful, who will not suffer you to be tempted above that ye are able; but will with the temptation also make a way to escape, that ye may be able to bear it" (1 Corinthians 10:13).

Then the final promise: "God shall be with you forever and ever." Isn't that what we are all striving for? To return to His eternal presence and live there forever. This formula seems to be able to be summed up in one short sentence: "Hang on and enjoy the ride."

POINTS TO PONDER

Psalm 139:7–12

Whither shall I go from thy spirit? or whither shall I flee from thy presence?

If I ascend up into heaven, thou art there: if I make my bed in hell, behold, thou art there.

If I take the wings of the morning, and dwell in the uttermost parts of the sea;

Even there shall thy hand lead me, and thy right hand shall hold me.

If I say, Surely the darkness shall cover me; even the night shall be light about me.

Yea, the darkness hideth not from thee; but the night shineth as the day: the darkness and the light are both alike to thee.

2 Corinthians 12:7–10

And lest I should be exalted above measure through the abundance of the revelations, there was given to me a thorn in the flesh, the messenger of Satan to buffet me, lest I should be exalted above measure.

For this thing I besought the Lord thrice, that it might depart from me.

And he said unto me, My grace is sufficient for thee: for my strength is made perfect in weakness. Most gladly therefore will I rather glory in my infirmities, that the power of Christ may rest upon me.

Therefore I take pleasure in infirmities, in reproaches, in necessities, in persecutions, in distresses for Christ's sake: for when I am weak, then am I strong.

Ether 12:27:

And if men come unto me I will show unto them their weakness. I give unto men weakness that they may be humble; and my grace is sufficient for all men that humble themselves before me; for if they humble themselves before me, and have faith in me, then will I make weak things become strong unto them.

Endure to the end to be saved (Matthew 24:13)

But he that shall **endure unto the end**, the *same shall be saved* (see also Mark 13:13; 1 Nephi 13:37; 1 Nephi 22:31; 2 Nephi 9:24; 2 Nephi 31:16; 2 Nephi 31:20; 2 Nephi 33:4; Omni 1:26; 3 Nephi 15:9; Mormon 9:29; D&C 14:7; D&C 18:22; D&C 20:25, 29; JST, Mark 13:13).

Endureth not—hewn down, not saved because of justice of the Father (3 Nephi 27:17)

And he that **endureth not unto the end**, the same is he that is also *hewn down and cast into the fire, from whence they can no more return, because of the justice of the Father.*

2 Timothy 4:5:

But watch thou in all things, endure afflictions.

James 1:12

Blessed *is* the man that endureth temptation: for when he is tried, he shall receive the crown of life, which the Lord hath promised to them that love him.

Doctrine and Covenants 121:7–8

My son, peace be unto thy soul; thine adversity and thine afflictions shall be but a small moment;

And then, if thou endure it well, God shall exalt thee on high; thou shalt triumph over all thy foes.

Doctrine and Covenants 136:31

My people must be tried in all things, that they may be prepared to receive the glory that I have for them, even the glory of Zion; and he that will not bear chastisement is not worthy of my kingdom.

Doctrine and Covenants 136:28–31

If thou art merry, praise the Lord with singing, with music, with dancing, and with a prayer of praise and thanksgiving.

If thou art sorrowful, call on the Lord thy God with supplication, that your souls may be joyful.

Fear not thine enemies, for they are in mine hands and I will do my pleasure with them.

My people must be tried in all things, that they may be prepared to receive the glory that I have for them, even the glory of Zion; and he that will not bear chastisement is not worthy of my kingdom.

10

OVERCOMING ADDICTIONS

For a God who knows the end from the beginning, it is impossible to believe that He was unaware of the challenges His children would face during the days leading up to the Second Coming. In fact, over 2500 years ago, Nephi, as he writes his concluding counsel to us, describes our day. He said: "They wear stiff necks and high heads; yea, and because of pride, and wickedness, and abominations, and whoredoms, they have all gone astray save it be a few, who are **the humble followers of Christ**; nevertheless, **they are led, that in many instances they do err because they are taught by the precepts of men**" (2 Nephi 28:14). Even the "humble followers of Christ" are not exempt from some of the pain of the latter days because they buy into the "precepts of men" rather than wholly accepting what the Lord has revealed.

It is always disappointing to hear of a Latter-day Saint therapist tell a struggling Saint that the addiction they have has no known cure and will be with them for the rest of their lives. I wonder if they have read what Paul wrote to the Saints in Philippi: "I can do all things through Christ which strengtheneth me" (Philippians 4:13) or what the Lord revealed through Joseph Smith in D&C 50:35: "And by giving heed and doing these things which ye have received, and which ye shall hereafter receive—and the kingdom is given you of the Father, **and power to overcome all things which are not ordained of him.**"

In order to truly conquer the flesh or the world, we must understand who we are and never allow what has happened (and is happening) to us to define us. This is an attainable goal the Savior gave to the Saints in this dispensation when He said: "For verily I say unto you, I will that ye should overcome the world; wherefore I will have compassion upon you" (D&C 64:2).

Who are you, really? Paul taught, "For in him we live, and move, and have our being; as certain also of your own poets have said, For we are also his offspring" (Acts 17:28). It is a given fact that offspring have the genetic capability of growing up to be like their parents; therefore we must view ourselves as having the genetic capability of growing up to be like God, our Father.

What happens to all mortals on earth came as a result of the Fall of Adam. Alma, in explaining the purpose of earth life and our need for a Savior, said: "Therefore, as the soul could never die, and the fall had brought upon all mankind a spiritual death as well as a temporal, that is, they were cut off from the presence of the Lord, it was expedient that mankind should be reclaimed from this spiritual death. Therefore, as they had become carnal, sensual, and devilish, by nature, this probationary state became a state for them to prepare; it became a preparatory state" (Alma 42:9–10). Let's make sure we get started right as we discover the Lord's formula for overcoming undesirable additions.

First, we are literal children of exalted parents with the capacity to grow and develop to become like them. **Second**, because of the Fall of Adam (or by nature—see Mosiah 3:16)) we become carnal, sensual, and devilish with the command, the time, and the resources necessary to overcome those weaknesses so we can again dwell in the presence of God. **Third**, God has provided all of the helps necessary to perfect ourselves—including a Savior who has made an infinite Atonement to cleanse us "after all we can do" (see 2 Nephi 25:23). **Fourth**, our progress toward overcoming the world is slowed or stopped because we embrace the "precepts of men" rather than relying wholly upon the grace (divine enabling power) of God.

Now for the formula: First, let's take a closer look at D&C 50:35: "And by giving heed and doing these things which ye have received, and which ye shall hereafter receive—and the kingdom is given you of the Father, **and power to overcome all things which are not ordained of**

him." There seems to be two prerequisites to receiving the divine power necessary to overcome all things that are offensive to God: 1) We must give heed to those things which we have received. That seems an apparent reference to canonized scriptures. 2) We must be willing to accept and act upon those things "which ye shall hereafter receive." That seems to indicate future scripture and prophetic counsel from our living leaders.

Although it can be challenging to keep abreast of everything the First Presidency and the Twelve Apostles are saying and writing, we can be assured that they are seeing not only world conditions but our individual challenges with vision reserved for those sustained as "seers" (see Mosiah 8:13–18). We need have no fear that the adversary will try to introduce some new addiction that will escape the knowledge of our God-ordained leaders.

Anyone who has tried to overcome an addictive problem and fallen back into the same black hole knows how discouraging it is and how hopeless it can make one feel. The Savior gave a parable that seems to have application. In Matthew 12:43–45 is recorded:

> When the unclean spirit is gone out of a man, he walketh through dry places, seeking rest, and findeth none.
>
> Then he saith, I will return into my house from whence I came out; and when he is come, he findeth *it* empty, swept, and garnished.
>
> Then goeth he, and taketh with himself seven other spirits more wicked than himself, and they enter in and dwell there: and the last *state* of that man is worse than the first. Even so shall it be also unto this wicked generation.

In order to cast out the undesirable habit or addiction, one must replace it with something desirable or the addiction will return with greater vengeance than previously experienced. The mind does not seem capable of having nothing on center stage. Either we consciously choose what act plays there, or the adversary is more than willing to provide one.

Likely there is not a person on earth who has reached the age of accountability who has not picked up some undesirable habit, addiction, or condition that needs to be overcome before we can comfortably dwell in the presence of God. There seems to be one place where the formula for overcoming addictive behavior is addressed in an easily understood, straightforward way. Let's read the scripture and then dissect it in order to make the direct connection. Can we agree that whoever has an addiction is in bondage? That will make these verses more easily understood.

> Behold what great destruction did come upon them; and also because of their iniquities they were brought into bondage.
>
> And were it not for the interposition of their all–wise Creator, and this because of their sincere repentance, they must unavoidably remain in bondage until now.
>
> But behold, he did deliver them because they did humble themselves before him; and because they cried mightily unto him he did deliver them out of bondage; and thus doth the Lord work with his power in all cases among the children of men, extending the arm of mercy towards them that put their trust in him. (Mosiah 29:18–20)

I suspect everyone would agree that if there wasn't an initial violation of a commandment or over-indulgence in an activity (drinking, drugs, pornography, gaming, Facebooking, and so on) that the present frustration of trying to reclaim your life wouldn't seem so impossible.

The next statement is sobering: "And were it not for the interposition of their all–wise Creator, and this because of their sincere repentance, they must unavoidably remain in bondage until now." The word "interposition" literally means to stand between two opposing or antagonistic foes. Perhaps this is one reason why the Savior said:

> I am the vine, ye *are* the branches: He that abideth in me, and I in him, the same bringeth forth much fruit: for **without me ye can do nothing.**
>
> If a man abide not in me, he is cast forth as a branch, and is withered; and men gather them, and cast *them* into the fire, and they are burned.
>
> **If ye abide in me, and my words abide in you, ye shall ask what ye will, and it shall be done unto you.** (John 15:5–7)

How many frustrated people battling addictions on their own have discovered the truth of what the Savior said: "Without Him, we can do NOTHING"? So how do we get Him to "interpose"? First, He says we must "humble ourselves." When the Lord accepted Solomon's temple He said: "If my people, which are called by my name, shall humble themselves, and pray, and seek my face, and turn from their wicked ways; then will I hear from heaven, and will forgive their sin, and will heal their land" (2 Chronicles 7:14). "Land" could very well be your heart, your mind, your body, your attitude, or anything else that needs fixing.

The first step in overcoming any undesirable weakness is to identify and admit we have a problem that needs more help than we have strength.

Then the Lord says we must repent. An entire chapter will be devoted to repenting and then recognizing when forgiveness has been granted. But the basic principle of repentance is to turn from doing wrong and start doing what is right.

The Lord reveals a direct cause and effect relationship of repenting (changing direction) and humbly seeking His help: "Because they cried mightily unto him he did deliver them out of bondage" (Mosiah 29:20). Another chapter will deal in more depth about how to get an answer to prayer. For the purpose of this chapter, a few scriptures and some "Points for Further Consideration" (at the end of the chapter) will suffice.

In D&C 6:36 the Lord directs: "Look unto me in every thought; doubt not, fear not." The adversary has his greatest success when he can turn our attention away from the Lord. In D&C 10:5 the Lord connects focusing on Him in prayer with overcoming temptation: "Pray always, that you may come off conqueror; yea, that you may conquer Satan, and that you may escape the hands of the servants of Satan that do uphold his work."

Following is the account of the serpent tempting Eve, which illustrates the necessity of not focusing our attention on that which the Lord has forbidden. Here is the account. We will look for applicable elements later.

> And he said unto the woman: Yea, hath God said—Ye shall not eat of every tree of the garden? (And he spake by the mouth of the serpent.)
>
> And the woman said unto the serpent: We may eat of the fruit of the trees of the garden;
>
> But of the fruit of the tree which thou beholdest in the midst of the garden, God hath said—Ye shall not eat of it, neither shall ye touch it, lest ye die.
>
> And the serpent said unto the woman: Ye shall not surely die;
>
> For God doth know that in the day ye eat thereof, then your eyes shall be opened, and ye shall be as gods, knowing good and evil.
>
> And when the woman saw that the tree was good for food, and that **it became pleasant to the eyes, and a tree to be desired to make her wise,** she took of the fruit thereof, and did eat, and also gave unto her husband with her, and he did eat. (Moses 4:7–12)

It is instructive to note that the tree of the knowledge of good and evil was not secreted in some obscure part of the Garden of Eden but was in the very "midst" or middle—likely a place where they had to pass every day. As the adversary always does, he tried to determine if the Lord had set any restrictions or put anything off limits. Naively the woman declared that they had freedom to eat whatever they wanted to. However, being totally truthful, she apparently viewed the fruit which had been forbidden and so declared it to Satan. He contradicted what the Lord said about dying and then held out to her the most desirable of all goals—to become like God (the very object of our existence). Verse 12 gives the real insight. It wasn't until the woman focused her attention on the forbidden fruit that it became "pleasant to the eyes, and a tree to be desired to make her wise" (Genesis 3:8).

So it is with every temptation that leads to the loss of our freedom to control our own destiny. If we expose ourselves frequently enough (sometimes once is enough!) and for a long enough period of time (again, sometimes a single exposure is enough to cause addition!), we will eventually give in and become a slave to the forbidden. By keeping our thoughts and prayers constantly focused on the Lord and His plan for our eternal happiness, we leave very little room for the adversary to trap us into his prisons.

Hence in his final counsel to his son Helaman, Alma instructs:

> Preach unto them repentance, and faith on the Lord Jesus Christ; teach them to humble themselves and to be meek and lowly in heart; **teach them to withstand every temptation of the devil, with their faith on the Lord Jesus Christ.**
>
> Teach them to never be weary of good works, but to be meek and lowly in heart; for such shall find rest to their souls.
>
> O, remember, my son, and learn wisdom in thy youth; yea, learn in thy youth to keep the commandments of God. (Alma 37:33–35)

Let's return to our evaluation of Mosiah 29:17–19. The final element of breaking out of bondage or overcoming addiction is "extending the arm of mercy towards them that put their trust in him." When we refuse to honestly believe that the Lord can and will "interpose" between us and our addiction, between us and the adversary, we block Him from giving us the relief we so desire.

It is most interesting to note the one phrase I have not emphasized yet: **"and thus doth the Lord work with his power in all cases among the children of men."**

One more circling around. If we want to break free of any undesirable addiction, behavior, attitude, or personality character, we must first realize that we are literally the offspring of divine parents and hence have all of the genetic DNA necessary to become like Them.

We are born into a fallen world and by nature (see reference below). We are brought into an environment where sin and evil predominate. That is not without divine approval. Ether 12:27 states: "And if men come unto me I will show unto them their weakness. **I give unto men weakness** that they may be humble; and my grace is sufficient for all men that humble themselves before me; for if they humble themselves before me, and have faith in me, **then will I make weak things become strong unto them.**"

Note carefully that the Lord revealed that "I give unto men weakness" in order to humble them. And upon conditions of humility, faith, and coming to Christ, *He* will make weak things become strong. What a wonderful time to put the Lord to the test by pleading for Him to interpose between us and our weakness. Turning away from those elements that have caused us to struggle (repenting), focusing our attention on the Lord (crying mightily to Him), trusting that He will extend His grace (divine enabling power) in our behalf, and freeing us by His almighty power from any and all "things that are not ordained of God" (D&C 50:35).

Will we still continue to struggle with the challenges of mortality? I suspect we will, but winning one major battle after another gives one the confidence that "[we] can do all things through Christ which strengtheneth [us]" (Philippians 4:13).

POINTS FOR FURTHER CONSIDERATION

James 4:10

Humble yourselves in the sight of the Lord, and he shall lift you up.

1 Peter 5:6

Humble yourselves therefore under the mighty hand of God, that he may exalt you in due time.

Alma 13:28–29

But that ye would humble yourselves before the Lord, and call on his holy name, and watch and pray continually, that ye may not be tempted above that which ye can bear, and thus be led by the Holy Spirit, becoming humble, meek, submissive, patient, full of love and all long-suffering;

Having faith on the Lord; having a hope that ye shall receive eternal life; having the love of God always in your hearts, that ye may be lifted up at the last day and enter into his rest.

Ether 12:27–28

And if men come unto me I will show unto them their weakness. I give unto men weakness that they may be humble; and my grace is sufficient for all men that humble themselves before me; for if they humble themselves before me, and have faith in me, then will I make weak things become strong unto them.

Behold, I will show unto the Gentiles their weakness, and I will show unto them that faith, hope and charity bringeth unto me—the fountain of all righteousness.

Doctrine and Covenants 104:82

And inasmuch as ye are humble and faithful and call upon my name, behold, I will give you the victory.

Doctrine and Covenants 112:10

Be thou humble; and the Lord thy God shall lead thee by the hand, and give thee answer to thy prayers.

Mosiah 3:16

And even if it were possible that little children could sin they could not be saved; but I say unto you they are blessed; for behold, *as in Adam*, or **by nature**, they fall, even so the blood of Christ atoneth for their sins.

Using Satan against Satan

Establish the practice that when you first notice a temptation, thank Satan for reminding you to initiate a strategy to counteract the temptation. It might be as simple as saying: "Thanks, Satan, for reminding me to read another chapter in the Book of Mormon, say a prayer asking for divine assistance, reread my patriarchal blessing, memorize a passage of scripture, call and talk to a spiritually strong friend, and so on."

Soon you will discover that Satan recognizes that tempting you in previously effective areas results in your taking steps away from his enslaving influence. He will stop tempting in that area and likely shift to another area where he might have more success. Give it a try and see if that tactic works for you!

11

GAINING EXALTATION

Because God's stated objective is to exalt His children (see Moses 1:39), it should be obvious that He would clearly outline the pathway back to His eternal presence. Although denied by a great many people, every person born on earth has the Light of Christ gifted to them. John testified: "That was the true Light, which lighteth every man that cometh into the world" (John 1:9). Lehi, in his final instructions to his family, said, "And men are instructed sufficiently that they know good from evil" (2 Nephi 2:5).

That initial knowledge, in many societies and among many individuals, is rapidly extinguished by the influence of the adversary and by the false traditions of men. "And that wicked one cometh and taketh away light and truth, through disobedience, from the children of men, and because of the tradition of their fathers" (D&C 93:39).

We will consider, however, a person who is born into a good Christian home and is taught to exercise faith in Christ. What does the progression on the pathway to perfection look like for that person?

The account of Cornelius (a gentile) receiving a witness or manifestation of the Holy Ghost before he was baptized is a New Testament example of what our missionaries witness on a daily basis. Luke records Peter as saying, "Can any man forbid water, that these should not be baptized, which have received the Holy Ghost as well as we?" (Acts 10:47).

There is a difference between a witness or manifestation of the Holy Ghost and the Gift of the Holy Ghost, which can only be received after baptism. Unless the individual acts on the witness and continues toward baptism, the Holy Ghost will not remain with them. In part this is what Joseph Smith explains in D&C 130:23: "A man may receive the Holy Ghost, and it may descend upon him and not tarry with him." Read Doctrine and Covenants 39–40 as a modern-day example of one who had a manifestation of the Spirit but then turned away—James Covill.

In Moroni 8:25 we begin to learn the prerequisites to baptism: "And the **first fruits of repentance is baptism**; and **baptism cometh by faith unto the fulfilling the commandments**; and the fulfilling the commandments bringeth remission of sins." Nephi also clearly pointed out the pathway to return to the presence of God. "Wherefore, do the things which I have told you I have seen that your Lord and your Redeemer should do; for, for this cause have they been shown unto me, that ye might know the gate by which ye should enter. For **the gate by which ye should enter is repentance and baptism by water**; and then cometh a remission of your sins by fire and by the Holy Ghost" (2 Nephi 31:17).

The Lord outlined seven requirements to qualify for baptism: "All those who (1) *humble* themselves before God, and (2) *desire* to be baptized, and (3) come forth with *broken hearts and contrite spirits,* and (4) witness before the church that they have *truly repented* of all their sins, and (5) are willing to *take upon them the name of Jesus Christ,* (6) having a determination to *serve him to the end,* and (7) truly *manifest by their works that they have received of the Spirit of Christ* unto the remission of their sins, shall be received by **baptism** into his Church" (D&C 20:37, emphasis and numbers added). This is a good standard to frequently assess whether we could still qualify for baptism today.

Receiving the Holy Ghost (which is frequently described as "baptism by fire") is the next step. Nephi outlined what we must do to qualify: "Wherefore, my beloved brethren, I know that if ye shall (1) *follow the Son, with full purpose of heart,* (2) *acting no hypocrisy and no deception before God, but with real intent,* (3) *repenting of your sins,* witnessing unto the Father that ye are (4) *willing to take upon you the name of Christ, by baptism*-yea, by following your Lord and your Savior down into the water, according to his word, behold, then shall ye receive the Holy Ghost; yea, then cometh the **baptism of fire** and of the Holy Ghost; and then can ye speak with the tongue of angels, and shout praises unto the Holy One of Israel" (2 Nephi 31:13, emphasis and numbers added).

The physical acts of baptism and confirmation, as essential as they are, alone do not constitute what the scriptures term as "being born again." Evidently Alma the Younger had been baptized some years before, but his behavior did not mirror what a converted saint would act like. After a life-changing interview with an angel and three days and nights of near-death repentance, he makes this statement: "And the Lord said unto me: Marvel not that all mankind, yea, men and women, and all nations, kindreds, tongues and people, must be **born again**; yea, born of God, *changed from their carnal and fallen state, to a state of righteousness, being redeemed of God, becoming his sons and daughters*" (Mosiah 27:25; emphasis added).

When Adam inquired of the Lord as to the necessity of repentance and baptism, the Lord answered by outlining a number of essential doctrine. Then in Moses 6:59–60 He says:

> That by reason of transgression cometh the fall, which fall bringeth death, and inasmuch as ye were born into the world by water, and blood, and the spirit, which I have made, and so became of dust a living soul, even so ye must be born again into the kingdom of heaven, of water, and of the Spirit, and be cleansed by blood, even the blood of mine Only Begotten; that ye might be sanctified from all sin, and enjoy the words of eternal life in this world, and eternal life in the world to come, even immortal glory;
>
> For by the **water ye keep the commandment; by the Spirit ye are justified, and by the blood ye are sanctified.**

We are baptized as a sign to heaven and earth that we will keep the commandments (see "Points for Further Consideration" at the end of the chapter). By the Spirit we are justified, and by the blood of Christ we are sanctified. There are two verses in Doctrine and Covenants 20 that point the direction we must take after baptism and receiving the Holy Ghost: "And we know that justification through the grace of our Lord and Savior Jesus Christ is just and true; And we know also, that sanctification through the grace of our Lord and Savior Jesus Christ is just and true, to all those who love and serve God with all their mights, minds, and strength" (D&C 20:30–31).

In order to benefit us, we must understand what those terms mean and how they help us progress toward exaltation. To be "just or justified" means to be without divine condemnation. In other words, the presence of the Spirit is God's way of testifying that we are going in the right direction and moving fast enough to eventually qualify for eternal life. In Doctrine and Covenants 111:8 the Lord revealed: "And the place where it is my will that you should tarry, for the main, shall be signalized unto you by the peace and power of my Spirit, that shall flow unto you." When we enjoy the presence of the Spirit, in spite of the fact we are far from perfect, we can know that we are doing as well as the Lord expects us to do given the amount of light and knowledge He has given us.

One of Satan's most successful tools is to discourage mankind into thinking they are lost forever because they are not totally perfect. The testimony of the Spirit should and must be more powerful than the lies of the adversary or our own judgment on ourselves. Too often Latter-day Saints condemn themselves unjustly because of perceived (or real) weaknesses when the Lord is testifying by the presence of His Spirit that we are doing all He expects of us at that time.

Sanctification, the process of purifying or cleansing, is just that—a process. The Lord defines the process of sanctification by saying: "Nevertheless they did fast and pray oft, and did wax stronger and stronger in their humility, and firmer and firmer in the faith of Christ, unto the filling their souls with joy and consolation, yea, even to the purifying and the sanctification of their hearts, **which sanctification cometh because of their yielding their hearts unto God**" (Helaman 3:35).

It is gratifying to know that we are the ones who dictate the speed and the extent of our own sanctification. The more we are willing to "yield our hearts unto God," the quicker the process proceeds. The more we stubbornly insist on doing our own thing and in our own way, the slower the process moves.

The Lord gives a great challenge and promise in Doctrine and Covenants 88:68: "Therefore, sanctify yourselves that your minds become single to God, and the days will come that you shall see him; for he will unveil his face unto you, and it shall be in his own time, and in his own way, and according to his own will." This promise will be considered later on.

Two verses help us understand that the Lord will help us know where He wants us to improve next and how we will know. In Doctrine and Covenants 66:3 the Lord says: "Verily I say unto you, my servant William, that you are clean, but not all; repent, therefore, of those things which are not pleasing in my sight, saith the Lord, **for the Lord will show them unto you.**" Then in Philippians 3:15 Paul explains: "Let us therefore, as many as be perfect, be thus minded: and if in any thing ye be otherwise minded, God shall reveal even this unto you."

Over the years we continue to identify and eliminate those characteristics and attitudes that are not Christlike. We identify them by the Lord revealing them unto us. We overcome them one at a time. It may be possible to determine our general place on the pathway to perfection by using Peter's teachings:

> And beside this, giving all diligence, add to your faith virtue; and to virtue knowledge;
>
> And to knowledge temperance; and to temperance patience; and to patience godliness;
>
> And to godliness brotherly kindness; and to brotherly kindness charity.
>
> For if these things be in you, and abound, they make *you that ye shall* neither *be* barren nor unfruitful in the knowledge of our Lord Jesus Christ.
>
> But he that lacketh these things is blind, and cannot see afar off, and hath forgotten that he was purged from his old sins.
>
> Wherefore the rather, brethren, give diligence to make your calling and election sure: for if ye do these things, ye shall never fall. (2 Peter 1:5–10)

We start with our faith in the Savior, the Father, and Their plan of salvation for us. That faith motivates us to rid ourselves of all ungodliness. Virtue is the very best of everything. So, the refining process includes our speech, our interaction with others, our recreation, our business dealings, and so on.

In order to understand more what Godlike qualities are, we search for more knowledge, each time refining our behavior to be more virtuous or Christlike. The Lord promises us: "God shall give unto you knowledge by his Holy Spirit, yea, by the unspeakable gift of the Holy Ghost, that has not been revealed since the world was until now" (D&C 121:26).

To our knowledge we add temperance. Extremes are seen as undesirable and we seek moderation instead.

As we realize that we are far from perfect ourselves and are still a work in progress, we extend that same tolerance to others demonstrating more patience with their weaknesses. As we begin to be more patient with others, we find ourselves becoming more Godlike ourselves.

To that more patient, Godlike behavior toward others, we add brotherly kindness, even extending tolerance and compassion toward those who are less than deserving. As we adopt a more Godlike attitude toward all of mankind, no matter what their current condition, we find ourselves growing in charity—the pure love of Christ. Is charity His love for us or our love of Him or our ability to love as He loves? Probably all three.

When we arrive or even approach that status, the revelatory windows of heaven seem to open, and we learn more how to become like Christ. He begins to share to a greater degree His knowledge with us.

The next step on our pathway to exaltation is what Peter ended with: "Wherefore the rather, brethren, give diligence to make your calling and election sure." Joseph Smith taught: "**More sure word of prophecy** means a *man's knowing that he is sealed up unto eternal life, by revelation and the spirit of prophecy, through the power of the Holy Priesthood*" (D&C 131:5). Although much more could be written about this step, perhaps this is sufficient for our study.

Somewhere along the line the Lord sees that the person has basically passed the tests of mortality and will not fall. At that point the promise given by the Savior to His early apostles can be fulfilled: "He that hath my commandments, and keepeth them, he it is that loveth me: and he that loveth me shall be loved of my Father, and **I will love him, and will manifest myself to him.** Jesus answered and said unto him, If a man love me, he will keep my words: and my Father will love him, and **we will come unto him, and make our abode with him**" (John 14:21, 23). This transcendent spiritual experience is often referred to as "the Second Comforter." The Savior reiterated that promise in Doctrine and Covenants 88:68: "Therefore, sanctify yourselves that your minds become single to God, and the days will come that you shall see him; for he will unveil his face unto you, and it shall be in his own time, and in his own way, and according to his own will."

More is written in the chapter on seeing God. For this chapter, we will conclude by citing what the Lord said to Joseph Smith (and is available to each of us): "For I am the Lord thy God, and will be with thee even unto the end of the world, and through all eternity; for verily I seal upon you your exaltation, and prepare a throne for you in the kingdom of my Father, with Abraham your father" (D&C 132:49).

Notably I have not talked about what is necessary to make an ordinance valid. I also have omitted addressing priesthood and temple ordinances—all of which will be addressed in the chapters on priesthood and marriage. A careful reading will reveal that performing the ordinances will actually be detrimental unless the person lives by the conditions of the covenants made. The sequence from spiritual infancy to exaltation has been outlined in enough clarity (hopefully) that you can see what the Lord requires to re-enter His presence.

POINTS FOR FURTHER CONSIDERATION

Baptism is a sign to God and man (3 Nephi 7:25)

Therefore, there were ordained of Nephi, men unto this ministry, that all such as should come unto them should be **baptized with water**, and this *as a witness and a testimony before God, and unto the people*, that they had repented and received a remission of their sins (see also Mosiah 18:13).

Just and True—those sealed by the Holy Spirit of Promise (D&C 76:53)

And who overcome by faith, and are *sealed by the Holy Spirit of promise*, which the Father sheds forth upon all those who are **just and true**.

Just man (Ezekiel 18:5–9)

Do that which is lawful and right, and hath not eaten upon the mountains, neither hath lifted up his eyes to the idols of the house of Israel, neither hath defiled his neighbour's wife, neither hath come near to a menstruous woman, and hath not oppressed any, but hath restored to the debtor his pledge, hath spoiled none by violence, hath given his bread to the hungry, and hath covered the naked with a garment; He that hath not given forth upon usury, neither hath taken any increase, that hath withdrawn his hand from iniquity, hath executed true judgment between man and man, hath walked in my statutes, and hath kept my judgments, to deal truly; he is **just**.

Just to live by faith (Galatians 3:11)

But that no man is justified by the law in the sight of God, it is evident: for, The **just shall live by faith** (see also Habakkuk 2:4; Romans 1:17; Hebrews 10:38; JST, Romans 1:17).

Justified because spirit is upon him (Moses 6:34)

Behold **my Spirit is upon you**, *wherefore all thy words will I justify*; and the mountains shall flee before you, and the rivers shall turn from their course; and thou shalt abide in me, and I in you; therefore walk with me.

Justified by belief (Acts 13:39)

And by him **all that believe are justified** from all things, from which ye could not be justified by the law of Moses.

Justified by the blood of Christ (Romans 5:9)

Much more then, being now **justified** *by his blood*, we shall be saved from wrath through him (see also Galatians 2:17).

Justified by a call from God (Romans 8:30)

Moreover whom he did predestinate, them he also called: and **whom he called, them he also justified**: and whom he justified, them he also glorified.

Justified by faith and works, through grace (Romans 4:16)

Therefore ye are **justified of faith and works, through grace**, to the end the promise might be sure to all the seed; not to them only who are of the law, but to them also who are of the faith of Abraham; who is the father of us all.

Sanctified in Christ by the grace of God (Moroni 10:33)

And again, if ye by the grace of God are perfect in Christ, and deny not his power, then are **ye sanctified in Christ** *by the grace of God*, through the shedding of the blood of Christ, which is in the covenant of the Father unto the remission of your sins, that ye become holy, without spot.

Sanctified by the blood of Christ (Moses 6:60)

For by the water ye keep the commandment; by the Spirit ye are justified, and by the **blood ye are sanctified** (see also John 17:19; Acts 26:18; Romans 15:16; 1 Thessalonians 4:3; 2 Thessalonians 2:13; Hebrews 10:29; 1 Peter 1:2; Alma 5:54; 13:11–12; 3 Nephi 27:20; Moroni 10:33; D&C 43:9; 84:33 ; 88:21; 88:35; Moses 6:59–60; Moses 7:45; JST, Genesis 6:62; JST, Genesis 6:63; JST, Genesis 7:52)

Sanctified by faith (Acts 26:18)

To open their eyes, and to turn them from darkness to light, and from the power of Satan unto God, that they may receive forgiveness of sins, and inheritance among them which are **sanctified** *by faith* that is in me.

Sanctified by the glory of God (Exodus 29:43)

And there I will meet with the children of Israel, and the tabernacle shall be **sanctified** *by my glory*.

Sanctified by God the Father (Jude 1:1)

Jude, the servant of Jesus Christ, and brother of James, to them that are **sanctified** *by God the Father,* and preserved in Jesus Christ, and called.

Sanctified by the Spirit (the Holy Ghost) (Romans 15:16)

That I should be the minister of Jesus Christ to the Gentiles, ministering the gospel of God, that the offering up of the Gentiles might be acceptable, being **sanctified** *by the Holy Ghost* (see also Alma 5:54; Alma 13:12; 3 Nephi 27:20; D&C 84:33).

Sanctified by the blood of Christ (Hebrews 10:10)

By the which will **we are sanctified** *through the offering of the body of Jesus Christ* once for all.

Sanctified by the law of my church (D&C 43:9)

And thus ye shall become *instructed in the law of my church,* and be **sanctified** *by that which ye have received,* and ye shall bind yourselves to act in all holiness before me (see also D&C 88:34).

Sanctified by the word of God and prayer (1 Timothy 4:5)

For it is **sanctified** *by the word of God and prayer.*

Sanctified (people in the celestial kingdom) (D&C 88:2)

Behold, this is pleasing unto your Lord, and the angels rejoice over you; the alms of your prayers have come up into the ears of the Lord of Sabaoth, and are recorded in the book of the names of the **sanctified,** *even them of the celestial world.*

Who is sanctified? (D&C 84:33)

For *whoso is faithful unto the obtaining these two priesthoods of which I have spoken, and the magnifying their calling* are **sanctified** by the Spirit unto the renewing of their bodies.

Sanctify yourself to be given eternal life (D&C 133:62)

And unto him that repenteth and **sanctifieth himself** before the Lord *shall be given eternal life.*

Sanctify yourselves (D&C 43:11)

Purge ye out the iniquity which is among you; **sanctify yourselves** before me (see also Leviticus 11:44; Leviticus 20:7; Numbers 11:18; Joshua 3:5; Joshua 7:13; 1 Samuel 16:5; 1 Chronicles 15:12; 2 Chronicles 35:6; D&C 43:16; D&C 88:68; D&C 88:74; D&C 133:4).

12

BEING A SUCCESSFUL MISSIONARY

Volumes have been written on missionary work (four by myself). This chapter is devoted strictly to elements designated by the Lord through His chosen prophets which have made certain individuals more successful at sharing the gospel than others.

With the privileges of discipleship comes certain responsibilities. The Lord said: "Behold, I sent you out to testify and warn the people, and it becometh every man who hath been warned to warn his neighbor" (D&C 88:81). Too often the adversary conjures up the mental image of angrily arguing with those who oppose the Church. However, in Doctrine and Covenants 38:41 our method of teaching is outlined: "And let your preaching be the warning voice, every man to his neighbor, in mildness and in meekness."

The challenge for summarizing a formula for missionary work is that the entire Doctrine and Covenants is the greatest missionary preparation manual ever written. Before the Church was organized, the Lord gave a list of qualifications for those desiring to share the gospel. The most famous section dealing with missionary work is Doctrine and Covenants 4 where the Lord said: "And faith, hope, charity and love, with an eye single to the glory of God, qualify him for the work. Remember faith, virtue, knowledge, temperance, patience, brotherly kindness, godliness, charity, humility, diligence" (D&C 4:5–6).

Those qualifications aren't just for missionary work. They are also characteristics that Peter said were necessary for making one's "calling and election sure" (see 2 Peter 1:5–10).

Hyrum Smith recognized the value of the revelations his younger brother, Joseph, was receiving and wanted to immediately share with others. The Lord outlined the sequence and the direction that effort was to take:

> Verily, verily, I say unto you, even as you desire of me so it shall be done unto you; and, if you desire, you shall be the means of doing much good in this generation.
>
> Say nothing but repentance unto this generation. Keep my commandments, and assist to bring forth my work, according to my commandments, and you shall be blessed. . . . Behold, I command you that you need not suppose that you are called to preach until you are called.
>
> Wait a little longer, until you shall have my word, my rock, my church, and my gospel, that you may know of a surety my doctrine. . . . Seek not to declare my word, but first seek to obtain my word, and then shall your tongue be loosed; then, if you desire, you shall have my Spirit and my word, yea, the power of God unto the convincing of men (D&C 11:8–9, 15–16, 21).

The entire section holds numerous keys for sharing the gospel.

To John Whitmer and Peter Whitmer Jr., in answer to their inquiry about what is the most valuable thing they could do, the Lord revealed: "And now, behold, I say unto you, that the thing which will be of the most worth unto you will be to declare repentance unto this people, that you may bring souls unto me, that you may rest with them in the kingdom of my Father" (D&C 15:6; 16:6).

To Joseph Knight Sr. and all who want to be on the Lord's first team in this last dispensation the Lord said: "Behold, I speak unto you, and also **to all those who have desires to bring forth and establish this work**; And no one can assist in this work except he shall be humble and full of love, having faith, hope, and charity, being temperate in all things, whatsoever shall be entrusted to his care" (D&C 12:7–8).

In many of the missionary oriented scriptures the stated prerequisite is desire. Without the desire to help spread the gospel, one becomes a burden to the work. So important is the spreading of the gospel that the Lord promises:

"Behold, I send you out to reprove the world of all their unrighteous deeds, and to teach them of a judgment which is to come. And whoso receiveth you, there I will be also, for I will go before your face. I will be on your right hand and on your left, and my Spirit shall be in your hearts, and mine angels round about you, to bear you up" (D&C 84:87–88).

Multitudes of missionaries can attest that they felt an increased closeness to the Lord while serving. All who diligently serve come to know the Lord better. Remember the Lord said, while serving His three-year mortal mission, "And this is life eternal, that they might know thee the only true God, and Jesus Christ, whom thou hast sent" (John 17:3).

Likewise, King Benjamin asked a probing question: "For how knoweth a man the master whom he has not served, and who is a stranger unto him, and is far from the thoughts and intents of his heart" (Mosiah 5:13)?

One might question how we are to find those who are being prepared to accept the gospel. The Lord said: "And ye are called to bring to pass the gathering of mine elect; for mine elect hear my voice and harden not their hearts" (D&C 29:7).

Our charge is not to convert the entire world but to make available the gospel to those who are prepared to receive it. Further answering the question "How will we recognize those who are prepared?" the Lord revealed: "And there are none that doeth good except those who are ready to receive the fulness of my gospel, which I have sent forth unto this generation" (D&C 35:12).

Few indeed would be those missionaries who are called who feel they are fully prepared and qualified. However, the Lord explains the caliber of those He calls and His reason for selecting them: "Wherefore, I call upon the **weak** things of the world, those who are **unlearned** and **despised**, to thrash the nations by the power of my Spirit; And their arm shall be my arm, and I will be their shield and their buckler; and I will gird up their loins, and they shall fight manfully for me; and their enemies shall be under their feet; and I will let fall the sword in their behalf, and by the fire of mine indignation will I preserve them" (D&C 35:13–14).

Missionaries are frequently asked if they have graduated from a theological seminary. It seems the Lord does not want people converted to the messenger but to the message. Multitudes of missionaries and their families can attest to the divine protection missionaries have received.

Perhaps it is of interest to note that occasionally a missionary is killed while serving. Although rare, the question is always asked why the Lord didn't protect them. Since our objective in teaching people is to help them gain eternal life, it is of value to note what the Lord said about those who die in His service: "And whoso layeth down his life in my cause, for my name's sake, shall find it again, even life eternal" (D&C 98:13). Just a side note: It is statically proven that missionaries have a significantly lower fatality rate than their non-missionary counterparts (*Deseret News*, Sept. 4, 2013).

From those early days of the Restoration, there has been a reluctance to open our mouths and share what we know. In Doctrine and Covenants 33:8–10, three times the Lord commands and promises: "Open your mouths and they shall be filled."

Almost a year and a half after the Church was restored, the Lord continued to urge the missionaries to share what they had received: "But with some I am not well pleased, for they will not open their mouths, but they hide the talent which I have given unto them, because of the fear of man. Wo unto such, for mine anger is kindled against them. And it shall come to pass, if they are not more faithful unto me, it shall be taken away, even that which they have" (D&C 60:2–3).

Part of the emerging formula on how to share the gospel comes with a list of promised blessings:

> Hearken, O ye who have given your names to go forth to proclaim my gospel, and to prune my vineyard.
>
> Behold, I say unto you that it is my will that you should go forth and not tarry, neither be idle but labor with your might—
>
> Lifting up your voices as with the sound of a trump, proclaiming the truth according to the revelations and commandments which I have given you.
>
> And thus, if ye are faithful ye shall be laden with many sheaves, and crowned with honor, and glory, and immortality, and eternal life. (D&C 75:2–5)

Just being away from home for eighteen months or two years does not constitute serving an honorable mission. First mentioned is that the Lord wants us to serve. Eight months after the Church was organized the Lord gave this commandment:

> And now this calling and commandment give I unto you concerning **all men**—
>
> That as many as shall come before my servants Sidney Rigdon and Joseph Smith, Jun., embracing this calling and commandment, shall

> be ordained and sent forth to preach the everlasting gospel among the nations—
>
> Crying repentance, saying: Save yourselves from this untoward generation, and come forth out of the fire, hating even the garments spotted with the flesh.
>
> And this commandment shall be given unto the elders of my church, that **every man** which will embrace it with singleness of heart may be ordained and sent forth, even as I have spoken. (D&C 36:4–7)

Through living prophets, we understand that not every young man may be able to serve. However, there are multitudes of young men who could serve if they would make the effort to be prepared, ready, and willing when the call comes.

The Lord is particularly sensitive about wasting time while serving as a full-time missionary. In section 75, He commands us not to idle away our time. Four months earlier He had admonished His missionaries: "Behold, they have been sent to preach my gospel among the congregations of the wicked; wherefore, I give unto them a commandment, thus: Thou shalt not idle away thy time, neither shalt thou bury thy talent that it may not be known" (D&C 60:13).

The command is definite that we are to teach the revelations of the Restoration and the commandments the Lord has given. In order to be qualified, we must start younger and be more diligent in studying the revelations and commandments. In the Lord's preface to the Doctrine and Covenants (D&C 1), He commanded: "Search these commandments, for they are true and faithful, and the prophecies and promises which are in them shall all be fulfilled" (D&C 1:37). Yet it was a rare treat when I served as a mission president to learn that an incoming missionary had even read the Doctrine and Covenants once. Many had not read (on their own) the entire Book of Mormon. How can we teach what we don't know?

Many of our young missionaries are looking forward to serving with a great deal of enthusiasm, as well they should be given that the Lord commanded:

> Lift up your heart and rejoice, for the hour of your mission is come; and your tongue shall be loosed, and you shall declare glad tidings of great joy unto this generation.
>
> You shall declare the things which have been revealed to my servant, Joseph Smith, Jun. You shall begin to preach from this time forth, yea, to reap in the field which is white already to be burned.

> Therefore, thrust in your sickle with all your soul, and your sins are forgiven you, and you shall be laden with sheaves upon your back, for the laborer is worthy of his hire. Wherefore, your family shall live. (D&C 31:3–5)

I have been a personal witness (both for myself and other missionaries) that the Lord really does loosen the tongue of His servants. Those who scoff at the "gift of tongues or the interpretation of tongues" (see D&C 46:24–25) need only observe how effectively our missionaries teach in foreign languages after a few months of practice, while others who are not missionaries struggle for years to gain a rudimentary understanding of the language.

Why teach the doctrine of the Restoration? The Lord told Joseph Smith more than a year before the Church was restored: "But this generation shall have my word through you" (D&C 5:10).

One of the unparalleled blessings promised for faithful missionary service is the remission of our sins—"your sins are forgiven you" (D&C 31:5 above). The Lord reiterated that promise in Doctrine and Covenants 62:3: "Nevertheless, ye are blessed, for the testimony which ye have borne is recorded in heaven for the angels to look upon; and they rejoice over you, and your sins are forgiven you."

Another great promised blessing is that because of your diligent service "your family shall live." Following up on that great promise the Lord revealed to Joseph Smith and Sidney Rigdon (and also to all of us) who were away from their families while they were serving a mission: "Verily, thus saith the Lord unto you, my friends Sidney and Joseph, your families are well; they are in mine hands, and I will do with them as seemeth me good; **for in me there is all power.** Therefore, follow me, and listen to the counsel which I shall give unto you" (D&C 100:1–2).

Certainly, we do not have all power, but the Savior does. So, we give all of our "heart, might, mind, and strength" (D&C 4:2) and He promises to use His unlimited power to bless our families. Not a bad trade.

In that same revelation (D&C 100) the Lord instructs and promises:

> Therefore, verily I say unto you, lift up your voices unto this people; **speak the thoughts that I shall put into your hearts,** and you shall not be confounded before men;
>
> For it **shall** be given you in the very hour, yea, in the very moment, what ye shall say.

> But a commandment I give unto you, that ye shall declare whatsoever thing ye declare in my name, in solemnity of heart, in the spirit of meekness, in all things.
>
> And I give unto you this promise, that inasmuch as ye do this the Holy Ghost shall be shed forth in bearing record unto all things whatsoever ye shall say. (D&C 100:5–8)

"Shall" is a condition that does not presently exist but will in the future. The "future," according to this block of scriptures, is "in the very moment" you need it. Likely all of us feel unprepared to meet the challenges of those who have studied for years to debunk and destroy the Church. However, the Lord promised His help when He said: "Again I say, hearken ye elders of my church, whom I have appointed: Ye are not sent forth to be taught, but to teach the children of men the things which I have put into your hands by the power of my Spirit; And ye are to be taught from on high. Sanctify yourselves and ye shall be endowed with power, that ye may give even as I have spoken" (D&C 43:15–16).

Perhaps the Lord was prefiguring our day when the need for senior missionaries is so great. He told Martin Harris: "Leave thy house and home, except when thou shalt desire to see thy family" (D&C 19:36).

To John Murdock, who had lost his wife and had entrusted his children to others, the Lord said: "And after a few years, if thou desirest of me, thou mayest go up also unto the goodly land, to possess thine inheritance; Otherwise thou shalt continue proclaiming my gospel until thou be taken" (D&C 99:7–8).

That may sound a little extreme for our time, but it certainly gives us insight as to how important the Lord sees missionary work.

The Lord is also aware that there are family and other circumstances that preclude full-time missionary service. He revealed: "And again, verily I say unto you, that every man who is obliged to provide for his own family, let him provide, and he shall in nowise lose his crown; and let him labor in the church. Let every man be diligent in all things. And the idler shall not have place in the church, except he repent and mend his ways" (D&C 75:28–29).

With the number of stay-at-home missions the Church has provided, there is no reason a couple or a person cannot serve in some way according to the health, the time, and the means the Lord has given us.

There are three promises given to missionaries who serve with all of the hearts, mights, minds, and strength which we should note: 1) "that ye may stand blameless before God at the last day"; 2) "that he perisheth not" (will not burn at the Second Coming); and 3) "bringeth salvation to his soul" (D&C 4:2, 4).

Some of the most famous verses in the restoration scriptures are found in D&C 18:14–16:

> Wherefore, you are called to cry repentance unto this people.
>
> And if it so be that you should labor all your days in crying repentance unto this people, and bring, save it be one soul unto me, how great shall be your joy with him in the kingdom of my Father!
>
> And now, if your joy will be great with one soul that you have brought unto me into the kingdom of my Father, how great will be your joy if you should bring many souls unto me!

Even at the peril of making this chapter too long, we must emphasize this vital lesson that Paul wrote to his "son in the faith," Timothy:

> Thou therefore, my son, be strong in the grace that is in Christ Jesus.
>
> And the things that thou hast heard of me among many witnesses, the same commit thou to faithful men, who shall be able to teach others also.
>
> Thou therefore endure hardness, as a good soldier of Jesus Christ.
>
> No man that warreth entangleth himself with the affairs of *this* life; that he may please him who hath chosen him to be a soldier.
>
> And if a man also strive for masteries, *yet* is he not crowned, except he strive lawfully.
>
> **The husbandman that laboureth must be first partaker of the fruits.**
>
> Consider what I say; and the Lord give thee understanding in all things. (2 Timothy 1–7)

For emphasis, consider these points contained in those verses:

Teach what you have been taught so others can continue to teach, thus causing a "snowball" effect carrying your influence far beyond those you can personally teach.

You will have very little power or influence unless you connect with that endless power supply—Jesus Christ.

Leave all your worldly cares behind when you go on your mission. Focus on sharing the gospel. Then you will be acceptable to the Savior and empowered by Him.

The next point (bolded above) is very important and will likely be the determining factor of how successful we are as missionaries. **You must first**

experience the gospel yourself before you can, with power, teach it to others. For example, how can you teach people to get an answer to prayer if you have never recognized an answer yourself? How can you teach people to repent and receive forgiveness of their sins if you have never repented and experienced the soul-thrilling effects of being forgiven?

From my early missionary days decades ago, I came to cherish Mormon's characterization of himself and those who serve: "Behold, I am a disciple of Jesus Christ, the Son of God. I have been called of him to declare his word among his people, that they might have everlasting life" (3 Nephi 5:13).

My hope is that we may all experience that joy that comes as we lose our lives in the service of the Master. One final note that summarizes what we must do to be effective missionaries: "But purify your hearts before me; and then go ye into all the world, and preach my gospel unto every creature who has not received it" (D& C112:28).

13

GETTING ANSWERS TO PRAYER

One of the most comforting lifelines given by God for the comfort and direction of His children during their mortal separation from Him is prayer. Although many people choose not to take advantage of that resource, many people do. However, being unaware of the elements constituting the formula for receiving answers to prayers, or the format the answers come in, many people are frustrated. Some people, failing to recognize answers they are receiving, stop praying all together.

This chapter is written in an attempt to increase our awareness of how Heavenly Father answers prayers. Undoubtedly you will be able to add additional elements of the formula, but this is at least a start.

In the year before the Church was restored, Oliver Cowdery had become acquainted with Joseph Smith. Having been convinced by a previous vision that Joseph had the plates from which the Book of Mormon was to be translated, Oliver desired to be part of the restoration process. He traveled from Palmyra, New York, to Harmony, Pennsylvania, where Joseph Smith was living. He arrived on April 5 and began acting as a scribe on April 7. Desiring a further witness that the enterprise he was engaging in was true, he requested Joseph to inquire of the Lord for a reconfirmation. Doctrine and Covenants 6 is the Lord's response. Herein lies the beginning of one of the most straightforward formulas the Lord has revealed.

Beginning in verse 14 the Lord said: "Verily, verily, I say unto thee, blessed art thou for what thou hast done; for thou hast inquired of me, and behold, **as often as thou hast inquired thou hast received instruction of my Spirit**. If it had not been so, thou wouldst not have come to the place where thou art at this time."

The first element of the formula is the Lord's declaration that He answers every sincere prayer. If we start our investigation with that foundational information, we are more apt to look for an answer.

The second element of the formula is that **answers to prayer always motivates the person to do something**. Oliver had been prompted to travel more than one hundred miles to meet the Prophet Joseph Smith. The Lord reiterated at the end of verse 14 that had it not been for the answer to his previous prayer, Oliver would not have made the arduous journey to meet Joseph Smith.

Third, **the Lord is responding to an inquiry**: "for thou hast inquired of me." I wonder if the Lord is reiterating what He revealed through the ancient Apostle James: "Yet **ye have not, because ye ask not**. Ye ask, and receive not, because ye ask amiss, that ye may consume *it* upon your lusts" (James 4:2–3).

The fourth element of the formula from Doctrine and Covenants 6:14 **should cause us to constantly look for our requested answer** "as often as thou hast inquired thou hast received instruction of my Spirit." Every sincere pray will be answered, but "it shall be in his own time, and in his own way, and according to his own will" (D&C 88:68). This appears to be the same as the first element, but instead of looking for an open vision (which the Lord uses to answer prayers at times), we must become more sensitive to the promptings of the Spirit.

The fifth element is found in verse 15: "Behold, thou knowest that thou hast inquired of me and **I did enlighten thy mind**; and now I tell thee these things that thou mayest know that thou hast been enlightened by the Spirit of truth."

Not only did the Lord explain that He had enlightened Oliver's mind but added the emphasis that he and all of God's children need to be constantly vigilant to the **enlightened thoughts** that come after we have offered a fervent, sincere prayer.

Perhaps Oliver thought he had received the entire formula and would never question again, but the Lord drove the point home in verses 22 and

23 of the same section: "Verily, verily, I say unto you, if you desire a further witness, cast your mind upon the night that you cried unto me in your heart, that you might know concerning the truth of these things. Did I not speak **peace to your mind concerning the matter?** What greater witness can you have than from God?"

The sixth element of the formula is "**peace to your mind**"—and it is labeled by the Lord Himself as the greatest witness from Him. While it is true that the devil could withdraw so that external conditions surrounding us would become calm or peaceful, the adversary does not have the power to bring "peace to the mind" or that internal peace that Paul referred to in Philippians 4:7: "And the peace of God, which passeth all understanding, shall keep your hearts and minds through Christ Jesus."

You may have wondered, as many have, how Joseph Smith on his way to Carthage Jail to be martyred could say, "I am going like a lamb to the slaughter; but I am calm as a summer's morning" (D&C 135:4). Once you have experienced that peace of mind that comes from God, knowing that Satan cannot duplicate it by merely withdrawing his influence, you begin to understand that all hell can be swirling around you and yet you can be at total peace.

At this point Oliver seems pretty confident that he understands prayer and how to recognize it. Then just two sections later he seems to be asking again for additional enlightenment. As the Lord promised, He reveals His will "line upon line, precept upon precept. Here a little and there a little" (see Isaiah 28:10, Isaiah 28:13; 2 Nephi 28:30; D&C 98:12; D&C 128:21).

In section 8:2–3 the Lord explains: "Yea, behold, I will tell you **in your mind** *and* **in your heart**, by the Holy Ghost, which shall come upon you and which shall dwell in your heart. Now, behold, **this is the spirit of revelation**; behold, this is the spirit by which Moses brought the children of Israel through the Red Sea on dry ground."

In this section and the one immediately following (D&C 9) the Lord takes the formula from an elementary level to an advanced course of instruction. The Lord had already introduced the necessity of being aware of what our minds are doing as we search for answers to prayers. Now He added the other domain: the heart. One might question the necessity of having both domains factored into the answer. Could it be that either you or the adversary can manipulate one domain or the other but neither you nor the adversary can manipulate both domains at once or it would negate the "spirit of revelation"?

It seems instructive that the Lord would refer to Moses using God's power to part the waters of the Red Sea so the children of Israel could pass through on dry ground. I have wondered how Moses even thought of the idea of parting the sea since it hadn't been done before. If these two verses are taken as an explanation, we can see that Moses likely mulled over his options given the Red Sea in front of them and the approaching armies of Pharaoh closing in from the rear. He may have considered using the pillar of fire and darkness to forestall the armies while the children of Israel marched around the sea. Not a very good solution since the Red Sea is huge. He may have thought of building rafts to float across the sea where the armies could not follow. Again, not a good solution given the scarcity of trees in that area. It may have been in frustration that he pondered the unthinkable—part the sea and walk through. However, whatever his thought processes were, when he came up with that solution, as impractical as it was to human logic, he knew by "peace in the mind" **and** the "burning of the bosom" that he had arrived at the solution God had in mind.

Recall also that the brother of Jared was required by the Lord to come up with a solution to the problem of crossing the great waters in darkness. The Lord had solved the most pressing problem (no air), but the brother of Jared was expected to become an active participant in finding a solution to the second problem (see Ether 2:9– 3:6).

Knowing of the impending failure of Oliver to translate, nevertheless the Lord gave him the privilege of trying. Oliver tried, commenced, failed, and then questioned why, when the Lord had promised that he could translate. The Lord used that failure to teach Oliver and all of us about a serious mistake we make in getting answers to prayers and then continuing to expand the formula for receiving an answer to prayers.

In Doctrine and Covenants 9:5 we learn that Oliver did commence to translate and then failed. "And, behold, it is because that you did not continue as you commenced, when you began to translate, that I have taken away this privilege from you."

In verse 7 the Lord explains: "Behold, you have not understood; you have supposed that I would give it unto you, when you took no thought save it was to ask me."

Too often, when approaching the most important decision of their entire lives (who to marry), many faithful LDS students would become frustrated that God didn't just tell them who to marry. It became evident that there was an eternal principle they had not fully understood: "whoever must eventually stand judgment for the decision must be free to make the decision." King Mosiah, in changing the form of government from kings to judges, made each person responsible for their own decisions: "Every man expressed a willingness to answer for his own sins . . . and they were exceedingly rejoiced because of the liberty which had been granted unto them" (Mosiah 29:38, 39). Too often many of the students I taught at BYU wanted the bishop, the stake president, their parents, their friends, or even me to tell them who to marry.

In verses 8 and 9 of section 9 the Lord clarifies the process for receiving His divine confirmation:

> But, behold, I say unto you, that you must study **it** out in your mind; then you must ask me if **it** be right, and if **it** is right I will cause that your bosom shall burn within you; therefore, you shall feel that **it** is right.
>
> But if **it** be not right you shall have no such feelings, but you shall have a stupor of thought that shall cause you to forget the thing which is wrong; therefore, you cannot write that which is sacred save it be given you from me.

This is so important that we will take a few minutes to analyze what the Lord revealed. First, He states that we must "study it out in our minds." What is that "it"? Whatever problem or plan we are facing. This is where we collect all of the input we can. We talk with experts, friends, parents, and Church leaders. We listen to talks, read books, consult the internet (with caution), or any other resource available. One possible way you can tell when you have gathered enough counsel is that it begins to become repetitive.

Then (and this is what is most often overlooked) **WE** must make a decision. With that decision fully and solidly in place, we must "ask [God] if it be right." What is that "**it**"? The decision we, through our own intellectual efforts, have determined is right. If our decision meets with divine approval, He will "cause that your bosom shall burn within you, therefore, you shall **feel** that it is right." Why didn't He say, "You will **know** that it is right"? Because, through your own intellectual analysis you have come to an intellectual decision that you are heading in the right direction. Now the Lord adds the affective or feeling part of the spirit of revelation (remember: the spirit of revelation is the mind *and* the heart).

What if the decision you came up with is not correct? Verse 9 says that you "shall have no such feelings" but you shall have a "stupor of thought that shall cause you to forget (or turn your heart away) from your incorrect decision. Students frequently asked what a "stupor of thought" is like. For me it is a breakdown in the logic I used to come to the incorrect decision. What was so clear and logical before now doesn't seem so clear and logical. But, most interestingly, my heart is turned away so that I lose interest in that which was very desirable before.

Undoubtedly one of the most frequently reiterated scriptural invitations is "ask and ye shall receive" (see D&C 4:7; Matthew 7:7; Luke 11:9–10; John 16:24; 3 Nephi 14:7; 3 Nephi 27:29; D&C 42:62; D&C 49:26; D&C 66:9; D&C 88:63; D&C 103:31; D&C 103:35; JST, Matthew 7:12). Surely a loving Heavenly Father would not give us that injunction that frequently without His being willing to answer our sincere prayers.

In the section named by the Lord "the Law of the Lord to the Church" (D&C 42), He expanded His invitation to ask Him for answers to some of life's greatest mysteries. In verse 61 He said: "If thou shalt ask, thou shalt receive revelation upon revelation, knowledge upon knowledge, that thou mayest know the mysteries and peaceable things—that which bringeth joy, that which bringeth life eternal."

Sometimes we may be frustrated because we have hit a mental wall and don't even know what to pray for. The ancient Apostle Paul gave this timely advice: "Likewise the Spirit also helpeth our infirmities: for we know not what we should pray for as we ought: but the Spirit itself maketh intercession for us with groanings which cannot be uttered. And he that searcheth the hearts knoweth what *is* the mind of the Spirit, because he maketh intercession for the saints according to the will of God" (Romans 8:26–27).

Perhaps an appropriate practice in such times of mental uncertainty would be to preface our prayers with a plea for the Spirit to make intercession for us so that we align our pleadings with the will of the Father.

While serving as a mission president, I was surprised at the number of humble, faithful missionaries who doubted that they had ever received an answer to their prayers. It may be enlightening to list some of the ways the Lord answers prayer. This list should be but a beginning point as we search the scriptures looking specifically at the variety of ways the Lord has communicated with His children in the past—and will continue in the future.

Recognizing how the Spirit impacts you

1. Gives feelings of love, joy, peace, patience, meekness, gentleness, faith, and hope (D&C 6:23, D&C 11:12–14; Romans 15:13; Galatians 5:22–23).
2. Gives ideas in the mind and feeling sin the heart (D&C 8:2–3).
3. Occupies the mind and presses on the feelings (D&C 128:1).
4. Helps scriptures have a powerful effect (Joseph Smith—History 1:11–12).
5. Gives good feelings to teach if something is true (D&C 9:8–9).
6. Enlightens the mind (Alma 32:28; D&C 6:14–15; 1 Corinthians 2:9–11).
7. Replaces darkness with light (Alma 19:6).
8. Strengthens the desire to avoid evil and obey the commandments (Mosiah 5:2–5).
9. Teaches truth and brings all things to remembrance (John 14:26).
10. Gives feelings of peace and comfort (John 14:27).
11. Guides to truth and shows things to come (John 16:13).
12. Reveals truth (Moroni 10:5).
13. Guides and protects from deception (D&C 45:57).
14. Glorifies and bears record of God the Father and Jesus Christ (2 Nephi 31:18; D&C 20:27; John 16:14).
15. Guides the words of humble teachers (D&C 42:16; D&C 84:85; D&C 100:5–8; Luke 12:11–12).
16. Recognized and corrects sin (John 16:8).
17. Gives gifts of the Spirit (Moroni 10:8–17; D&C 46:8–26; 1 Corinthians 12).
18. Helps to perceive or discern the thoughts of others (Alma 10:17; Alma 12:3; Alma 18:16, 20, 32, 35).
19. Tells what to pray for (Romans 8:26; 3 Nephi 19:24; D&C 46:28, 30; D&C 50:29–30).
20. Tells what to do (1 Nephi 4:6; 2 Nephi 32:1–5; D&C 28:15; Helaman 5:18).
21. Teaches us where to go (D&C 79:2; Helaman 5:18).
22. Helps the righteous speak with power and authority (1 Nephi 10:22; Alma 18:35).
23. Testifies of the truth (D&C 21:9; D&C 100:8; John 15:26).
24. Sanctifies and brings remission of sins (2 Nephi 31:17; Alma 13:12; 3 Nephi 27:20).

25. Carries truth unto the heart of the listener (1 Nephi 2:16–17; 2 Nephi 33:1; Alma 24:8).
26. Enhances skills and abilities (1 Nephi 1:1–3; Exodus 31:3–5).
27. Constrains or restrains (1 Nephi 7:15; 2 Nephi 28:1; 2 Nephi 32:7; Alma 14:11; Mormon 3:16; Ether 12:2).
28. Edifies both teacher and students (D&C 50:13–22).
29. Gives comfort (D&C 88:3; John 14:26).
30. Helps understand scriptures like never before (Joseph Smith—History 1:74).

There is power of people uniting in prayer. The Lord taught: "Again I say unto you, That if two of you shall agree on earth as touching any thing that they shall ask, it shall be done for them of my Father which is in heaven. For where two or three are gathered together in my name, there am I in the midst of them" (Matthew 18:19–20, see also D&C 6:32).

In our hurry-up world, too often we forget to pray. However, Nephi put a far more sinister cause on our neglect. He said:

> And now, my beloved brethren, I perceive that ye ponder still in your hearts; and it grieveth me that I must speak concerning this thing. For if ye would hearken unto the Spirit which teacheth a man to pray ye would know that ye must pray; **for the evil spirit teacheth not a man to pray, but teacheth him that he must not pray.**
>
> But behold, I say unto you that ye must pray always, and not faint; that ye must not perform any thing unto the Lord save in the first place ye shall pray unto the Father in the name of Christ, that he will consecrate thy performance unto thee, that thy performance may be for the welfare of thy soul. (2 Nephi 32:8–9)

Praying before performing the daily required tasks can add an eternal dimension to what could otherwise be routine. How many "good ideas" could be "great ideas" if tweaked by the Spirit after our fervent prayers?

In a rapidly darkening world, even the faithful Saints fear that we will be engulfed in the mire of an imploding world and wonder if we will be able to withstand the evil of the day. Another chapter will be devoted to this idea in some detail. But for here, Alma's plea for his people seems to be relevant to our discussion:

> But that ye would humble yourselves before the Lord, and call on his holy name, and **watch and pray continually, that ye may not be**

> **tempted above that which ye can bear,** and thus be led by the Holy Spirit, becoming humble, meek, submissive, patient, full of love and all long-suffering;
>
> Having faith on the Lord; having a hope that ye shall receive eternal life; having the love of God always in your hearts, that ye may be lifted up at the last day and enter into his rest. (Alma 13:28–29)

Add to this plea the admonition of the Lord in Doctrine and Covenants 10:5, which states: "Pray always, that you may come off conqueror; yea, that you may conquer Satan, and that you may escape the hands of the servants of Satan that do uphold his work."

Far from leaving us alone to fight against a seasoned adversary who has enjoyed more than six thousand years' experience tempting and destroying countless sons and daughters of God, the Lord has said: "Draw near unto me and I will draw near unto you; seek me diligently and ye shall find me; ask, and ye shall receive; knock, and it shall be opened unto you" (D&C 88:63).

Although we will discuss in detail forgiving others in another chapter, the Savior gave this powerful counsel:

> Therefore I say unto you, What things soever ye desire, when ye pray, **believe that ye receive *them*, and ye shall have *them*.**
>
> And when ye stand praying, forgive, if ye have ought against any: that your Father also which is in heaven may forgive you your trespasses.
>
> But if ye do not forgive, neither will your Father which is in heaven forgive your trespasses. (Mark 11:24–26)

POINTS FOR FURTHER CONSIDERATION

Ask anything according to God's will—He hears (1 John 5:14)

> And this is the confidence that we have in him, that, **if we ask any thing according to his will,** *he heareth us.*

Ask anything (anyone) in faith, receive answer (Mormon 9:21)

> Behold, I say unto you that **whoso believeth in Christ, doubting nothing,** *whatsoever he shall ask the Father in the name of Christ it shall be granted him; and this promise is unto all, even unto the ends of the earth* (see also verse 25).

Ask believing, and you will receive it if it's right (3 Nephi 18:20)

And **whatsoever ye shall ask** the Father in my name, **which is right, believing** that ye shall receive, *behold it shall be given unto you.*

Ask anything (expedient) will receive (D&C 88:64)

Whatsoever ye ask the Father in my name it shall be given unto you, **that is expedient for you.**

Ask anything (not expedient) will turn to condemnation (D&C 88:65)

And **if ye ask anything that is not expedient** for you, *it shall turn unto your condemnation.*

Ask in faith, believing, ye will receive (Enos 1:15)

Wherefore, I knowing that the Lord God was able to preserve our records, I cried unto him continually, for he had said unto me: **Whatsoever thing ye shall ask in faith, believing that ye shall receive in the name of Christ,** *ye shall receive it.*

14

CONTROLLING SELF AND CONFLICT RESOLUTION

Progressively from our birth in the pre-earth life, through those countless eons of time, to our appearance on earth, we have been learning and growing en route to becoming like our Heavenly Parents. Through exercising our agency in the premortal life, many became "noble and great ones" (see Abraham 3:22). Since noble and great are comparative terms, we must assume there some were not so noble and not so great.

In order to complete the curriculum designed for our exaltation, it was necessary to come to earth to get a body. Being born into a telestial or fallen world, and because our bodies are made up of the materials common to this earth, it stands to reason that our celestial spirits would find it challenging to control our telestial bodies.

Paul lamented over this battle between the spirit and the body:

> For I know that in me (that is, in my flesh,) dwelleth no good thing: for to will is present with me; but *how* to perform that which is good I find not.
>
> For the good that I would I do not: but the evil which I would not, that I do.
>
> Now if I do that I would not, it is no more I that do it, but sin that dwelleth in me. (Romans 7:18–20)

This is the first time in our eternal existence where we have had a physical body. Controlling it at all times and under all circumstances is no simple matter. Paul further explains: "This I say then, Walk in the Spirit, and ye shall not fulfill the lust of the flesh. For the flesh lusteth against the Spirit, and the Spirit against the flesh: and these are contrary the one to the other: so that ye cannot do the things that ye would" (Galatians 5:16–17).

Paul contrasts for us the challenges we face in the flesh and the fruits of the Spirit.

> Now the **works of the flesh** are manifest, which are *these;* Adultery, fornication, uncleanness, lasciviousness,
>
> Idolatry, witchcraft, hatred, variance, emulations, wrath, strife, seditions, heresies,
>
> Envyings, murders, drunkenness, revellings, and such like: of the which I tell you before, as I have also told *you* in time past, that they which do such things shall not inherit the kingdom of God.
>
> But the **fruit of the Spirit** is love, joy, peace, longsuffering, gentleness, goodness, faith,
>
> Meekness, temperance: against such there is no law. (Galatians 5:19–23)

We could devote the entire chapter to analyzing the pitfalls and the blessings outlined in those verses, but we will assume a wise reader will ponder and take whatever precautions are necessary to avoid the "works of the flesh" and strive for the "fruits of the Spirit."

Of all sins man can commit, the most grievous is denying the Holy Ghost—which is "unpardonable" (see Alma 39:5). Next is murder. Since the vast majority of mankind does not have the knowledge and experience to commit the unpardonable sin, the Savior gives particular note to that which leads to murder—which, for a member of the Church is "unforgiveable" (see D&C 42:19).

In the Sermon on the Mount the Lord helps us avoid the path that leads to our taking someone else's life.

> Ye have heard that it was said by them of old time, Thou shalt not kill; and whosoever shall kill shall be in danger of the judgment:
>
> But I say unto you, That **whosoever is angry with his brother** without a cause shall be in danger of the judgment: and whosoever shall say to his brother, Raca, shall be in danger of the council: but whosoever shall say, Thou fool, shall be in danger of hell fire.
>
> Therefore if thou bring thy gift to the altar, and there rememberest that thy brother hath ought against thee;

> Leave there thy gift before the altar, and go thy way; first be reconciled to thy brother, and then come and offer thy gift. (Matthew 5:21–24)

Also of note is that in delivering this sermon to the Nephites, the Savior omits the phrase "without a cause" (see 3 Nephi 12:22).

How are we to control our anger? Solomon said, "A soft answer turneth away wrath: but grievous words stir up anger" (Proverbs 15:1).

If we mistakenly think that a soft answer indicates we are weak, Solomon counsels further: "He that is slow to anger is better than the mighty; and he that ruleth his spirit than he that taketh a city" (Proverbs 16:32).

Holding on to a grudge or anger only provides fertile ground for the devil to plant his seeds of destruction in us. Paul taught the Ephesians, "Be ye angry, and sin not: let not the sun go down upon your wrath: Neither give place to the devil" (Ephesians 4:26–27).

Paul gives great counsel for controlling ourselves as we strive to become more Christlike: "Let all bitterness, and wrath, and anger, and clamour, and evil speaking, be put away from you, with all malice: And be ye kind one to another, tenderhearted, forgiving one another, even as God for Christ's sake hath forgiven you" (Ephesians 4:31–32).

Nephi saw our day and warned us against one of Satan's most effective tools: "For behold, at that day shall he rage in the hearts of the children of men, and stir them up to anger against that which is good" (2 Nephi 28:20).

Perhaps the word of the resurrected Savior to the Nephites is sufficient to cement the disapproval of the Lord against contention and arguments: "For verily, verily I say unto you, he that hath the spirit of contention is not of me, but is of the devil, who is the father of contention, and he stirreth up the hearts of men to contend with anger, one with another. Behold, this is not my doctrine, to stir up the hearts of men with anger, one against another; but this is my doctrine, that such things should be done away" (3 Nephi 11:29–30).

It should be relatively easy to detect when the spirit of contention is creeping into a conversation. The Spirit of the Lord withdraws immediately. What should one do if that happens? Stop immediately, recognize what is happening, and either change the discussion or disengage from the contentious situation.

James puts great emphasis on controlling one's tongue. "For in many things we offend all. If any man offend not in word, the same is a perfect man, and able also to bridle the whole body" (James 3:2).

The entire third chapter of James deserves our careful attention. However, we will limit ourselves to the following verses:

> Even so the tongue is a little member, and boasteth great things. Behold, how great a matter a little fire kindleth!
>
> And the tongue *is* a fire, a world of iniquity: so is the tongue among our members, that it defileth the whole body, and setteth on fire the course of nature; and it is set on fire of hell.
>
> For every kind of beasts, and of birds, and of serpents, and of things in the sea, is tamed, and hath been tamed of mankind:
>
> But the tongue can no man tame; *it is* an unruly evil, full of deadly poison. (James 3:5–8)

In today's world, there seems to be no shortage of people who want to "toot their own horn" or be puffed up with pride and self-importance. Paul warned: "For I say, through the grace given unto me, to every man that is among you, not to think *of himself* more highly than he ought to think; but to think soberly, according as God hath dealt to every man the measure of faith" (Romans 12:3).

Jacob, in the Book of Mormon, issued this caution which has particular application in our day of advanced learning: "O that cunning plan of the evil one! O the vainness, and the frailties, and the foolishness of men! When they are learned they think they are wise, and they hearken not unto the counsel of God, for they set it aside, supposing they know of themselves, wherefore, their wisdom is foolishness and it profiteth them not. And they shall perish. But to be learned is good if they hearken unto the counsels of God" (2 Nephi 9:28–29).

It is an easy matter to get drawn into endless arguments with people of corrupt minds. Paul cautioned: "He is proud, knowing nothing, but doting about questions and strifes of words, whereof cometh envy, strife, railings, evil surmisings, Perverse disputings of men of corrupt minds, and destitute of the truth, supposing that gain is godliness: **from such withdraw thyself**" (1 Timothy 6:4–5).

In today's world of affluence, the following caution helps us avoid becoming spiritually insensitive and thus putting our eternal destiny in jeopardy: "But wo unto the rich, who are rich as to the things of the world. For because they are rich they despise the poor, and they persecute the meek, and their hearts are upon their treasures; wherefore, their treasure is their god. And behold, their treasure shall perish with them also" (2 Nephi 9:30).

Alma 5 is one of the most thought-provoking chapters anywhere in scriptures. In it, Alma, the head of the Church in his day, asks dozens of questions urging the people to take inventory of where they stand. Here are just a few of those "personal priesthood interview" questions we might benefit from asking ourselves.

> Behold, are ye stripped of pride? I say unto you, if ye are not ye are not prepared to meet God. Behold ye must prepare quickly; for the kingdom of heaven is soon at hand, and such an one hath not eternal life.
>
> Behold, I say, is there one among you who is not stripped of envy? I say unto you that such an one is not prepared; and I would that he should prepare quickly, for the hour is close at hand, and he knoweth not when the time shall come; for such an one is not found guiltless.
>
> And again I say unto you, is there one among you that doth make a mock of his brother, or that heapeth upon him persecutions?
>
> Wo unto such an one, for he is not prepared, and the time is at hand that he must repent or he cannot be saved! (Alma 5:28–31)

Here is another important key to controlling self and controlling whatever situation you may find yourself in: "And every man that striveth for the mastery is temperate in all things" (1 Corinthians 9:25).

When striving to progress spiritually toward our goal of becoming more Christlike, we would be wise to take Peter's formula as a guide:

> And beside this, giving all diligence, add to your faith virtue; and to virtue knowledge;
>
> And to knowledge temperance; and to temperance patience; and to patience godliness;
>
> And to godliness brotherly kindness; and to brotherly kindness charity.
>
> For if these things be in you, and abound, they make *you that ye shall* neither *be* barren nor unfruitful in the knowledge of our Lord Jesus Christ. (2 Peter 1:5–8)

In taking control of ourselves, there seems to be a common thread of advice that comes from various prophets over a wide span of dispensations. Alma said:

> And now my beloved brethren, I have said these things unto you that I might awaken you to a sense of your duty to God, that ye may walk blameless before him, that ye may walk after the holy order of God, after which ye have been received.

> And now I would that ye should be humble, and be submissive and gentle; easy to be entreated; full of patience and long-suffering; being temperate in all things; being diligent in keeping the commandments of God at all times; asking for whatsoever things ye stand in need, both spiritual and temporal; always returning thanks unto God for whatsoever things ye do receive.
>
> And see that ye have faith, hope, and charity, and then ye will always abound in good works. (Alma 7:22–24)

Paul writes some of the most condensed advice of any prophet. In Romans 12:9–21, he writes:

> Let love be without dissimulation [sincere, unfeigned, real—footnote explanation]. Abhor that which is evil; cleave to that which is good.
>
> Be kindly affectioned one to another with brotherly love; in honour preferring one another;
>
> Not slothful in business; fervent in spirit; serving the Lord;
>
> Rejoicing in hope; patient in tribulation; continuing instant in prayer;
>
> Distributing to the necessity of saints; given to hospitality.
>
> Bless them which persecute you: bless, and curse not.
>
> Rejoice with them that do rejoice, and weep with them that weep.
>
> Be of the same mind one toward another. Mind not high things, but condescend to men of low estate. Be not wise in your own conceits.
>
> Recompense to no man evil for evil. Provide things honest in the sight of all men.
>
> If it be possible, as much as lieth in you, live peaceably with all men.
>
> Dearly beloved, avenge not yourselves, but *rather* give place unto wrath: for it is written, Vengeance *is* mine; I will repay, saith the Lord.
>
> Therefore if thine enemy hunger, feed him; if he thirst, give him drink: for in so doing thou shalt heap coals of fire on his head.
>
> Be not overcome of evil, but overcome evil with good.

Without question, the Lord is our Great Exemplar. At the conclusion of His visit to the Nephites He said: "Verily, verily, I say unto you, this is my gospel; and ye know the things that ye must do in my church; for the works which ye have seen me do that shall ye also do; for that which ye have seen me do even that shall ye do; Therefore, if ye do these things blessed are ye, for ye shall be lifted up at the last day" (3 Nephi 27:21–22).

And then as though to punctuate His commandment, He said: "Therefore, what manner of men ought ye to be? Verily I say unto you, even as I am" (3 Nephi 27:27).

One of the most rewarding times I have enjoyed over a lifetime is reading the scriptures (especially the four Gospels and 3 Nephi), looking specifically for how the Savior acted in all situations. Then, trying to follow His example, although my efforts fall forever short, the rewards are tangible and visibly observable.

I have marveled how no one was ever able to "make the Savior mad"—His anger as He cleansed the temple once at the beginning of His ministry and once near the end was a calculated move. He was in perfect control as He paused to braid a whip—hardly something a person who loses control because of anger would do (see John 2:15).

It is a challenge to determine when the Savior used harshness and was somewhat sarcastic in answering questions and when He demonstrated His infinite patience and compassion. To those who questioned in sincerity, He was ever compassionate. To those who attempted to entrap Him, His answers were cutting and sharp.

It is rewarding to identify His compassion for the one and yet how thoughtful He was in meeting the immediate needs of the hungry multitudes. It will require a lifetime and more to mine all of the elements of His Christlike character. The challenge "come follow me" is an invitation to open the revelatory windows of heaven and "learn of me, and listen to my words; walk in the meekness of my Spirit, and you shall have peace in me" (D&C 19:23). May we all be wise enough to take seriously His invitation.

15

RECEIVING FORGIVENESS FOR SINS

Feeling abandoned in a hostile world without any divine guidance is probably the most painful state a person could find himself in. While it is true that Adam's transgression resulted in both physical and spiritual death, Christ's Atonement provided the avenue by which both deaths can be overcome.

Does that mean we are destined to wander throughout our mortal life without divine guidance? Certainly not! However, Isaiah stated the reason for our individual separation from God: "Behold, the Lord's hand is not shortened, that it cannot save; neither his ear heavy, that it cannot hear: But your iniquities have separated between you and your God, and your sins have hid *his* face from you, that he will not hear" (Isaiah 59:1–2).

Paul stated the obvious when referring to all of mankind: "For all have sinned, and come short of the glory of God" (Romans 3:23).

In this dispensation the Lord gave four succinct reasons the Saints had not received pardon for their sins: "Behold, thus saith the Lord unto my people—you have many things to do and to repent of; for behold, your sins have come up unto me, and are **not pardoned, because** (1) you seek to counsel in your own ways. (2) And your hearts are not satisfied. (3) And ye obey not the truth, but (4) have pleasure in unrighteousness" (D&C 56:14–15, emphasis and numbers added).

This is a great place to begin to identify potential reasons we have not received forgiveness of sins. Once we are assured that these four reasons are not our roadblocks, we are prepared to proceed.

How can an individual overcome that spiritual death which forces a separation between us and God? Thankfully, the Lord has given the formula. Now we need to discover and apply it.

After praying all day and into the night, pleading for a remission of his sins, Enos received a revelation that his sins had been forgiven him. When he questioned how that was possible, the Lord revealed:

> And there came a voice unto me, saying: Enos, **thy sins are forgiven thee**, and thou shalt be blessed.
>
> And I, Enos, knew that God could not lie; wherefore, my guilt was swept away.
>
> And I said: Lord, **how is it done?**
>
> And he said unto me: **Because of thy faith in Christ**, whom thou hast never before heard nor seen. And many years pass away before he shall manifest himself in the flesh; wherefore, go to, thy faith hath made thee whole. (Enos 1:5–8)

There are many examples of individuals and groups receiving a remission of their sins, but perhaps one more will suffice to set us on a quest to discover the elements in the law of forgiveness. After delivering the message an angel had given him concerning the Savior, King Benjamin's people had the following experience:

> And now, it came to pass that when king Benjamin had made an end of speaking the words which had been delivered unto him by the angel of the Lord, that he cast his eyes round about on the multitude, and behold they had fallen to the earth, for the fear of the Lord had come upon them.
>
> And they had viewed themselves in their own carnal state, even less than the dust of the earth. And they all cried aloud with one voice, saying: O have mercy, and apply the atoning blood of Christ that we may receive forgiveness of our sins, and our hearts may be purified; for we believe in Jesus Christ, the Son of God, who created heaven and earth, and all things; who shall come down among the children of men.
>
> And it came to pass that after they had spoken these words the Spirit of the Lord came upon them, and they were filled with joy, having received a remission of their sins, and having peace of conscience, because of the

> exceeding faith which they had in Jesus Christ who should come, according to the words which king Benjamin had spoken unto them. (Mosiah 4:1–3)

Note the beginning elements of this marvelous formula: First they recognized the contrary position that their sins had placed them in with God. Next, they recognized that they needed divine help to overcome their fallen condition. Then they pleaded that the atoning blood of Christ be applied to them that they could be forgiven of their sins and purified so the negative prospects of being eternally excluded from God's presence would not be realized. The result was that the Spirit of the Lord came upon them, giving them peace of conscience "because of the Spirit of the Lord Omnipotent, which has wrought a mighty change in us, or in our hearts, that we have no more disposition to do evil, but to do good continually" (Mosiah 5:2). The immersion in the Spirit erased any desire to do evil and put them on a course of desiring to do good continually.

Hopefully, all of us have had experiences when the Spirit was with us in an almost tangible manifestation. Reflect on how you felt at that time. I presume you had no disposition to do evil but were highly motivated to do good. It isn't until the presence of the Spirit wanes that the temptations of the devil are more difficult to resist.

How can a person determine whether he has repented of his sins? The Lord revealed: "Behold, he who has repented of his sins, the same is forgiven, and I, the Lord, remember them no more. By this ye may know if a man repenteth of his sins—behold, he will confess them and forsake them" (D&C 58:42–43).

First a person must acknowledge to himself that he has sinned. Next, confession is to the Lord, to the offended person, and where major sin is involved, to the authorized priesthood leader. Attending the confession, one can know if the level of confession is acceptable to the Lord by the lightening of the burden of sin. Often it is almost a visible reaction.

Now a word of caution. Once that experience has happened and the burden has been lifted, know for sure that the adversary will try to convince you that you are just making it up in your mind and that you need to confess again. People who are sincere in wanting to be forgiven run the risk of falling into the trap of "confessionitis." Confess, have the burden lightened, listen to Satan's lies that they left one element out, confess again, have the burden lightened, listen to Satan again tell them their confession was not complete or adequate, confess again. The cycle is endless.

Once you have had the burden lifted, refuse to listen to Satan's lies. Move confidently ahead in your diligent effort to forsake your sins.

For anyone who has attempted numerous times to forsake (quit, abandon) sin and has fallen back into transgression, discouragement and despair are common companions. A feeling of helplessness and adopting a "what's the use" attitude is difficult to avoid. However, the Lord knew that His people would continue to struggle with weaknesses until they finally succeeded in arriving where King Benjamin's people were. He therefore revealed:

> Therefore I say unto you, Go; and whosoever transgresseth against me, him shall ye judge according to the sins which he has committed; and if he confess his sins before thee and me, and repenteth in the sincerity of his heart, him shall ye forgive, and I will forgive him also.
>
> Yea, and **as often as my people repent will I forgive them their trespasses against me.**
>
> And ye shall also forgive one another your trespasses; for verily I say unto you, he that forgiveth not his neighbor's trespasses when he says that he repents, the same hath brought himself under condemnation. (Mosiah 26:29–31)

As long as we keep trying, the Lord is willing to continue to forgive us and help us gain strength to permanently overcome. However, another element of the formula is mentioned here but reiterated numerous times in the scriptures. That is our responsibility to forgive others of the wrongs they do to us.

Combining answer to prayers with forgiveness of our sins the Savior taught:

> Therefore I say unto you, What things soever ye desire, when ye pray, believe that ye receive *them*, and ye shall have *them*.
>
> And when ye stand praying, forgive, if ye have ought against any: that your Father also which is in heaven may forgive you your trespasses.
>
> But if ye do not forgive, neither will your Father which is in heaven forgive your trespasses. (Mark 11:24–26)

The most forceful requirement to forgive others is found in Doctrine and Covenants 64:8–11, which contains instructions of several of the elements of the law of forgiveness:

> My disciples, in days of old, sought occasion against one another and forgave not one another in their hearts; and for this evil they were afflicted and sorely chastened.

> Wherefore, I say unto you, that ye ought to forgive one another; for he that forgiveth not his brother his trespasses standeth condemned before the Lord; for there remaineth in him the greater sin.
>
> I, the Lord, will forgive whom I will forgive, but of you it is required to forgive all men.
>
> And ye ought to say in your hearts—let God judge between me and thee, and reward thee according to thy deeds.

These points are so critical we need to take the time to list them. In verse 8 the Lord informs the Latter-day Saints that His disciples who travelled with Him during His mortal ministry didn't always get along. Although lip service was given that they forgave one another, they still harbored ill feelings in their hearts. The result was that they were "afflicted and sorely chastened" (D&C 64:8). Saying we forgive but continuing to hold hard feelings against one who has wronged us will bring the same afflictions and chastisements as they received anciently—truth doesn't change.

Verse 9 is difficult to understand if serious sins have been committed against you. However, a closer look may provide at least a partial explanation. The Lord sees the end from the beginning. He has no veil of forgetfulness between Him and the transgressor. He sees what has happened to him up to that point in his life with all of the contributing factors. He sees the state of mind the person was in when he transgressed. He sees what will happen to him in the future as a direct result of his transgression. He knows the immediate and eternal consequences of his transgression. He knows when he will have qualified to receive divine forgiveness. We don't know any of those things. So, when we refuse to forgive, we place ourselves in the place of the Lord, which by scriptural definition is blasphemy (see John 10:33), a greater sin than anything a person can do to us.

Verse 10 explains that the Lord holds the key to forgiveness—not us. It is a divine requirement that we forgive all men. But how are we to do that? He explains in verse 11: "Leave judgment in the hands of God and rest assured that the divine scales of justice will be perfectly balanced—by the Lord. He really doesn't need our help in meting out punishment. Life becomes so much simpler and enjoyable if we follow the Lord's admonition revealed in D&C 82:23: "Leave judgment alone with me, for it is mine and I will repay. Peace be with you; my blessings continue with you."

We could perhaps end this discussion here, but over a lifetime of teaching I have seen the struggle people have in forgiving themselves.

Although numerous talks have been given in general conference by apostles and prophets, yet the message seems to have a difficult time making it into the heads and hearts of the people.

Let's look at what the formula says. In Romans 6:3–6 Paul explains:

> Know ye not, that so many of us as were baptized into Jesus Christ were baptized into his death?
>
> Therefore we are buried with him by baptism into death: that like as Christ was raised up from the dead by the glory of the Father, even so we also should walk in newness of life.
>
> For if we have been planted together in the likeness of his death, we shall be also *in the likeness* of *his* resurrection:
>
> **Knowing this, that our old man is crucified with *him*, that the body of sin might be destroyed**, that henceforth we should not serve sin.

Since the weekly partaking of the sacrament is renewing of the baptismal covenant, based upon our sincere repentance, weekly we can rid ourselves of the "old man of sin." Alma the Younger, after three days and nights of repenting in pain that brought him near to death, said:

> For, said he, I have repented of my sins, and have been redeemed of the Lord; behold I am born of the Spirit.
>
> And the Lord said unto me: Marvel not that all mankind, yea, men and women, all nations, kindreds, tongues and people, **must be born again; yea, born of God**, changed from their carnal and fallen state, to a state of righteousness, being redeemed of God, becoming his sons and daughters;
>
> And **thus they become new creatures**; and unless they do this, they can in nowise inherit the kingdom of God.
>
> I say unto you, unless this be the case, they must be cast off; and this I know, because I was like to be cast off.
>
> Nevertheless, after wading through much tribulation, repenting nigh unto death, the Lord in mercy hath seen fit to snatch me out of an everlasting burning, and I am born of God.
>
> My soul hath been redeemed from the gall of bitterness and bonds of iniquity. I was in the darkest abyss; but now I behold the marvelous light of God. My soul was racked with eternal torment; but I am snatched, and my soul is pained no more. (Mosiah 27:24–29)

If true repentance results in our "crucifying the old man of sin" and becoming "a new creature in Christ," then are we still the old, sinful person?

As a young man I remember a Sunday School teacher driving nails into a board while explaining that each nail represented sins we commit. Then he extracted the nails, explaining that this is what repentance did. All of us recognize now that the demonstration is flawed in that the nail holes still remain. Is that really what repentance does? Even if we fill the holes with putty and shellac the board, does that truly represent what the Atonement does for us? Or does the Atonement give us a brand-new board?

I assume we all recognize that the Atonement gives us a brand-new board. Then why would we continue to make the near-fatal mistake that Lot's wife did in looking back (see Genesis 19:26)? The Lord Himself cautioned us to "remember Lot's wife" (Luke 17:32).

Too often, when inappropriately questioned about past sins, the repentant, new creature in Christ—out of a misunderstanding of what true honest repentance does—re-identifies himself with the crucified "old man of sin." In so doing, are we not denying the efficacy of the Atonement of Christ in making us new creatures?

Over a lifetime of attending lectures, talks, youth conferences, and symposia, I have heard speakers refer to their past sins in an attempt to help their audience avoid similar sins. I have also witnessed the "backfire" effects on more than one occasion. The young listener looks at the presenter and says to himself, "He turned out okay. If he can sin and still be that good, maybe I can do the same!" Hidden from the young person is the pain and suffering, the remorse and regret the speaker went through before becoming a "new creature in Christ." Also unnoted are the number of individuals who decided to take that sinful path and never made it back and are still wandering on forbidden paths, experiencing the natural consequences of their poor choices, and living without the companionship of the Holy Ghost in their lives.

A second "backfire" frequently observed when the speaker refers to his sinful past is the reaction of the audience in "tuning him out" because they see him as hypocritical—teaching one thing and having lived something entirely opposite.

One may question why Alma the Younger recounted his sinful experience to his sons as part of his final instruction. Even though he referred to the incident, the details of his state which is merely mentioned as his being "the vilest of sinners" (see Mosiah 28:4) is not mentioned. His case was so widely known that it would have served no useful purpose to ignore that it happened. But one cannot deny the change that took place in his life. He was likely one of a few who were translated prior to the birth of the Savior. However, as one scours the scriptures and the lives of the Latter-day prophets and apostles, it becomes evident that re-identifying with youthful transgressions is not a common practice.

Each individual must gain a personal testimony that the Atonement of Christ literally makes them a new creature—not just painted to look nice but one totally separate and apart from the old man of sin. Although some consequences of the "old man of sin" may linger, the inner man can and must accept the Savior's power to make him a "new creature in Christ."

POINTS FOR FURTHER CONSIDERATION

D&C 64:7

Nevertheless, he (Joseph Smith) has sinned; but verily I say unto you, I, the Lord, forgive sins unto those **who confess their sins before me and ask forgiveness**, who have not sinned unto death.

Read and ponder **Romans 6** with regard to "crucifying the old man of sin."

Forgive or not be forgiven (Matthew 6:14–15)

For **if ye forgive men their trespasses**, your *heavenly Father will also forgive you*: But **if ye forgive not men their trespasses**, *neither will your Father forgive your trespasses* (see also 3 Nephi 13:14–15).

Forgive others, the Lord forgives you (D&C 82:1)

Verily, verily, I say unto you, my servants, that **inasmuch as you have forgiven one another** your trespasses, *even so I, the Lord, forgive you.*

Forgive sins (who gains?) (D&C 6:2)

I, *the Lord*, **forgive sins**, and am merciful *unto those who confess their sins with humble hearts.*

Forgiven as oft as repented (Moroni 6:8)

But as **oft as they repented and sought forgiveness, with real intent**, *they were forgiven* (see also Mosiah 26:30–31).

Who is forgiven? (D&C 1:31)

Nevertheless, he that *repents and does the commandments* of the Lord shall be **forgiven**.

Forgiveness of sins (who shall not have) (D&C 84:41)

But *whoso breaketh this covenant* [Oath and covenant of the Priesthood] *after he hath received it, and altogether turneth therefrom,* shall **not have forgiveness of sins** in this world nor in the world to come.

New Creature (2 Corinthians 5:17)

Therefore if *any man be in Christ,* he is a **new creature** old things are passed away; behold all things are become new.

Repent and sanctify self to be given eternal life (D&C 133:62)

And unto him that **repenteth and sanctifieth himself** before the Lord *shall be given eternal life.*

Repent—Don't give up, people may and come to Christ (3 Nephi 18:32)*

Nevertheless, ye shall not cast him out of your synagogues, or your places of worship, for unto such shall ye continue to minister; for **ye know not but what they will return and repent,** and come unto me with full purpose of heart, *and I shall heal them;* and ye shall be the means of bringing salvation unto them.

Repent or cannot dwell with God (Moses 6:57)

Wherefore teach it unto your children, that all men, everywhere, **must repent,** or **they can in nowise** inherit the kingdom of God, for no unclean thing can dwell there, or **dwell in his presence;** for, in the language of Adam, Man of Holiness is his name, and the name of his Only Begotten is the Son of Man, even Jesus Christ, a righteous Judge, who shall come in the meridian of time.

Repent or suffer (D&C 19:4, 17)

And surely every man **must repent or suffer,** for I, God, am endless . . . But if they **would not repent they must suffer** even as I.

Ways God invites people to repent (D&C 43:25)

How oft have I called upon you by the (1) *mouth of my servants,* and by the (2) *ministering of angels,* and by (3) *mine own voice,* and by the (4) *voice of thunderings,* and by the (5) *voice of lightnings,* and by the (6) *voice of tempests,* and by the (7) *voice of earthquakes,* and (8) *great hailstorms,* and by the (9) *voice of famines* and (10) *pestilences of every kind,* and by the (11) *great sound of a trump,* and by the (12) *voice of judgment,* and by the (13) *voice of mercy all the day long,* and by the (14) *voice of glory and honor* and the (15) *riches of eternal life,* and would have saved you with an everlasting salvation, but ye would not (numbers and italics added)!

Repentance (and suffering) in spirit prison (D&C 138:57–59)

I beheld that the faithful elders of this dispensation, when they depart from mortal life, continue their labors in the preaching of the gospel of repentance and redemption, through the sacrifice of the Only Begotten Son of God, among those who are in darkness and under the bondage of sin in the great world of the spirits of the dead. 58 The **dead who repent** will be redeemed, through obedience to the ordinances of the house of God, 59 And **after they have paid the penalty of their transgressions,** and are washed clean, shall receive a reward according to their works, for they are heirs of salvation.

Repentance declared (Helaman 12:22)

For this cause *that men might be saved,* hath **repentance been declared.**

Repentance—declaring is of most worth (D&C 15:6; 16:6)

And now, behold, I say unto you, that the thing which will be of the *most worth* unto you will be **to declare repentance unto this people,** that you may bring souls unto me, that you may rest with them in the kingdom of my Father.

Repentance—results of failure to (D&C 1:33)

And he that **repents not,** from him *shall be taken even the light which he has received;* for my Spirit shall not always strive with man, saith the Lord of Hosts.

16

FINDING A MATE/ TRUE FRIEND

It is safe to say that we almost always choose our mates from our circle of friends. Since finding an eternal companion is a top priority of our mortal stay, it seems logical that the Lord would give us some guidance for achieving that greatest of all blessings.

It can be a painful experience to discover that many you consider to be friends are really "fair weather friends," meaning that as long as things are going well, they stand by you, but when difficult times come, they are nowhere to be found. Wise King Solomon understood that and said: "A friend loveth at all times, and a brother is born for adversity" (Proverbs 17:17).

A point is made in this chapter contrasting friends with true friends because the former are plentiful; the latter are rare and prized. Solomon again helps us determine the difference between the two groups: "Many will entreat the favour of the prince: and every man is a friend to him that giveth gifts" (Proverbs 19:6).

Of the true friend Solomon observed: "A man that hath friends must shew himself friendly: and there is a friend that sticketh closer than a brother" (Proverbs 18:24).

The first element of a formula for finding true friends is be a true friend. According to what King Solomon said, it is easy to recognize a true friend because they will stick by you during good times and bad. What a great time to evaluate how many people would call us their true friends.

It may seem that I am emphasizing the wisdom of King Solomon more than I should, but given his prominence and wealth, he was in a prime position to see both friends and true friends and point the difference between the two groups. He further counsels: "Ointment and perfume rejoice the heart: so doth the sweetness of a man's friend by hearty counsel. Thine own friend, and thy father's friend, forsake not; neither go into thy brother's house in the day of thy calamity: for better is a neighbour that is near than a brother far off" (Proverbs 27:9–10).

It is interesting to note that Solomon counsels to stick close to not only your own true friends but your father's true friends. Additionally, his counsel that a neighbor is better than a distant brother suggests the need for a close proximity for true friends to be of immediate help in times of trouble. I don't know if he would modify that counsel given today's means of travelling anywhere in the world in a matter of hours.

James, half-brother of the Lord, draws an interesting contrast. First, what constitutes a true friend of God? "And the scripture was fulfilled which saith, Abraham believed God, and it was imputed unto him for righteousness: and **he was called the Friend of God"** (James 2:23).

Truly believing in God and following His commandments, no matter how difficult, constitutes the prerequisite of becoming a "friend to God" (just prior to this verse James had recounted how Abraham had been willing to sacrifice Isaac). Abraham's righteousness in seeking to know God's will and following it qualified him to be called "the friend of God." That would be a model for us to follow as well.

Two chapters later James described another kind of friendship that separates us from God: "Ye adulterers and adulteresses, know ye not that the friendship of the world is enmity with God? **whosoever therefore will be a friend of the world is the enemy of God**" (James 4:4).

Part of our expanding definition of true friendship has to do with our relationship to God and eternal principles and not to the vain and transitory things of the world.

What is the danger of making friends with worldly type people? Proverbs 22:24 states: "Make no friendship with an angry man; and with a furious man thou shalt not go: Lest thou learn his ways, and get a snare to thy soul."

How does one qualify to become a friend to God? Jesus answered that question Himself: "Greater love hath no man than this, that a man lay down his life for his friends. **Ye are my friends, if ye do whatsoever I command you**" (John 15:13–14).

Once we have made sacred covenants and are striving to keep them, the Savior says: "Ye are they whom my Father hath given me; ye are my friends" (D&C 84:63).

The Savior puts friendship and service in perspective: "Verily, I say unto my servant Joseph Smith, Jun., or in other words, I will call you friends, for you are my friends, and ye shall have an inheritance with me—I called you servants for the world's sake, and ye are their servants for my sake" (D&C 93:45–46).

All of this may seem strange as we move into seeking to find an eternal companion. However, there is one verse that takes on added significance when viewed in this context. Doctrine and Covenants 88:40 states that likes attract: "For intelligence cleaveth unto intelligence; wisdom receiveth wisdom; truth embraceth truth; virtue loveth virtue; light cleaveth unto light; mercy hath compassion on mercy and claimeth her own; justice continueth its course and claimeth its own; judgment goeth before the face of him who sitteth upon the throne and governeth and executeth all things."

When we interface with the world, it is difficult not to become worldly. If we take verse 40 at face value, then finding a mate should be relatively easy. All we do is figure out what qualities we want in a mate, incorporate those characteristics into our personality, radiate them, and interface with potential mates. When we find one that has the same goal, characteristics and attributes, there will be an automatic attraction.

That is not to say we are ready at that point to be married, but we can begin a dating relationship that will naturally evolve into courtship. Along the way, we will become "true friends" as described above.

Paul gave some timely advice when he taught: "Be ye not unequally yoked together with unbelievers: for what fellowship hath righteousness with unrighteousness? and what communion hath light with darkness" (2 Corinthians 6:14)?

Welding two individuals together not only of different sexes but also from different backgrounds is challenging at best. The more differences we have, the more challenging it is to fulfill the Lord's injunction: "Behold, this I have given unto you as a parable, and it is even as I am. I say unto you, be one; and if ye are not one ye are not mine" (D&C 38:27).

Perhaps we should review an eternal principle: "Whoever must stand judgment for the decision, must be free to make the decision." If we agree, then we can see the fallacy in asking the Lord to decide who we should marry. He will not stand judgment for that decision—we must.

Having taught college-aged students for many years, I saw the frustration as they dated and then, fearing that they would make a mistake, insisted that God give them a revelation on who they should marry.

In Doctrine and Covenants 9:7 the Lord points out the error of that train of thinking: "Behold, you have not understood; you have supposed that I would give it unto you, when you took no thought save it was to ask me."

He carefully leads His sons and daughters through the step by step process of determining the rightness of their choice.

> But, behold, I say unto you, that (1) **you must study it out in your mind**; (2) then you must ask me if **it** be right, and (3) if **it** is right I will cause that your bosom shall burn within you; therefore, you shall feel that it is right.
>
> But (4) if it be not right you shall have no such feelings, (5) but you shall have a stupor of thought that shall cause you to forget the thing which is wrong; therefore, you cannot write that which is sacred save it be given you from me. (D&C 9:8–9, numbers and emphasis added)

First, studying it out in your mind suggests that you share mutual experiences. It is helpful to see each other in the morning, at mid-day, in the evening, when feeling good, when not feeling well, when everything is going well, when nothing is going well, when you are alone, when you are in a group, when you are at church, when you are at a party, when you are with family, when you are with strangers, when you with children, when you are with adults, and so on. All of this takes time and patience.

When decision-making time is approaching, get all the counsel you desire—but don't ask others (including God) to make the final decision for you. In my experience I saw far too often parents and siblings wanting to step in and make the decision for the prospective bride or groom. Often there were no concrete reasons for their suggestions to break off the relationship—only a "bad feeling." While not discounting their input, it should be only one part of the larger gathering of counsel and facts.

Once you have weighed all the pros and cons, *you* make the decision. It needs to be a solid decision. James said: "But let him ask in faith, nothing wavering. For he that wavereth is like a wave of the sea driven with the wind and tossed. For let not that man think that he shall receive any thing of the Lord. A double minded man is unstable in all his ways" (James 1:6–8).

I have witnessed more vacillating men and women lose their chance for a great marriage because one or the other could not make a decision and stick with it. Acting in faith does not mean jumping without looking. Alma taught, "And now as I said concerning faith—faith is not to have a perfect knowledge of things; therefore if ye have faith ye hope for things which are not seen, which are true" (Alma 32:21). I have witnessed the frustration and heartache when one of the couple cannot make and stick to a decision. After some time, the on-again, off-again cycle becomes too much to tolerate and the couple separates.

After making a firm decision, you must ask God if **it** (the decision you made through counsel, experience, and mental exertion) is right.

If **it** (the decision you have made) is right, you will have the promised "burning of the bosom" (which is different for each person); therefore you will **feel** that it is right. Why doesn't it say "you will *know* it is right"? Because you already have the intellectual confirmation through your study that you have made the right decision. Now the Lord is adding the affective or feeling witness. In Doctrine and Covenants 8:2–3 the Lord explained that **the mind AND the heart** constituted what He referred to as "the spirit of revelation."

If you have made an incorrect decision, rather than the confirming feeling there will be an empty feeling.

You will experience a "stupor of thought" that shall cause you to forget or turn your heart away from your decision. Some people describe the "stupor of thought" as a breakdown in the logic you used to come to the decision you did. Experience will help you determine what that stupor of thought feels like to you. Subsequently your enthusiasm for the relationship or the proposal will wane and your heart will be turned away from the mistaken decision.

One aspect of the Lord's formula that is difficult to remember is to keep the end in mind. He revealed: "But ye are commanded in all things to ask of God, who giveth liberally; and that which the Spirit testifies unto you even so I would that ye should do in all holiness of heart, walking uprightly before me, **considering the end of your salvation**, doing all things with prayer and thanksgiving, that ye may not be seduced by evil spirits, or doctrines of devils, or the commandments of men; for some are of men, and others of devils" (D&C 46:7).

Kneeling at an altar in a temple to be married is a great first step. Then comes the challenge of "enduring to the end"—a friend suggested we say "joyfully enduring to the end" since the first statement often gives the impression of drudgery.

Establishing, during the dating and courtship, the principles upon which true friendship and harmony in marriage are built lessens the chances of a catastrophic blow-up after marriage when each is surprised by habits or beliefs their spouse has that they were unaware of. Far too many marriages are built on the physical attraction the couple feels for each other. After the honeymoon is over and the newness of the physical wanes, what remains are the elements of true friendship.

We can identify what those elements of true friendship are that we need to build upon by referring to the Savior's example. Luke records: "And Jesus increased in wisdom and stature, and in favour with God and man" (Luke 2:52).

The four areas we build a foundation on for our marriage that will last through the eternities are wisdom—intellectual oneness and like interests; stature—physical activities and likes; favor with God—spiritual unity; and favor with man—social similarities.

Building upon a common solid foundation individually before marriage all but ensures success in marriage. In Helaman 5:12 Mormon records Helaman's counsel to his sons: "And now, my sons, remember, remember that it is upon the rock of our Redeemer, who is Christ, the Son of God, that ye must build your foundation; that when the devil shall send forth his mighty winds, yea, his shafts in the whirlwind, yea, when all his hail and his mighty storm shall beat upon you, it shall have no power over you to drag you down to the gulf of misery and endless wo, because of the rock upon which ye are built, which is a sure foundation, a foundation whereon if men build they cannot fall."

One word of caution as you progress toward marriage: expect satanic opposition. It appears that Satan is not hampered by a veil of forgetfulness between us and our pre-earth past. He can see the talents we were given, perhaps even knows the assigned tasks we accepted, and the potential we have to do serious harm to him and his kingdom. Therefore, he who is rightly called "the enemy to all righteousness" (see Mosiah 4:14) will do all in his power to disrupt and destroy your possible eternal marriage.

17

ANSWERING CHALLENGES OF DOCTRINE/FAITH

No single chapter in a book could adequately address the challenges (malicious and sincere) that have been made since the Church was restored. Since 1835 when E.D. Howe published *Mormonism Unveiled,* attacks have been made by anti-Mormon groups and individuals attempting to "prove" the Church is false. Someday it would be an amusing study to see how many of those "proofs" have been proven wrong. Everything from "no pre-Spanish horses" (disproved by discoveries in the LaBrea tar pits of California) to "no evidence of records written on metallic plates" (proven false by multiple recent discoveries in various places around the world), one after another honest truth-seeking people have come to see faith-destroying attacks for what they really are—mortal men being used by unseen devils to fight against God.

It is pathetically amusing to read the four Gospels and see how stubborn and determined the Jewish leaders were in Christ's day. In spite of the constant and various miracles the Savior performed, they refused to see the divine in Him. In fact, they actually said He had "Beelzebub, the prince of devils" (see Matthew 12:24, Mark 3:22).

This is a classic and extreme example of "you see what you look for." How can one looking for fault see the truth even in the sinless Son of God?

The same principle exists today—one can read the Book of Mormon determined to prove it false and never get a witness it is true. One could see an angel or the Savior Himself and have Him testify of the truth of His restored gospel and still (like the Jewish leaders) deny that testimony. Unless a person is sincere in his or her investigation of the gospel, there is little or no chance they will get the convincing witness of the Spirit that will put to rest forever the devilish attempts to deceive and destroy.

A few principles punctuated by examples may at least give the reader more confidence in knowing what the scriptures say not only on what to do but how to answer some difficult questions.

As in all cases, the Savior is the role model for answering questions—both sincere and malicious. During His mock trial before the Jewish leaders, He remained silent. Certainly, there is a time to answer and a time to ignore the challenge: "And when he was accused of the chief priests and elders**, he answered nothing.** Then said Pilate unto him, Hearest thou not how many things they witness against thee? And **he answered him to never a word**; insomuch that the governor marvelled greatly" Matthew 27:12–14).

Other times He asked them a question in response to their challenge: "And when he was come into the temple, the chief priests and the elders of the people came unto him as he was teaching, and said, By what authority doest thou these things? and who gave thee this authority? And Jesus answered and said unto them, **I also will ask you one thing**, which if ye tell me, I in like wise will tell you by what authority I do these things" (Matthew 21:23–24).

At other times He used a parable to illustrate the point and then ask them to answer their own question. For example, the parable of the good Samaritan was posed in response to a lawyer's inquiry "Who is my neighbor" when the Savior taught the two great commandments: love God and love your neighbor. Read Luke 10:25–37 for the whole story.

You might think, "Yes, that would be great if I had the intellect of the Savior, but He gave the scriptures through His chosen prophets and I can't remember where everything is written." Two scriptures in the Doctrine and Covenants address this concern. In D&C 84:85 the Lord says: "Neither take ye thought beforehand what ye shall say; but **treasure up in your minds continually the words of life**, and it shall be given you in the very hour that portion that shall be meted unto every man."

In Doctrine and Covenants 100:5–8 the Lord promises to prompt you what to say and the very moment that is most appropriate.

> Therefore, verily I say unto you, lift up your voices unto this people; speak the thoughts that I shall put into your hearts, and you shall not be confounded before men;
>
> For it shall be given you in the very hour, yea, in the very moment, what ye shall say.
>
> But a commandment I give unto you, that ye shall declare whatsoever thing ye declare in my name, in solemnity of heart, in the spirit of meekness, in all things.
>
> And I give unto you this promise, that inasmuch as ye do this the Holy Ghost shall be shed forth in bearing record unto all things whatsoever ye shall say.

Now for some principles and examples from personal experiences. During a long conversation I had with a minister about the gospel, the minister charged that the Book of Mormon was false because it said there was three days of darkness in the Americas but only three hours in Jerusalem at the crucifixion of the Savior.

Principle: For every challenge against the Church there is a similar situation in the Bible. Here is one example:

> When Pharoah refused to let the children of Israel go, Moses used the power of God in bringing plagues against them. Exodus 10:21–23 reads: And the Lord said unto Moses, Stretch out thine hand toward heaven, that there may be darkness over the land of Egypt, even darkness which may be felt.
>
> And Moses stretched forth his hand toward heaven; and there was a thick darkness in all the land of Egypt three days:
>
> They saw not one another, neither rose any from his place for three days: but all the children of Israel had light in their dwellings.

How could there be light with the Israelites but not with the Egyptians? I don't know but whatever God did in Egypt and Goshen, He certainly could to in Israel and America.

During two separate extended discussion with this very knowledgeable (but very anti-Mormon) minister, I had the opportunity to hear and answer many of his "strongest proofs." Noting that "the **devil is an enemy unto God, and fighteth against him continually"** (Moroni 7:12) one of the favorite targets of all anti-Mormon attacks is against the revealed doctrine that man's ultimate destiny is to become like God.

Principle: Even though an individual or the entire world rejects a revealed doctrine, that does not make the doctrine false.

The minister asked if I knew who first suggested that man could become a god. Having answered the question dozens of time while serving my first mission in Samoa, I knew exactly where he was going. I asked him to tell me. Rather gloatingly he opened his Bible to Genesis 3:4–5, which reads: "And the serpent said unto the woman, Ye shall not surely die: For God doth know that in the day ye eat thereof, then your eyes shall be opened, and ye shall be as gods, knowing good and evil."

I then asked, "Are you saying that anyone who suggests man can become like God is deceived by Satan?" He answered in the affirmative. I asked him to turn the page and read verse 22: "And the Lord God said, Behold, the man is become as one of us, to know good and evil."

In my youthful exuberance, I said: "I am so sorry that your God is deceived by Satan!" Not a good response since I was trying to maintain a congenial relationship. I went on to say, "The Lord Himself taught the potential of man to become a god." I referred him to John 10:30–36:

> I and my Father are one.
>
> Then the Jews took up stones again to stone him.
>
> Jesus answered them, Many good works have I shewed you from my Father; for which of those works do ye stone me?
>
> The Jews answered him, saying, For a good work we stone thee not; but for blasphemy; and because that thou, being a man, makest thyself God.
>
> **Jesus answered them, Is it not written in your law, I said, Ye are gods?**
>
> If he called them gods, unto whom the word of God came, and the scripture cannot be broken;
>
> Say ye of him, whom the Father hath sanctified, and sent into the world, Thou blasphemest; because I said, I am the Son of God?

Quickly the minister jumped to another hot topic—eternal marriage. He referred to Matthew 22:23–30, which says that the Sadducees, who do not believe in a resurrection, posed a situation of a man who had six brothers. According to the law of Moses, if a man died without having children, his brothers were to marry the wife and "raise up seed unto his brother." Each brother, in turn, married the widow and died without her having children. At last she died. The question, given to trap the Savior, was, "In the resurrection whose wife shall she be of the seven, they all had her?" The Savior points out the problem that all anti-Mormons—and many LDS people have: "Jesus answered and said unto them, Ye do err, **not knowing**

the scriptures, nor the power of God." In other words, you don't understand the plan of salvation nor do you understand the sealing power of the priesthood.

The very purpose for the six brothers marrying their brother's widow was to "raise up seed unto his brother." If there was no life after death, why raise up seed to him? If there was no eternal marriage, why raise up seed to a single man rather than to a husband and wife as God had established as the family pattern from the days of Adam and Eve? The question arises from verse 30: "For in the resurrection they neither marry, nor are given in marriage, but are as the angels of God in heaven."

That is a very true statement: When people have been resurrected and are assigned a kingdom of glory (in the resurrection), the time for marrying and being given in marriage is over. That has to happen before the resurrection.

The good minister didn't agree with my interpretation, so I pursued the matter further. I asked if he believed the Bible. He answered that he believed every word of it. I then responded that he believes in eternal marriage, which he vehemently denied. I asked him who was the first marriage. He thought I was being juvenile with him so he rather sarcastically answered, "Adam and Eve!" I then asked, "Who married them?" That question wasn't so easily answered. We reviewed Genesis 2:22–25, and he concluded that God had brought "the woman" to the man and after that she was always referred to as "the man and his wife."

I then asked him to turn to Ecclesiastes 3:14, which reads: "I know that, whatsoever God doeth, it shall be for ever: nothing can be put to it, nor any thing taken from it: and God doeth *it*, that *men* should fear before him."

He said that I perverted the scriptures worse than anyone he had ever talked with but had to admit that there was at least one eternal marriage—Adam and Eve. I then referred him to 1 Corinthians 11:11, which states: "Nevertheless neither is the man without the woman, neither the woman without the man, in the Lord." If we want to live eternally with the Lord, we will enter His presence as couples.

These examples are not given to demonstrate how smart I was but to show that the Bible itself teaches what God has restored in simplicity and plainness in these latter days.

Many Christians reject The Church of Jesus Christ of Latter-day Saints because we have additional scriptures, and they mistakenly feel the Bible is complete citing Revelation 22:18–19 as proof: "For I testify unto every man that heareth the words of the prophecy of this book, If any man shall add unto these things, God shall add unto him the plagues that are written in this book: And if any man shall take away from the words of the book of this prophecy, God shall take away his part out of the book of life, and out of the holy city, and *from* the things which are written in this book."

I have heard several methods of answering this challenge—some more effective than others. However, it is likely that the person questioning latter-day scriptures has been schooled by their minister or "informed" family member or friend that Latter-day Saints will try to use the construction of the Bible to weasel around this seemingly definite declaration. It is true, to anyone who wants to pick up a commentary on the Bible, that the Bible is a compilation of 66 individual manuscripts and that several of the canonized books were written after the book of Revelation. Refer to Adam Clarke's *Bible Commentary* (a non-LDS author) to verify that Revelation certainly was not the last book written.

The footnote for verse 18 refers you to Deuteronomy 4:2, which reads: "Ye shall not add unto the word which I command you, neither shall ye diminish *ought* from it, that ye may keep the commandments of the Lord your God which I command you."

Then, according to the restriction, they or their minister has placed on Revelation 22, everything from Deuteronomy 4 should be removed since it was added after the command not to add to nor diminish from. Obviously, Revelation must have reference to that book alone and not the entire Bible.

Additionally, it is helpful to note that Revelation 22 states that "man" shall not add to or diminish from. John does not attempt to limit God from adding or taking away. Others steadfastly maintain that the Bible is whole and complete as it now stands. Listed below are the books mentioned in the Bible but are not found in the canonized version. Chapter 29 in 2 Nephi is given as the Lord's response to those who say: "A Bible! A Bible! We have got a Bible, and there cannot be any more Bible" (2 Nephi 29:3). For those Christians who treasure God's word in the Bible, it remains a constant mystery why they would balk at receiving more of His word.

In his parting words to us, Mormon says: "Therefore repent, and be baptized in the name of Jesus, and lay hold upon the gospel of Christ, which shall be set before you, not only in this record but also in the record which shall come unto the Gentiles from the Jews, which record shall come from the Gentiles unto you. For behold, this (the Book of Mormon) is written for the intent that ye may believe that (the Bible); and if ye believe that (the Bible) ye will believe this (the Book of Mormon) also; and if ye believe this (the Book of Mormon) ye will know concerning your fathers, and also the marvelous works which were wrought by the power of God among them" (Mormon 7:8–9, explanation of "this" and "that" added).

The ultimate challenge, however, to any accusation against the Church was given by Moroni as he closed the portion of the Book of Mormon plates that we have:

> Behold, I would exhort you that when ye shall read these things, if it be wisdom in God that ye should read them, that ye would remember how merciful the Lord hath been unto the children of men, from the creation of Adam even down until the time that ye shall receive these things, and ponder it in your hearts.
>
> And when ye shall receive these things, I would exhort you that ye would ask God, the Eternal Father, in the name of Christ, if these things are not true; and if ye shall ask with a sincere heart, with real intent, having faith in Christ, he will manifest the truth of it unto you, by the power of the Holy Ghost.
>
> And by the power of the Holy Ghost ye may know the truth of all things. (Moroni 10:3–5)

Think of that promise. It would be beyond ludicrous for Joseph Smith to pen such a "provable" test at the conclusion of a fake manuscript. Any honest, sincere seeker of truth can put it to the test. If he or she is willing to read, ponder, and receive the teachings of the Book of Mormon and then ask God (as James 1:5 instructs) if it is true. If they are sincere and really want to know, they will get the undeniable manifestation from the Holy Ghost. Joseph Smith or any other man cannot fulfill that promise.

After a lifetime of answering both sincere and antagonistic questions, I am convinced that God has provided the answers to almost all of the challenges to His restored gospel. Those yet remaining will be revealed:

> Yea, verily I say unto you, in that day when the Lord shall come, he shall reveal all things—
>
> Things which have passed, and hidden things which no man knew, things of the earth, by which it was made, and the purpose and the end thereof—
>
> Things most precious, things that are above, and things that are beneath, things that are in the earth, and upon the earth, and in heaven. (D&C 101:32–34)

The fact that you or I or any other human being cannot presently answer a challenging question certainly does not mean that God doesn't know the answer. Given the hundreds of anti-Mormon questions on the internet, in books, articles, and circulated verbally that have been answered, it does not require a great deal of faith to believe the rest will also be answered. It is disappointing but not surprising to note how many anti-Mormons continue to use questions that have long since been answered but are not familiar to those they try to influence.

Mortality provides the environment where we can learn to "live by faith" (see Romans 1:17) rather than by sight. God never intended the gospel to be proven solely in a scientific laboratory—as the first means of proof. Science is ever changing as new discoveries are made. God's truth (the gospel) is eternal and never changes. Concerning not being willing to exercise faith, Paul said, "But without faith it is impossible to please him: for he that cometh to God must believe that he is, and that he is a rewarder of them that diligently seek him" (Hebrews 11:6).

A word of warning to those who attempt to destroy the faith of Latter-day Saints or anyone else. This is best explained by one of the most revered Jewish leaders of his time as recorded in Acts 5:34–39:

> Then stood there up one in the council, a Pharisee, named Gamaliel, a doctor of the law, had in reputation among all the people, and commanded to put the apostles forth a little space;
>
> And said unto them, Ye men of Israel, take heed to yourselves what ye intend to do as touching these men.
>
> For before these days rose up Theudas, boasting himself to be somebody; to whom a number of men, about four hundred, joined themselves: who was slain; and all, as many as obeyed him, were scattered, and brought to nought.
>
> After this man rose up Judas of Galilee in the days of the taxing, and drew away much people after him: he also perished; and all, *even* as many as obeyed him, were dispersed.
>
> And now I say unto you, **Refrain from these men, and let them alone: for if this counsel or this work be of men, it will come to nought:**
>
> **But if it be of God, ye cannot overthrow it; lest haply ye be found even to fight against God.**

What a dreadful day lies ahead for those who have made it their life's mission to destroy peoples' faith and tear down God's true Church. I have often wondered what their reaction will be when the Savior Himself testifies that the gospel He restored is true.

POINTS FOR FURTHER CONSIDERATION

Lost Scriptures (mentioned but not found in Bible)
Wars of the Lord (Numbers 21:14)
Jasher (Joshua 10:13; 2 Samuel 1:18)
Acts of Solomon (1 Kings 11:41)
Samuel the Seer (1 Chronicles 29:29)
Nathan the Prophet (2 Chronicles 9:29)
Shemaiah the Prophet (2 Chronicles 12:15)
Iddo the Prophet (2 Chronicles 13:22)
Jehu (2 Chronicles 20:34)
The Sayings of the Seers (2 Chronicles 33:19)
Enoch (Jude 1:14)
Book of Remembrance (Moses 6:5)
Another Epistle to the Corinthians (1 Corinthians 5:9)
Another Epistle to the Ephesians (Ephesians 3:3)
Epistle from Laodicea (Colossians 4:16)

18

PREPARING FOR THE SECOND COMING

On a hot August Sunday afternoon, I was sitting at the back of our non-air-conditioned chapel, hoping to endure another "boring" sacrament meeting. I must have been in my mid-teens and, although not a "bad kid," I certainly was not highly motivated by religious teachings.

The speaker, a high councilor, was waxing eloquent as I dozed with my head resting on the back of the bench in front of me. I was awakened by the high councilor slapping his hand on the pulpit and saying, "Prepare for the Second Coming or you will burn!"

In my boyish mind I figured if anyone would qualify to burn, I would. So, I said to myself, "Okay, Brother High Councilor, how am I supposed to prepare?" He never bothered to answer the question. As I listened to numerous talks and presentations in the following months and years, I discovered that everyone talked about the Second Coming, the signs, and the actual appearances, but virtually no one said anything about how to prepare other than offering broad generalizations.

I decided I would have to find the answer myself. That quest started what has become a lifelong feast of searching the scriptures for answers.

It must have been some years later that I discovered the Lord's answer to my question of how to prepare in one half of one verse: "And at that day, when I shall come in my glory, shall the parable be fulfilled which I spake concerning the ten virgins. For they that are **(1) wise and have (2) received the truth, and (3) have taken the Holy Spirit for their guide, and (4) have not been deceived**—verily I say unto you, they shall not be hewn down and cast into the fire, but shall abide the day" (D&C 45:56–57, numbers and emphasis added).

How simple! Now all I had to do was identify what the Lord said about those four simple qualifying conditions, make sure they were part of my life, and then stop worrying.

Wise

At the conclusion of the Sermon on the Mount in Matthew 7:24–27 the Lord drew the contrast between the foolish and the wise when He said:

> Therefore whosoever heareth these sayings of mine, and doeth them, I will liken him unto a wise man, which built his house upon a rock:
>
> And the rain descended, and the floods came, and the winds blew, and beat upon that house; and it fell not: for it was founded upon a rock.
>
> And every one that heareth these sayings of mine, and doeth them not, shall be likened unto a foolish man, which built his house upon the sand:
>
> And the rain descended, and the floods came, and the winds blew, and beat upon that house; and it fell: and great was the fall of it.

Sounds like if I am serious about preparing for His Second Coming, I should study Matthew 5–7 (also 3 Nephi 12–14) and make sure my life is aligned with the principles He taught.

Received the truth

There are several definitions in the scriptures of "truth." The first and most important definition is found in John 14:6: *"I [Christ]* am the way, the **truth** and the life." In John 17:17 the Lord declares: "*Thy word* is **truth**." If we are going to fully prepare for His Second Coming, we must be willing to accept Him as our unwavering example, we must learn to treasure and trust His word (scriptures, words of latter-day prophets), and we must prepare for the ridicule of the world when we take what they want to label as old fashioned and out-of-date (see 1 Nephi 8:25–28).

The Lord gives some additional direction to the Nephites just before departing from them: "Verily, verily, I say unto you, this is my gospel; and ye know the things that ye must do in my church; for **the works which ye have seen me do that shall ye also do**; for that which ye have seen me do even that shall ye do; Therefore, if ye do these things blessed are ye, for ye shall be lifted up at the last day" (3 Nephi 27:21–22).

What did Jesus do? Luke records in Acts 10:38: "How God anointed Jesus of Nazareth with the Holy Ghost and with power: who went about doing good, and healing all that were oppressed of the devil; for God was with him."

Perhaps preparing for the Second Coming is not all that difficult if we make it a lifetime practice of doing good and ministering to those in need. One additional thought: In spite of the fact that the world is continually trying to change the definitions of everything from what marriage is to the legalization of what God has forbidden, God's truth *never* changes. He said: "And truth is knowledge of things as they are, and as they were, and as they are to come; And whatsoever is more or less than this is the spirit of that wicked one who was a liar from the beginning" (D&C 93:24–25).

Have taken the Holy Spirit for their guide

The first step to getting the Holy Spirit is to accept the ordinance of baptism, and then receive the right to the Gift of the Holy Ghost by the laying on of hands by one having authority (see Articles of Faith 1:4).

If we live worthy to keep the Spirit with us, we can receive the promptings or direction we need to know what we should do. In D&C 111:8 the Lord revealed: "And the place where it is my will that you should tarry, for the main, shall be signalized unto you by the peace and power of my Spirit, that shall flow unto you."

So as long as I am heading in the right general direction ("for the main"), the presence of the Spirit indicates that I am doing all the Lord requires of me (to that point in time) and am moving in the right direction and at the right speed to accomplish His will concerning me.

Additionally, the Spirit will do a multitude of things for us, but here are just a few:

> And now, verily, verily, I say unto thee, put your trust in that Spirit which leadeth to do good—yea, to do justly, to walk humbly, to judge righteously; and this is my Spirit.
>
> Verily, verily, I say unto you, I will impart unto you of my Spirit, which shall enlighten your mind, which shall fill your soul with joy;
>
> And then shall ye know, or by this shall you know, all things whatsoever you desire of me, which are pertaining unto things of righteousness, in faith believing in me that you shall receive. (D&C 11:12–14)

The Savior also gave this promise: "But the Comforter, which is the Holy Ghost, whom the Father will send in my name, he shall teach you all things, and bring all things to your remembrance, whatsoever I have said unto you" (John 14:26).

So far nothing seems to be so difficult that any sincere person is incapable of doing. But the fourth condition—we may need some help to understand.

Have not been deceived

In today's world where lying seems to be an acceptable form of speech, how can one avoid being deceived? Add to that an adversary and his followers who have enjoyed over six thousand years of deceiving and destroying Heavenly Father's spirit sons and daughters. Apparently, Joseph Smith asked the same question: How am I to avoid being deceived? The very next day after the Lord revealed Doctrine and Covenants 45, the Lord answered the question in D&C 46:8: "Wherefore, beware lest ye are deceived; and **that ye may not be deceived seek ye earnestly the best gifts**, always remembering for what they are given."

Rather than diving into a discussion on deception, we will postpone that for another chapter where the Lord's directives will be investigated in greater detail. For this chapter, it would be well to read all of Doctrine and Covenants 46, Moroni 10, and 1 Corinthians 12. Consider re-reading your patriarchal blessing for direction on what your gifts may be, and then be confident in approaching the Lord to ask for whatever gift you feel would assist you in being better prepared for His Second Coming.

Probably the most frequently asked question concerning this topic is, "When will the Second Coming happen?" The Lord made it abundantly clear that no one will be able to pinpoint the day or the hour, although He promised to reveal it to His servants (the prophets)—see Amos 3:7—before it actually occurs. The generation and general time period can be known. In the Lord's Q & A of the book of Revelation when asked about the time of the Second Coming, He revealed: "Q. When are the things to be accomplished, which are written in the 9th chapter of Revelation? A. They are to be accomplished **after the opening of the seventh seal, before the coming of Christ**" (D&C 77:13). All indicators suggest we are living during that time.

A frequent admonition is, "Be ye therefore ready also: for the **Son of man cometh at an hour when ye think not**" (Luke 12:40). In Matthew

25:13 the Savior said: "Watch therefore, for ye know **neither the day nor the hour** *wherein the Son of man cometh.*"

One of the dangers outlined by the Savior is that when His Second Coming does not happen within the timeframe anticipated by some of His saints, they will begin to indulge in the forbidden things of the world only to discover too late, the spiritually fatal mistake they have made. He said in Doctrine and Covenants 63:54: "And until that hour there will be foolish virgins among the wise; and at that hour cometh an **entire separation of the righteous and the wicked**; and in that day will I send mine angels to pluck out the wicked and cast them into unquenchable fire."

There will be many signs (some are listed below) that will precede the Second Coming. However, there is one final thrust which will be made that you and I can participate in. The Lord said:

> And they shall hear of wars, and rumors of wars.
>
> Behold I speak for mine elect's sake; for nation shall rise against nation, and kingdom against kingdom; there shall be famines, and pestilences, and earthquakes, in divers places.
>
> And again, because iniquity shall abound, the love of men shall wax cold; but he that shall not be overcome, the same shall be saved.
>
> And again, **this Gospel of the Kingdom shall be preached in all the world, for a witness unto all nations, and then shall the end come,** or the destruction of the wicked. (Joseph Smith—Matthew 1:28–31)

What an opportunity to play on the Lord's first team in the final seconds of the fourth quarter of the Super Bowl of all time. What a terrible tragedy to put worldly things ahead of spiritual things and be found standing on the sidelines while this most glorious of all events transpires before our very eyes. Now really is the time to answer the question: "Who's on the Lord's side who?" If there are mid-course corrections to be made, wouldn't today be a good day to make them?

Latter-day prophets have repeatedly reiterated what Paul said about us: "And hath made of one blood all nations of men for to dwell on all the face of the earth, and **hath determined the times before appointed, and the bounds of their habitation**" (Acts 17:26). The Lord not only knows when we will live on earth but how far we will travel during our lifetime. There is no question in my mind that you are a person of destiny. Now you just have to live worthily so your foreordained missions can be fulfilled in the Lord's due time.

Like Queen Esther of Old Testament fame (see Esther 4:14), we have been saved "for such a time as this." Although the Lord can do

His own work, He has allowed us to participate in the greatest event since His resurrection. Like Queen Esther, our future assignments may be life-threatening. But the Lord has comfortingly revealed, "For I, the Lord, rule in the heavens above, and among the armies of the earth; and in the day when I shall make up my jewels, all men shall know what it is that bespeaketh the power of God" (D&C 60:4).

The faithful need has no fear that events now and, in the future, will swirl out of control and frustrate the plan of God. Both He and our Father know when He will return again and nothing will change that. The only question remaining is, which team will we be playing on when the actual Second Coming occurs?

POINTS FOR FURTHER CONSIDERATION

Sermon on the Mount

Luke 6; 3 Nephi 12–14

Second Coming—signs preceding foretold

Matthew 24; Mark 13:1–37; Luke 12:37–48; 17:20–37; 21:5–38; D&C 29:14–21; 43:20–34; 45; 63:32–35; 87; 88:86–95; 101:23–35; 133; Joseph Smith—Matthew; JST, Matthew 24

Second Coming—no one knows day or hour

Matthew 24:36,42, 50; Mark 13:32; Luke 12:46; D&C 39:21; D&C 49:7; D&C 124:10; D&C 133:11; Joseph Smith—Matthew 1:40; JST, Matthew 24:43

Second Coming—destruction at (D&C 101:24–25)

And **every corruptible thing**, both of *man*, or of the *beasts* of the field, or of the *fowls* of the heavens, or of the *fish* of the sea, that dwells upon all the face of the earth, **shall be consumed**; And also that of *element* shall **melt with fervent heat**; and all things shall become new, that my knowledge and glory may dwell upon all the earth.

Second Coming—cause of burning, presence of Christ (D&C 133:41)

And it shall be answered upon their heads; for the **presence of the Lord** shall be as the *melting fire* that burneth, and as the fire which *causeth the waters to boil* (see also 2 Nephi 12:10; Isaiah 2:10).

Second Coming—all to see Christ together (D&C 101:23)

And prepare for the revelation which is to come, when the veil of the covering of my temple, in my tabernacle, which hideth the earth, shall be taken off, and **all flesh shall see me together.**

Second Coming draws nigh (D&C 106:4)

And again, verily I say unto you, the **coming of the Lord draweth nigh**, and *it overtaketh the world as a thief in the night.*

Second Coming (who will be burned) (1 Nephi 22:23)

For the time speedily shall come that *all churches which are built up to get gain, and all those who are built up to get power over the flesh, and those who are built up to become popular in the eyes of the world, and those who seek the lusts of the flesh and the things of the world, and to do all manner of iniquity; yea, in fine, all those who belong to the kingdom of the devil* are they who need fear, and tremble, and quake; they are those who must be brought low in the dust; **they are those who must be consumed as stubble**; and this is according to the words of the prophet.

The problem with members who stop preparing (Luke 12:45–48)

But and if that servant say in his heart, My lord delayeth his coming; and shall begin to beat the menservants and maidens, and to eat and drink, and to be drunken;

The lord of that servant will come in a day when he looketh not for *him*, and at an hour when he is not aware, and will cut him in sunder, and will appoint him his portion with the unbelievers.

And that servant, which knew his lord's will, and prepared not *himself*, neither did according to his will, shall be beaten with many *stripes*.

But he that knew not, and did commit things worthy of stripes, shall be beaten with few *stripes*. For unto whomsoever much is given, of him shall be much required: and to whom men have committed much, of him they will ask the more.

19

DETECTING AND OVERCOMING SATAN

This may seem like an unlikely topic to discuss in a book devoted to formulas for success. However, without some caution this chapter could evolve into an entire book. Let's start with a thought-provoking question that initially may elicit the wrong response: Is the devil an essential part of God's plan for the salvation of His children? Many very bright college-aged students answer, "Yes, absolutely!" A follow-up question isn't so easily answered: "In other words an omniscient, omnipotent Being is beholding to a rebellious spirit son to make His plan work?" A third question creates even more food for thought: "If mortals must be tempted in order to pass the tests of mortality, how will those who will be born, live, and die during the Millennium pass their tests since Satan will be bound?" With very little mental effort, the question poses itself in the form of, "Is there a devil on other worlds?" Or is the fact that Satan and his angels were cast out of heaven on this world (see Revelation 12:9) what causes the premortal Savior to explain to Enoch as he showed him the future history of this world: "Wherefore, I can stretch forth mine hands and hold all the creations which I have made; and mine eye can pierce them also, and among all the workmanship of mine hands there has not been so great wickedness as among thy brethren" (Moses 7:36).

Although interesting and thought-provoking, the answer to these questions is ancillary to our discussion and must be postponed to a later time. But it is a given fact that the devil and his angels are here on this earth and are intensifying their efforts to enslave and destroy mankind more than ever before. Why is that so? John the Revelator, seeing our day in vision, wrote: "Therefore rejoice, ye heavens, and ye that dwell in them. Woe to the inhabiters of the earth and of the sea! for the devil is come down unto you, having great wrath, because he knoweth that he hath but a short time" (Revelation 12:12).

Although the following list of Satan's tactics and objectives is not comprehensive, one can benefit by recognizing who we are fighting and some of the plays in their game-plan. One tactic that is almost unbelievable but very evidently successful in our day was seen and described by Nephi over 2500 years ago. He wrote:

> For behold, at that day shall he rage in the hearts of the children of men, and stir them up to anger against that which is good.
>
> And others will he pacify, and lull them away into carnal security, that they will say: All is well in Zion; yea, Zion prospereth, all is well—and thus the devil cheateth their souls, and leadeth them away carefully down to hell.
>
> And behold, others he flattereth away, and telleth **them there is no hell; and he saith unto them: I am no devil, for there is none**—and thus he whispereth in their ears, until he grasps them with his awful chains, from whence there is no deliverance. (2 Nephi 28:20–22)

Denying the existence of a devil or a place of punishment (hell), the devil and his angels can go about without fear of detection doing exactly what Peter warned: "Be sober, be vigilant; because your adversary the devil, as a roaring lion, walketh about, seeking whom he may devour" (1 Peter 5:8) .

In addition to warning us of Satan's ploy that he doesn't exist, Nephi said the devil would rage in people's hearts and stir them up to anger against anything that is good. One needs only watch, listen to, or read the news to see the fulfillment of that prophecy. Not only on the national and international stage are terrorists trying to destroy anything and everything that is good with no viable replacement, but on the individual and family level atrocities are being committed daily as well.

Nephi continues his prophecy, explaining that others will be succored into believing that we can kick back and relax since all of this violence is "over there and amongst other people" and does not directly involve us.

So important does the Lord see His warning to us about Satan's tactics that he devotes one of the early sections of the Doctrine and Covenants (section 10) to making us aware. Although the Lord is speaking directly about the book of Lehi (116 lost manuscript pages) Satan's tactic that was successfully used then is being employed daily among us: "And, on this wise, the devil has sought to lay a cunning plan, that he may destroy this work (you!); For he hath put into their hearts to do this, that **by lying** they may say they have caught you in the words which you have pretended to translate" (D&C 10:12–13, emphasis and additions added). Isaiah noted this same lying tactic when he penned: "**That make a man an offender for a word,** and lay a snare for him that reproveth in the gate, and turn aside the just for a thing of nought" (Isaiah 29:21).

The Lord further warns in section 10:

> Verily, verily, I say unto you, that Satan has great hold upon their hearts; he stirreth them up to iniquity against that which is good;
>
> And their hearts are corrupt, and full of wickedness and abominations; and they love darkness rather than light, because their deeds are evil; therefore they will not ask of me.
>
> Satan stirreth them up, that he may lead their souls to destruction. (D&C 10:20–22)

How has Satan been able to lead so many people to do everything from redefining marriage to legalizing abortion to excluding even the mention of God from our classrooms, and the list goes on and on? Not only are there those who advocate positions contrary to what God has revealed, but they become militant in demanding their "rights" while at the same time they try to deny others of their God-given rights.

Why the near constant opposition to the Church in the news, on the internet, and increasingly found on social media? It shouldn't be a surprise since the Lord said: "Yea, he stirreth up their hearts to anger against this work" (D&C 10:24).

Another practice which is revealed almost daily in the news media is a tactic Satan uses that the Lord foretold:

> Yea, he saith unto them: Deceive and lie in wait to catch, that ye may destroy; behold, this is no harm. And thus he flattereth them, and telleth them that it is no sin to lie that they may catch a man in a lie, that they may destroy him.
>
> And thus he flattereth them, and leadeth them along until he draggeth their souls down to hell; and thus he causeth them to catch themselves in their own snare.
>
> And thus he goeth up and down, to and fro in the earth, seeking to destroy the souls of men. (D&C 10:25–27)

Within far too many Church meetings as well as in every conceivable forum outside the Church, Satan uses another tactic very successfully: "And this I do that I may establish my gospel, that there **may not be so much contention**; yea, **Satan doth stir up the hearts of the people to contention concerning the points of my doctrine**; and in these things they do err, for they do wrest the scriptures and do not understand them" (D&C 10:63).

The list can be expanded to book length, but there are two overriding statements that may raise the warning flag for all of us. Satan is called "the enemy to all righteousness" five times in the scriptures. For example: "Yea, cry unto him against the devil, **who is an enemy to all righteousness**" (Alma 34:23). The second overriding concept is found in Moroni 7:12: "Wherefore, all things which are good cometh of God; and that which is evil cometh of the devil; for the **devil is an enemy unto God, and fighteth against him continually**, and *inviteth and enticeth to sin, and to do that which is evil continually.*" It should not be surprising to a Latter-day Saint that whenever he or she tries to do anything good or that will lead them toward their eternal goal of exaltation, they will experience satanic opposition. That will happen in marriages, families, wards, stakes, communities, as well as nations and worldwide.

For a continuing study of Satan and his tactics see "Points for Further Consideration" at the end of the chapter.

Overcoming Satan and his temptations

It is obvious from the above scriptures that the Lord knows there is a devil and realizes without divine direction His mortal children would not be able to withstand the increasingly difficult and sophisticated attacks of the adversary and his angels. Although a comprehensive investigation of what the Lord has revealed concerning detecting and overcoming satanic attacks is warranted, an in-depth evaluation of a twice repeated formula will suffice for this study.

In Ephesians 6:11–18 the Apostle Paul saw our day and gave us a warning. In Doctrine and Covenants 27:15–18 the Lord gave Joseph Smith the same warning again. We will cite Paul's formula in total and carefully look for the elements of the formula and how to apply them. Although I have taught "The Whole Armor of God" for nearly four decades to college-aged students, few seem to have any concept of what it means and how to apply it, although many can quote it verbatim.

> Put on the whole armour of God, that ye may be able to stand against the wiles of the devil.
>
> For we wrestle not against flesh and blood, but against principalities, against powers, against the rulers of the darkness of this world, against spiritual wickedness in high *places*.
>
> Wherefore take unto you the whole armour of God, that ye may be able to withstand in the evil day, and having done all, to stand.
>
> Stand therefore, having your loins girt about with truth, and having on the breastplate of righteousness;
>
> And your feet shod with the preparation of the gospel of peace;
>
> Above all, taking the shield of faith, wherewith ye shall be able to quench all the fiery darts of the wicked.
>
> And take the helmet of salvation, and the sword of the Spirit, which is the word of God:
>
> Praying always with all prayer and supplication in the Spirit, and watching thereunto with all perseverance and supplication for all saints. (Ephesians 6:11–18)

Paul realized that many of the adversaries we would face would not be mortal. Although in today's world we indeed are concerned with wars, terrorists, gangs, and evil persons, the subtler and equally as lethal foes we face are not seen. Paul, using the ever present Roman soldiers as visible object lessons, teaches how to stand in the final days leading up to the Second Coming.

Stand therefore, having your loins girt about with truth. Why would Paul start with the loins? Could it be that the greatest challenge to our successfully negotiating the challenges of the latter days will be against our use—and not misuse—of our procreative powers? Any review of the studies or polls concerning chastity or morality in our day clearly reveals that a growing majority of people (members not excluded) have diminished or dismissed all together the commandment to be morally clean. Movies, DVDs, the internet, books, television, and even commercials have moved from being suggestive to pornographic.

How are we to teach our children to avoid following the path of a self-destructing world? What is truth, and how can it protect our virtue? There are many definitions of truth. I have provided a list at the end of this chapter, but we will study two right now. The Savior said, "I am the way, the **truth** and the life" (John 14:6). Christ is the truth, and He is the way we can withstand all of the temptations we face. Alma taught his son, "Preach unto them repentance, and faith on the Lord Jesus Christ; teach them to humble themselves and to be meek and lowly in heart; **teach them to withstand every temptation of the devil, with their faith on the Lord Jesus Christ**" (Alma 37:33).

Let's also expand our understanding of what the Lord revealed in Doctrine and Covenants 93:24: "And **truth** is *knowledge of things as they are, and as they were, and as they are to come.*" Truth does not change with the changing times. What was wrong when God revealed it from Mt. Sinai is wrong today in spite of what governments legislate and mankind believes. God's commandments are not subject to popular vote or worldwide disagreement. Certainly, the Ten Commandments are not a true/false test or a multiple-choice test.

Let's take one example that seemed to help my college-aged students understand better. Most of them were searching for a spouse. When progressively talking them verbally through the steps of immorality starting with holding hands and ending with intercourse, I asked them to mentally raise their hand when their future mate (whom they supposedly had never met) was on a date with another person and started getting physically involved. Although I was not privy to when they raised their mental hand signalizing that they did not want their future mate going any further with another person, I would then say, "Now the truth is that it is totally hypocritical for you to expect a higher degree of morality of your future mate than you are willing to live as you date other people prior to finding your eternal companion." It was evident from the looks on their faces that they hadn't understood that truth does not change when applied to themselves compared to their future mates.

If we are determined to successfully endure to the Second Coming, we had better establish what the truth is and then do all in our power to apply those truths to our moral standing no matter what the world is willing to accept.

Next Paul teaches us to "**[put] on the breastplate of righteousness.**" The breastplate covers our vital organs—especially the heart. So, what is "righteousness," and why is it necessary to cover our heart with it in order to stand against the adversary? Perhaps it is easier to define "right." If we could agree with the definition "what God says is right is right and what God says is wrong is wrong," it makes this part of the formula much easier to find application. In an ever-changing world where right and wrong are all relative, James describes it best by saying: "For he that wavereth is like a wave of the sea driven with the wind and tossed" (James 1:6).

Although we need to treat those with a different sexual orientation with Christlike kindness, we should never try to modify what God has revealed from the beginning. Homosexuality has never been approved by God, and given that He is an unchangeable being, it isn't likely that He will change His mind anytime soon. The same is true with abortion, the legalization of drugs, the definition of marriage, and what is sure to be an ever-increasing number of other God-revealed issues. We would do well to follow the Lord's counsel given shortly after the Church was restored to those who wanted to dictate to Him the conditions upon which they wanted to join the Church. He said, "Seek not to counsel your God" (D&C 22:4).

Next Paul counsels us to make "**your feet shod with the preparation of the gospel of peace**." What is the gospel of peace? Perhaps it is easier to answer the question: "Who is the Prince of Peace?" Isaiah said: "For unto us a child is born, unto us a son is given: and the government shall be upon his shoulder: and his name shall be called Wonderful, Counsellor, The mighty God, The everlasting Father, **The Prince of Peace**" (Isaiah 9:6).

Now for a little deductive reasoning. What are feet used for? A logical answer might be to carry us toward our goal. Since the gospel was restored so that we might enjoy eternal glory with the Lord (the Prince of Peace) in the highest degree of the celestial kingdom, then we should be able to conclude that we can tell if our feet are shod with what would prepare us for exaltation by merely asking the question: "If I do this will it take me toward my eternal goal?" If the answer is "no," then don't do it.

The questions necessary to get a temple recommend to enter into a temple (also called the House of the Lord) is a great reminder of what is necessary to enter into God's presence. The unchangeable God would not have one standard for entering His earthly temple and a different one for entering into His eternal presence. So, when faced with any decision of life, it is a simple thing to question whether it would put in jeopardy your worthiness to enter the temple.

Next in Paul's explanation of the essentials to withstand the evil attacks of the adversary he says: "**Above all, taking the shield of faith.**" Where is a shield used? Not infrequently the students would answer, "Everywhere!" I would chide them by saying, "No wonder you kids get wounded so often. A shield is a secondary defensive weapon used wherever you are being attacked!" If you are morally challenged, use your shield to reinforce your understanding of the truth. If your conduct is under attack, use your shield of faith to hold fast to what the Lord has revealed in scriptures and through latter-day prophets. Perhaps the shield is put before the next piece of armor for a specific reason.

Paul then says, "And **take the helmet of salvation**." The intellectual challenge to the elements of the plan of salvation, the existence of God, the reality of a Christ, and everything else that so-called science can mount sometime requires the shield of faith to be able to "to quench all the fiery darts of the wicked."

For years scientists have scoffed at various teachings of the Church such as pre-Spanish horses in America, records kept on metallic plates, the harmfulness of tobacco and alcohol, and so on. Now each of those (and many, many more) have been proven by the scientific world to be exactly what the Lord revealed. Still there are those who mockingly laugh at the creation of the earth by an intelligent being, preferring to believe the astronomically impossible theories of spontaneous generation. All of this challenges the revealed truth that we lived as spirit children of God long before being born on earth. That earth life is part of a divine plan for the future exaltation of God's spirit children. That there is life after death and there will be a time of judgment. That man will literally be resurrected and live forever.

Through a very sad experience with a very close friend whose faith was destroyed as an atheistic professor assailed her testimony of the plan of salvation, I have come to realize through her teaching me that if one loses his or her testimony of the plan of salvation, like dominoes all of the other commandments fall. I am comfortable for the present in not knowing so many things that so-called scientist put forth as "proof positive" that the gospel is not correct. The Lord revealed: "Yea, verily I say unto you, **in that day when the Lord shall come, he shall reveal all things**—Things which have passed, and hidden things which no man knew, things of the earth, by which it was made, and the purpose and the end thereof—Things most precious, things that are above, and things that are beneath, things that are in the earth, and upon the earth, and in heaven" (D&C 101:32–34). As you continue to faithfully live the gospel, you will see that not infrequently what scientists taunt as "absolutely true" is proven false by further discoveries—all of which confirm what God has revealed from the beginning of time.

Before leaving the defensive part of the armor, it should be noted that one part of the body is conspicuously not covered—the back. To me that indicates that the trials, temptations, and fiery darts of the adversary cannot be avoided by running away. We must meet them face on. However, if all of these parts of the armor are firmly in place, we will still lose without an offensive weapon. Paul informed us that the offensive weapon is "the sword of the Spirit."

In an attempt to help students understand the necessity of living so that the Spirit could be their constant companion, I asked, "What do you think would happen if a person stepped onto a real battlefield where swords and shields were used without a sword or a shield?" Yet I watched so many (even returned missionaries) disqualify themselves from having the Spirit by the movies they watched, the internet sites they visited, or the games they played. As they started to question their faith, I could see far too many of them rationalize that they no longer embraced the faith that they had so vigorously proclaimed and defended on their missions.

There is no question as to why Paul ended his analogy with the plea to remember our prayers and to stay in close company with those of like faith (watching thereunto with all perseverance and supplication for all Saints). Even with all of the warnings and helps, we mortals find it difficult to go against an unseen foe who has enjoyed over six thousand years' experience tempting and destroying billions of sons and daughters of God. It would be unfair except that the Lord has promised,

> I will go before your face. I will be on your right hand and on your left, and my Spirit shall be in your hearts, and mine angels round about you, to bear you up. (D&C 84:88)

> But behold, verily, verily, I say unto you that mine eyes are upon you. I am in your midst and ye cannot see me;
>
> But the day soon cometh that ye shall see me, and know that I am; for the veil of darkness shall soon be rent, and he that is not purified shall not abide the day.
>
> Wherefore, gird up your loins and be prepared. Behold, the kingdom is yours, and **the enemy shall not overcome.** (D&C 38:7–9)

It is evident that the Lord knows perfectly well what we are going through and the opposition we are facing. In a section demonstrating His great concern for His Saints, the Lord said: "But now I tell it unto you, and ye are blessed, not because of your iniquity, neither your hearts of unbelief; for verily some of you are guilty before me, **but I will be merciful unto your weakness.** Therefore, be ye strong from henceforth; fear not, for the kingdom is yours" (D&C 38:14–15). We are not sent here to fail, and we will not fail if we will take advantage of the resources and the directions the Lord has provided for our salvation.

POINTS FOR FURTHER CONSIDERATION

The devil is the founder of secret combinations (Ether 8:25)

It [secret combinations] is built up by the **devil**, who is the *father of all lies;* even that same liar who *beguiled our first parents,* yea, even that *same liar who hath caused man to commit murder from the beginning.*

The devil is a murderer and a liar (John 8:44)

Ye are of your father the **devil**, and the lust of your father ye will do. *He was a murderer from the beginning, and abode not in the truth, because there is no truth in him.* When he speaketh a lie, he speaketh of his own: for he is a liar, and the father of it.

The devil appeared to Korihor as an angel (Alma 30:53)

But behold, the **devil hath deceived me; for he appeared unto me in the form of an angel.**

The devil doesn't know the mind of God (Moses 4:6)

And Satan put it into the heart of the serpent, (for he had drawn away many after him,) and he sought also to beguile Eve, **for he knew not the mind of God**, wherefore he sought to destroy the world.

The devil is the father of all lies (2 Nephi 2:18)

And because he had fallen from heaven, and had become miserable forever, he sought also the misery of all mankind. Wherefore, he said unto Eve, yea, even that old serpent, who is **the devil, who is the father of all lies**, wherefore he said: Partake of the forbidden fruit, and ye shall not die, but ye shall be as God, knowing good and evil (see also Ether 8:25; Moses 4:4; JST, Genesis 3:5)

The devil never persuades men to do good (Moroni 7:17)

But whatsoever thing persuadeth men to do evil, and believe not in Christ, and deny him, and serve not God, then ye may know with a perfect knowledge it is of the devil; **for after this manner doth the devil work, for he persuadeth no man to do good, no, not one**; neither do his angels; neither do they who subject themselves unto him.

The devil's power

And not choose eternal death, according to *the will of the flesh and the evil which is therein,* which **giveth the spirit of the devil power** to captivate, to bring you down to hell, that he may reign over you in his own kingdom (2 Nephi 2:29).

And thus we see how great the inequality of man is because of sin and transgression, and the **power of the devil,** *which comes by the cunning plans which he hath devised to ensnare the hearts of men* (Alma 28:13).

Behold, verily I say unto you, there are *hypocrites among you, who have deceived some,* which **has given the adversary power**; but behold such shall be reclaimed (D&C 50:7).

The devil will have power over his dominion before the Second Coming (D&C 1:35)

For I am no respecter of persons, and will that all men shall know that the day speedily cometh; the hour is not yet, but is nigh at hand, when peace shall be taken from the earth, and **the devil shall have power over his own dominion.**

The devil will not support his children in last days (Alma 30:60)

And thus we see the end of him who perverteth the ways of the Lord; and thus we see that the **devil will not support his children at the last day,** *but doth speedily drag them down to hell.*

The devil's objective

And because he had fallen from heaven, and had become miserable forever, he **sought also the misery of all mankind.** (2 Nephi 2:18)

Wherefore, men are free according to the flesh; and all things are given them which are expedient unto man. And they are free to choose liberty and eternal life, through the great Mediator of all men, or to choose captivity and death, according to the captivity and power of the **devil; for he seeketh that all men might be miserable like unto himself.** (2 Nephi 2:27)

Satan stirreth them up, **that he may lead their souls to destruction.** (D&C 10:22)

And thus he goeth up and down, to and fro in the earth, **seeking to destroy the souls of men.** (D&C 10:27)

And also Satan hath sought to deceive you, that **he might overthrow you.** (D&C 50:3)

Yea, how could you have given way to the enticing of him who is **seeking to hurl away your souls down to everlasting misery and endless wo?** (Helaman 7:16)

The **evil one** *who seeketh to destroy the souls of men* (Helaman 8:28; see also Moses 4:6; 2 Nephi 2:18, 28).

The devil's tactics

And he became Satan, yea, even the devil, the father of all lies, **to deceive and to blind men, and to lead them captive at his will,** even as many as would not hearken unto my voice. (Moses 4:4)

Verily, verily, I say unto you, that Satan has great hold upon their hearts; he **stirreth them up to iniquity against that which is good.** (D&C 10:20)

Yea, he **stirreth up their hearts to anger against this work.** (D&C 10:24)

Yea, he saith unto them: Deceive and lie in wait to catch, that ye may destroy; behold, this is no harm. And thus **he flattereth them,** and **telleth them that it is no sin to lie** that they may catch a man in a lie, that they may destroy him. (D&C 10:25)

And thus he flattereth them, and leadeth them along until he draggeth their souls down to hell; and thus he **causeth them to catch themselves in their own snare.** (D&C 10:26)

And thus **he goeth up and down, to and fro in the earth,** *seeking to destroy the souls of men.* (D&C 10:27)

And the children of men were numerous upon all the face of the land. And in those days Satan had great dominion among men, and **raged in their hearts;** and from thenceforth came **wars and bloodshed;** and a man's hand was against his own brother, in administering death, because of secret works, **seeking for power.** (Moses 6:15)

Satan makes war with Saints (D&C 76:29)

Wherefore, **he [Satan,** see verse 28] maketh **war with the saints of God,** and *encompasseth them round about.*

Doctrine and Covenants 27:15–18

The Whole Armor of God reiterated by the Lord as a warning and method of overcoming Satan's s temptations in the latter-days.

Truth

Thy word is **truth** (John 17:17).

The *Spirit* is **truth** (John 5:6).

Behold, my brethren, he that prophesieth, let him prophesy to the understanding of men; for the **Spirit speaketh the truth and lieth not.** Wherefore, it *speaketh of things as they really are, and of things as they really will be*; wherefore, these things are manifested unto us plainly, for the salvation of our souls. But behold, we are not witnesses alone in these things; for God also spake them unto prophets of old (Jacob 4:13).

For the *word of the Lord* is **truth**, and whatsoever is **truth** is light, and whosoever is light is Spirit, even the *Spirit of Jesus Christ* (D&C 84:45).

Behold, that which you hear is as the voice of one crying in the wilderness-in the wilderness, because you cannot see him-my voice, because my voice is Spirit; *my Spirit is* **truth;** truth abideth and hath no end; and if it be in you it shall abound (D&C 88:66).

A word beyond scripture: For those of you have been through the temple, it would be wise to return and do a session of initiatory ordinances and listen closely to the thirteen promises you were given and the power the garment holds.

20

GETTING POWER IN THE PRIESTHOOD

The formula for getting power in the priesthood is fairly simple. Applying the conditions is a challenge of a lifetime. Perhaps the best place to start is with the incomparable oath and covenant of the priesthood found in Doctrine and Covenants 84:33–44:

> For whoso is faithful unto the obtaining these two priesthoods of which I have spoken, and the magnifying their calling, are sanctified by the Spirit unto the renewing of their bodies.
>
> They become the sons of Moses and of Aaron and the seed of Abraham, and the church and kingdom, and the elect of God.
>
> And also all they who receive this priesthood receive me, saith the Lord;
>
> For he that receiveth my servants receiveth me;
>
> And he that receiveth me receiveth my Father;
>
> And he that receiveth my Father receiveth my Father's kingdom; therefore all that my Father hath shall be given unto him.
>
> And this is according to the oath and covenant which belongeth to the priesthood.
>
> Therefore, all those who receive the priesthood, receive this oath and covenant of my Father, which he cannot break, neither can it be moved.

> But whoso breaketh this covenant after he hath received it, and altogether turneth therefrom, shall not have forgiveness of sins in this world nor in the world to come.
>
> And wo unto all those who come not unto this priesthood which ye have received, which I now confirm upon you who are present this day, by mine own voice out of the heavens; and even I have given the heavenly hosts and mine angels charge concerning you.
>
> And I now give unto you a commandment to beware concerning yourselves, to give diligent heed to the words of eternal life.
>
> For you shall live by every word that proceedeth forth from the mouth of God.

As we analyze what the Lord has revealed, it should become evident that being entrusted with the priesthood—literally the power of God—is no light thing and should only be entered into if we have seriously considered not only the blessings but the responsibilities associated with the priesthood.

First, we must be faithful enough to receive the priesthood. Since baptism is a prerequisite to priesthood ordination, it seems apparent that we should be living the covenants we made in the waters of baptism, some of which include:

> Ye are desirous to come into the fold of God, and to be called his people, and are willing to bear one another's burdens, that they may be light;
>
> Yea, and are willing to mourn with those that mourn; yea, and comfort those that stand in need of comfort, and to stand as witnesses of God at all times and in all things, and in all places that ye may be in, even until death. (Mosiah 18:8–9)

Priesthood requires selfless service. Abinadi instructed wicked King Noah and his priests what priesthood meant: "And **thus being called by this holy calling, and ordained unto the high priesthood of the holy order of God**, *to teach his commandments unto the children of men*, that they also might enter into his rest" (Alma 13:6).

If we are living our baptismal covenants and are willing to devote whatever time is required in serving and teaching others, we are in line to receive the priesthood. Now the charge is that we must also magnify our calling. Many people define "magnify" as "to enlarge and expand"—both of which are correct definitions. But how can we enlarge something so powerful it can create worlds without number? Considering a magnifying glass, one can ignite grass or paper using the rays of the sun. Would you say that the magnifying glass increased the power of the sun? What actually happened was that it focused the rays of the sun. Could giving a priesthood blessing be similar to using a magnifying glass? By placing hands on the head of a sick or ailing person, the normal powers of the priesthood which are all about us are focused or concentrated on the individual.

The result of the righteous use of the priesthood is to sanctify the priesthood bearer to the point of renewing his body. Perhaps that is one reason we do not give ourselves priesthood blessings. In blessing others, the Lord sanctifies and blesses us.

Over time, as we righteously use the priesthood, we become "the sons of Moses." Moses was a prophet who received revelations for the children of Israel. We, in turn, by magnifying the priesthood, qualify to receive revelation, insight, inspiration, or prompting for those over whom we have stewardship.

Continuing, we become the sons of Aaron. Aaron was a priest who officiated in ordinances for the spiritual welfare of the people. We also are empowered with the insight and knowledge to minister to the spiritual needs of our family and those over whom we preside. Aaron was further charged with the temporal or physical welfare of the people. If we magnify our priesthood, we will have insights necessary to also provide for our family and other for whom we have stewardship.

Further, we become the "seed of Abraham." Abraham was a patriarch. A righteous father has the right to give a patriarchal blessing (a father's blessing) to his wife and children. Although he may desire to have it recorded for posterity's sake, the difference between the stake patriarch's blessing and a father's blessing is that the patriarch's blessing is kept permanently on the records of the Church, while the father's blessing may be kept in the family records.

We also become "the church and kingdom and the elect of God." Although each of those words have been applied to our earthly experience, they have also been applied to the eternal state of man.

How can one possibly learn to use that unlimited source of power without self-destructing? The Lord answers that question: "All they who receive this priesthood receive me, saith the Lord" (D&C 84:35). Through the prompting of His Spirit a faithful, humble priesthood bearer will be instructed how to use the priesthood. It should be noted that being a bearer of the priesthood does not mean one can force the

Lord to do something contrary to His will. It is a continual refining process to learn to recognize what the will of God is and then use the priesthood to accomplish God's will.

The account is recorded about Nephi, son of Helaman, when the Lord said to him:

> And it came to pass as he was thus pondering in his heart, behold, a voice came unto him saying:
>
> Blessed art thou, Nephi, for those things which thou hast done; for I have beheld how thou hast with unwearyingness declared the word, which I have given unto thee, unto this people. And thou hast not feared them, and hast not sought thine own life, but **hast sought my will**, and to keep my commandments.
>
> And now, because thou hast done this with such unwearyingness, behold, I will bless thee forever; and I will make thee mighty in word and in deed, in faith and in works; yea, **even that all things shall be done unto thee according to thy word, for thou shalt not ask that which is contrary to my will.** (Helaman 10:3–5)

A wise priesthood bearer constantly seeks to know the will of the Lord. Additional help comes in the form of priesthood leaders: "For he that receiveth my servants receiveth me" (D&C 84:36). A constant study of the teachings of living prophets and apostles will yield a wealth of direction on how to magnify our priesthood callings.

Since our eternal objective is to become like our Heavenly Father, the next promise has particular meaning:

> And he that receiveth me receiveth my Father;
>
> And he that receiveth my Father receiveth my Father's kingdom; therefore **all that my Father hath shall be given unto him.**
>
> And this is according to the oath and covenant which belongeth to the priesthood.
>
> Therefore, all those who receive the priesthood, receive this oath and covenant of my Father, which he cannot break, neither can it be moved. (D&C 84:37–40)

What does the Father have? All power, all knowledge, and the ability to create and people worlds eternally. Although the magnitude of that blessing is impossible to comprehend, the promise is made sure by an oath and covenant which the Father cannot break or modify. With that degree of surety, surely there must be consequences if we fail to keep our part of the agreement.

In a very sobering verse the Lord says: "But whoso breaketh this covenant after he hath received it, and altogether turneth therefrom, shall not have forgiveness of sins in this world nor in the world to come" (D&C 84:41). Whether that applies to every priesthood bearer who becomes less active in the Church is a point of question. Why would any man want to run the risk of being required to pay for his own sins merely to indulge in practices that limit or preclude the use of the priesthood?

To a male Church member who cowers away from receiving the priesthood because of the attendant responsibilities, the Lord says:

> And wo unto all those who come not unto this priesthood which ye have received, which I now confirm upon you who are present this day, by mine own voice out of the heavens; and even I have given the heavenly hosts and mine angels charge concerning you.
>
> And I now give unto you a commandment to beware concerning yourselves, to give diligent heed to the words of eternal life.
>
> For you shall live by every word that proceedeth forth from the mouth of God. (D&C 84:42–44)

Why would the Lord use such a harsh warning about not coming to the priesthood? Perhaps another part of Abinadi's teachings apply. Alma 13:3–5 reads:

> And this is the manner after which they were ordained—**being called and prepared from the foundation of the world according to the foreknowledge of God**, on account of their exceeding faith and good works; in the first place being left to choose good or evil; therefore they having chosen good, and exercising exceedingly great faith, are called with a holy calling, yea, with that holy calling which was prepared with, and according to, a preparatory redemption for such.
>
> And thus they have been called to this holy calling on account of their faith, while others would reject the Spirit of God on account of the hardness of their hearts and blindness of their minds, while, if it had not been for this they might have had as great privilege as their brethren.
>
> Or in fine, in the first place they were on the same standing with their brethren; thus this holy calling being prepared from the foundation of the world for such as would not harden their hearts, being in and through the atonement of the Only Begotten Son, who was prepared.

It appears that we had made an eternal commitment concerning the accepting and using of the priesthood. Failure to accept that draws forth a "wo" from the Savior. Reassuring us that we haven't taken on a responsibility that we can't fulfill, the Lord states that He has given the angels charge concerning us. However, He also gives us the charge that we need to take responsibility for our own actions. Up to the time we receive the Melchizedek Priesthood we have had parents, teachers, leaders, and so on to "herd" us in the right direction. Now the Lord says we must "beware concerning yourselves, to give diligent heed to the words of eternal life." Additionally, He warns about being "selectively obedient." We are to "live by every word that proceedeth forth from the mouth of God."

While the blessing associated with bearing the priesthood are incomparable, the attendant responsibilities are equally as daunting.

Now let us shift our attention to the prerequisites necessary to use the priesthood. In D&C 121:34–40 the Lord explains the challenges faced by priesthood bearers:

> Behold, there are many called, but few are chosen. And **why are they not chosen?** (What is the reason foreordained men fail to get and honor the priesthood?)
>
> Because their (1) hearts are set so much upon the things of this world, and (2) aspire to the honors of men, that **they do not learn this one lesson**—
>
> That the rights of the priesthood are inseparably connected with the powers of heaven, and that the powers of heaven cannot be controlled nor handled only upon the principles of righteousness. (emphasis and commentary added)

Here is a lesson on how to use the priesthood to become like our Heavenly Father. These principles of righteousness are the very ones on which the government of heaven is conducted.

"That they may be conferred upon us, it is true; but (1) when we undertake to cover our sins, or (2) to gratify our pride, our vain ambition, or (3) to exercise control or dominion or compulsion upon the souls of the children of men, in any degree of unrighteousness, behold, (a) the heavens withdraw themselves; (b) the Spirit of the Lord is grieved; and when it is withdrawn, (c) Amen to the priesthood or the authority of that man" (D&C 121:37; numbers and letters added).

The commentary is sobering. Three activities seem to be the major stumbling blocks to all priesthood bearers as numbered above (cover our sins; gratify our pride; exercise unrighteous dominion or compulsion). Then the three-lettered consequences happen almost before the priesthood bearer is aware (heaven withdraws—no divine guidance; the Spirit is withdrawn—no revelation; no power in the priesthood). The consequences of failing to recognize and fix the problem are equally as sobering:

> Behold, ere he is aware, (1) he is left unto himself, (2) to kick against the pricks, (3) to persecute the saints, and (4) to fight against God.
>
> We have learned by sad experience that it is the nature and disposition of almost all men, as soon as they get a little authority, as they suppose, they will immediately begin to exercise unrighteous dominion.
>
> Hence many are called, but few are chosen. (numbers added)

The grouping of "almost all men" causes one to wonder if the priesthood is really a blessing. Obviously, it is—especially to those who are willing to heed the Lord's warning and take the steps to avoid the pitfalls. Next the Lord outlines the eleven principles of righteousness that should be the manual of operation for everything we do using the priesthood—or in our everyday lives.

> No power or influence can or ought to be maintained by virtue of the priesthood, only by persuasion, by long-suffering, by gentleness and meekness, and by love unfeigned;
>
> By kindness, and pure knowledge, which shall greatly enlarge the soul without hypocrisy, and without guile—
>
> Reproving betimes with sharpness, when moved upon by the Holy Ghost; and then showing forth afterwards an increase of love toward him whom thou hast reproved, lest he esteem thee to be his enemy;
>
> That he may know that thy faithfulness is stronger than the cords of death.
>
> Let thy bowels also be full of charity towards all men, and to the household of faith, and let virtue garnish thy thoughts unceasingly. (D&C 121:41–45).

After teaching Doctrine and Covenants 121 to my BYU religion classes, I sat in my office reviewing how well I was doing in applying those eleven principles in my own life. I concluded that I was doing pretty well. As though an afterthought from the other side of the veil, I thought, "I ought to look up the antonyms just to see what the devil's counterfeits are." In the chart below, I discovered something that completely erased my smug attitude about how well I was doing. Yes, I had the beginnings of all eleven principles of righteousness, but I also had more than a little of many of the antonyms. See how you fare when you do the same evaluation:

11 Principles of Righteousness and Their Opposites
Doctrine and Covenants 121:41–45

Godly Principle	Satan's Opposing Influence
1. Persuasion	Force, duress, pressure, demanding, guilt trip
2. Long-suffering	Short fuse, intolerant, quick to anger, impatient, insistent, irritable, mean, always have to be right, stubborn, close-minded
3. Gentleness and meekness	Violence, defiance, mean-spirited, antagonistic, contentious
4. Love unfeigned	Forced affection, alienation, isolation, hatred
5. Kindness	Anger, cruelty, miserliness
6. Pure knowledge, which shall enlarge the soul without hypocrisy	Close-mindedness, false traditions, incorrect theories, false ideas, lack of understanding
7. Without guile	Trickery, deceit, insincerity, lack of honesty in dealings
8. Reproving Betimes with sharpness when moved upon by the Holy Ghost	Global anger, non-specific castigations, dredging up past, ungodly anger, rage, false accusations
9. Showing forth Afterward an increase of love toward him whom thou has reproved, lest he esteem thee to be his enemy	Withholding affections, continuing to punish, sulking, unwillingness to communicate, moodiness, irritable, melancholy, oppressive, pessimism
10. Let thy bowels also be full of charity towards all men, and to the household of faith (D&C 88:125–charity is the bond of perfectness and peace)	Tearing down, put down, condescending remarks, agitation, combative
11. Let virtue garnish thy thoughts unceasingly	Immoral, low, course, evil, fault-finding, worthless, imperfections, ineffectiveness

If we could successfully employ those eleven principles of righteousness in all we do, there are five promised blessings which would follow:

> (1) then shall thy confidence wax strong in the presence of God; and (2) the doctrine of the priesthood shall distil upon thy soul as the dews from heaven.
>
> (3) The Holy Ghost shall be thy constant companion, and (4) thy scepter an unchanging scepter of righteousness and truth; and (5) thy dominion shall be an everlasting dominion, and without compulsory means it shall flow unto thee forever and ever. (D&C 121:45–46, numbers added)

POINTS FOR FURTHER CONSIDERATION

Priesthood

Behold, I will lead thee by my hand, and I will take thee, to put upon thee *my name*, even the **Priesthood** of thy father, and my power shall be over thee (Abraham 1:18).

Priesthood (Melchizedek) all authority and offices are appendages to (D&C 107:5)

All other authorities or offices in the church are appendages to this **priesthood** [**Melchizedek,** see verse 4].

Priesthood of Aaron (D&C 13:1)

Priesthood of Aaron, which holds the *keys of the ministering of angels, and of the gospel of repentance, and of baptism by immersion for the remission of sins.*

1 Peter 2:5

Ye also, as lively stones, are built up a spiritual house, an holy priesthood, to offer up spiritual sacrifices, acceptable to God by Jesus Christ.

Doctrine and Covenants 84:19–25

And this greater priesthood administereth the gospel and holdeth the key of the mysteries of the kingdom, even the key of the knowledge of God.

Therefore, in the ordinances thereof, the power of godliness is manifest.

And without the ordinances thereof, and the authority of the priesthood, the power of godliness is not manifest unto men in the flesh;

For without this no man can see the face of God, even the Father, and live.

Now this Moses plainly taught to the children of Israel in the wilderness, and sought diligently to sanctify his people that they might behold the face of God;

But they hardened their hearts and could not endure his presence; therefore, the Lord in his wrath, for his anger was kindled against them, swore that they should not enter into his rest while in the wilderness, which rest is the fulness of his glory.

Therefore, he took Moses out of their midst, and the Holy Priesthood also.

Doctrine and Covenants 86:8–11

Therefore, thus saith the Lord unto you, with whom the priesthood hath continued through the lineage of your fathers—

For ye are lawful heirs, according to the flesh, and have been hid from the world with Christ in God—

Therefore your life and the priesthood have remained, and must needs remain through you and your lineage until the restoration of all things spoken by the mouths of all the holy prophets since the world began.

Therefore, blessed are ye if ye continue in my goodness, a light unto the Gentiles, and through this priesthood, a savior unto my people Israel. The Lord hath said it. Amen.

Doctrine and Covenants 113:7–8

Questions by Elias Higbee: What is meant by the command in Isaiah, 52d chapter, 1st verse, which saith: Put on thy strength, O Zion—and what people had Isaiah reference to?

He had reference to those whom God should call in the last days, who should hold the power of priesthood to bring again Zion, and the redemption of Israel; and to put on her strength is to put on the authority of the priesthood, which she, Zion, has a right to by lineage; also to return to that power which she had lost.

Moses 6:7

Now this same Priesthood, which was in the beginning, shall be in the end of the world also.

21

GAINING THE MOST FROM TEMPLE WORSHIP

A wise Latter-day Saint would not write specifically about what happens in the temple. This chapter, therefore, is devoted to general principles that deal with learning spiritual truths. There is no better place to learn to see the "big picture" of eternity than in the temple—that is, if you have eyes to see and ears to hear.

When Jesus started teaching in parables, His disciples questioned the reasoning behind that teaching method since it precluded many from learning those truths. Jesus responded by saying:

> Who hath ears to hear, let him hear.
>
> And the disciples came, and said unto him, Why speakest thou unto them in parables?
>
> He answered and said unto them, **Because it is given unto you to know the mysteries of the kingdom of heaven, but to them it is not given.**
>
> For whosoever hath, to him shall be given, and he shall have more abundance: but whosoever hath not, from him shall be taken away even that he hath.
>
> Therefore speak I to them in parables: because they seeing see not; and hearing they hear not, neither do they understand.

> And in them is fulfilled the prophecy of Esaias, which saith, By hearing ye shall hear, and shall not understand; and seeing ye shall see, and shall not perceive:
>
> For this people's heart is waxed gross, and their ears are dull of hearing, and their eyes they have closed; lest at any time they should see with their eyes, and hear with their ears, and should understand with their heart, and should be converted, and I should heal them.
>
> But blessed *are* your eyes, for they see: and your ears, for they hear. (Matthew 13:9–16)

Perhaps a statement in Doctrine and Covenants 41:1 sheds light on what the Savior was teaching. "Hearken and hear, O ye my people, saith the Lord and your God, **ye whom I delight to bless with the greatest of all blessings, ye that hear me; and ye that hear me not will I curse, that have professed my name, with the heaviest of all cursings."**

The gospel is only a blessing (in fact the greatest of all blessings) if we learn and live the commandments. If we embrace it and subsequently fail to live those saving principles, the gospel becomes the "heaviest of all cursings."

The same principle exists regarding the temple. It is the supernal blessing of God to His spirit children *if* we enter, learn, and live the covenants we make. However, just "going through the temple" without the "temple going through you" is not a blessing.

Preparing people for the temple is an ongoing challenge. When the age limit was lowered for missionary service, it was seen by all as a great blessing. However, it has also opened the doors of the temples to young men and women who need much more preparation to be able to understand and live the covenants they make. Isaiah saw the problem and proffered the solution: "Whom shall he teach knowledge? and whom shall he make to understand doctrine? them that are weaned from the milk, and drawn from the breasts. For precept must be upon precept, precept upon precept; line upon line, line upon line; here a little, and there a little" (Isaiah 28:9–10).

Thankfully that is the way understanding of the temple ordinances occurs—line upon line and precept upon precept. Unfortunately, in today's hurry-up, throw-away world, far too many temple goers' first time through is also their last time through. What a tragedy.

The key to growing in understanding of the temple is given by the Lord: "That which is of God is light; and he that receiveth light, and continueth in God, receiveth more light; and that light groweth brighter and brighter until the perfect day. And again, verily I say unto you, and I say it that you may know the truth, that you may chase darkness from among you" (D&C 50:24–25).

The more frequently we attend, really wanting to learn and grow, the greater is our love and appreciation of the temple.

What are we "growing toward"? In the dedicatory prayer of the Kirtland Ohio Temple in 1836, Joseph Smith prayed:

> And now we ask thee, Holy Father, in the name of Jesus Christ, the Son of thy bosom, in whose name alone salvation can be administered to the children of men, we ask thee, O Lord, to accept of this house, the workmanship of the hands of us, thy servants, which thou didst command us to build.
>
> For thou knowest that we have done this work through great tribulation; and out of our poverty we have given of our substance to build a house to thy name, **that the Son of Man might have a place to manifest himself to his people.** (D&C 109:4–5)

Earlier the Lord had commanded the Saints to build a temple and mentioned what the multiple purposes were:

> Behold, this is the tithing and the sacrifice which I, the Lord, require at their hands, that there may be a house built unto me **for the salvation of Zion**—
>
> For (1) a place of thanksgiving for all saints, and for (2) a place of instruction for all those who are called to the work of the ministry in all their several callings and offices;
>
> That they (3) may be perfected in the understanding of their ministry, in theory, in principle, and in doctrine, in all things pertaining to the kingdom of God on the earth, the keys of which kingdom have been conferred upon you.
>
> And inasmuch as my people build a house unto me in the name of the Lord, and do not suffer any unclean thing to come into it, that it be not defiled, **my glory shall rest upon it;**
>
> Yea, and my presence shall be there, for I will come into it, and all the pure in heart that shall come into it shall see God.
>
> But if it be defiled I will not come into it, and my glory shall not be there; for I will not come into unholy temples. (D&C 97:12–17, numbers and emphasis added)

The temple is specifically designated for the "salvation of Zion." If we know what we are looking for, it is much easier to identify it. Just attending the temple provides a very visually pleasing experience in a surreal environment—but there is much, much more.

First, it is a place of thanksgiving. Quietly sitting in the celestial room, without any distractions, one is able to mentally review blessings that might otherwise go unnoticed. At times, the most distressing and senseless trials we have or are still enduring in an instant are transformed into our greatest blessings as divine understanding distills upon us.

I fear I have been guilty many times of overlooking the hand of the Lord in helping me negotiate the challenges of life. The Lord revealed: "And in nothing doth man offend God, or against none is his wrath kindled, save those who confess not his hand in all things, and obey not his commandments" (D&C 59:21). Perhaps old age has its blessings. I am not nearly as prone now to hurry out of the temple as soon as the session is complete as I was in my younger years.

Second, the temple is a place of instruction in all of our callings. At first glance, one may think that refers to the bishop or Relief Society president or Sunday School teacher, which it does. However, those are all callings from which we will be released. The most important (and eternal) callings from which we will never be released are husband, wife, father, mother, and grandparents.

How many times have we lamented about our lack of understanding on how to cope with a difficult child or a troubled marriage? Have we resorted to the temple and received the divine assistance that the Lord promised?

Third, the temple is a "perfecting place" for every aspect of our lives because everything we do pertains to the kingdom of God on the earth. Whether we are working on personal perfection, family issues, employment challenges, Church callings, or understanding gospel principles and doctrine, the temple is "the Lord's university."

If we worthily attend the temple, the Lord promises that His glory will be there. "The glory of God is intelligence, or, in other words, light and truth. Light and truth forsake that evil one" (D&C 93:36–37). Because of this, there couldn't be a better place to grow in our understanding of God and His plan of salvation and also learn the principles necessary to identify and overcome the influences of the "evil one."

Eventually, as we discussed in the chapter on seeing God, the veil will be parted and you will be able to use what you learned in the endowment session to part the veil and enter the very presence of God.

It seems that many regular temple goers fail to realize why we need the initiatory ordinances. The Lord gives this explanation:

> And I give unto you, who are the first laborers in this last kingdom, a commandment that you assemble yourselves together, and organize yourselves, and prepare yourselves, and sanctify yourselves; yea, purify your hearts, and **cleanse your hands and your feet before me, that I may make you clean;**
>
> **That I may testify unto your Father, and your God, and my God, that you are clean from the blood of this wicked generation**; that I may fulfil this promise, this great and last promise, which I have made unto you, when I will. (D&C 88:74–75)

When will that time of the Savior testifying to the Father of our worthiness to re-enter the very presence of God actually occur? "When I will!" That is good enough for me.

Preparing people to re-enter the presence of God is not a modern-day objective of priesthood leaders. The Lord explains how Moses tried with the recently liberated slaves/children of Israel but failed:

> And this greater priesthood administereth the gospel and holdeth the key of the mysteries of the kingdom, even the key of the knowledge of God.
>
> Therefore, in the ordinances thereof, the power of godliness is manifest.
>
> And without **the ordinances** thereof, and the authority of the priesthood, the power of godliness is not manifest unto men in the flesh;
>
> **For without this no man can see the face of God, even the Father, and live.**
>
> Now this Moses plainly taught to the children of Israel in the wilderness, and sought diligently to sanctify his people that they might behold the face of God;
>
> But they hardened their hearts and could not endure his presence; therefore, the Lord in his wrath, for his anger was kindled against them, swore that they should not enter into his rest while in the wilderness, which rest is the fulness of his glory.
>
> Therefore, he took Moses out of their midst, and the Holy Priesthood also. (D&C 84:19–25)

One would hope that we (modern Israel) will not make the same mistake by hardening our hearts and refusing to embrace the ordinances of exaltation found in the temple. The Lord has given us so many mind-boggling promises that it is difficult to comprehend the magnitude of what is available if we are willing to pay the price of true discipleship.

> For thus saith the Lord—I, the Lord, am merciful and gracious unto those who fear me, and **delight to honor those who serve me** in righteousness and in truth unto the end.
>
> Great shall be their reward and eternal shall be their glory.
>
> And **to them will I reveal all mysteries**, yea, all the hidden mysteries of my kingdom from days of old, and for ages to come, will I make known unto them the good pleasure of my will concerning all things pertaining to my kingdom.
>
> Yea, **even the wonders of eternity** shall they know, and things to come will I show them, even the things of many generations.
>
> And their wisdom shall be great, and their understanding reach to heaven; and before them the wisdom of the wise shall perish, and the understanding of the prudent shall come to naught.
>
> For by my Spirit will I enlighten them, and by my power will I make known unto them the secrets of my will—yea, even those things which eye has not seen, nor ear heard, nor yet entered into the heart of man. (D&C 76:5–10)

It is disappointing to hear that some apostates have lied their way into the Lord's temples, recorded and filmed the endowment, and then posted it on anti-Mormon internet sites. It is pathetically amusing that, like with the Savior's use of parables, all they see is the story and cannot gain any insight into the hidden wisdom of the endowment. Paul addressed this same issue many years ago:

> Howbeit we speak wisdom among them that are perfect: yet not the wisdom of this world, nor of the princes of this world, that come to nought:
>
> But **we speak the wisdom of God in a mystery, *even* the hidden *wisdom*,** which God ordained before the world unto our glory:
>
> Which none of the princes of this world knew: for had they known *it*, they would not have crucified the Lord of glory.
>
> But as it is written, Eye hath not seen, nor ear heard, neither have entered into the heart of man, the things which God hath prepared for them that love him.
>
> But God hath revealed *them* unto us by his Spirit: for the Spirit searcheth all things, yea, the deep things of God.
>
> For what man knoweth the things of a man, save the spirit of man which is in him? even so the things of God knoweth no man, but the Spirit of God.

> Now we have received, not the spirit of the world, but the spirit which is of God; that we might know the things that are freely given to us of God.
>
> Which things also we speak, not in the words which man's wisdom teacheth, but which the Holy Ghost teacheth; comparing spiritual things with spiritual.
>
> But **the natural man receiveth not the things of the Spirit of God: for they are foolishness unto him: neither can he know *them*, because they are spiritually discerned.** (1 Corinthians 2:6–14)

If the anti-Mormons were to analyze and evaluate the endowment for a thousand years, they would never come to the deep, spiritual knowledge that is there. Likewise, the insincere who are social temple attenders will fail to enjoy the happiness reserved for the humble saints. Jacob made the following declaration:

> And whoso knocketh, to him will he open; and the wise, and the learned, and they that are rich, who are puffed up because of their learning, and their wisdom, and their riches—yea, they are they whom he despiseth; and save they shall cast these things away, and consider themselves fools before God, and come down in the depths of humility, he will not open unto them.
>
> **But the things of the wise and the prudent shall be hid from them forever—yea, that happiness which is prepared for the saints.** (2 Nephi 9:42–43)

It seems the keys to getting the most of our temple experience is to go worthily, to go often, and to go with an open mind willing to let the Spirit teach you. As you patiently fulfill your duty in the family and the Church, the Lord will magnify you until you evolve into a perfect, exalted being.

22

SUCCESSFULLY FOLLOWING THE PROPHETS

From the very beginning of man's mortal experience, the Lord established a dual avenue for communicating with His spirit children. One was by personal revelation to the individual for matters pertaining to him and his stewardship. The second was through prophets who would receive revelation for the entire world. This chapter will deal with the second source of divine guidance—prophets.

What is the divinely appointed purpose of prophets? Paul wrote:

> And he gave some, **apostles; and some, prophets; and some, evangelists; and some, pastors and teachers**; *For the perfecting of the saints, for the work of the ministry, for the edifying of the body of Christ*: Till we all come in the unity of the faith, and of the knowledge of the Son of God, unto a perfect man, unto the measure of the stature of the fulness of Christ: That we henceforth be no more children, tossed to and fro, and carried about with every wind of doctrine, by the sleight of men, and cunning craftiness, whereby they lie in wait to deceive. (Ephesians 4:11–14)

How long would prophets be necessary in God's plan? Paul said: "Til we all come to a unity of the faith." It doesn't take a PhD in theology to see that we are anything but at a unity of the faith. Therefore, the continuing need for prophets exists.

The first prophet was Adam. Although his memory of the pre-earth life was blocked when he was placed in the Garden of Eden, there is no indication that his memory of what transpired in the Garden was taken from him when he left the Garden. So, he was teaching his children by actual sight knowledge of what he had experienced. However, a vital key to our safety is revealed in the earliest record we have of what transpired:

> And in that day Adam blessed God and was filled, and began to prophesy concerning all the families of the earth, saying: Blessed be the name of God, for because of my transgression my eyes are opened, and in this life I shall have joy, and again in the flesh I shall see God.
>
> And Eve, his wife, heard all these things and was glad, saying: Were it not for our transgression we never should have had seed, and never should have known good and evil, and the joy of our redemption, and the eternal life which God giveth unto all the obedient.
>
> And Adam and Eve blessed the name of God, and they made all things known unto their sons and their daughters.
>
> And Satan came among them, saying: I am also a son of God; and he commanded them, saying: Believe it not; and they believed it not, and they loved Satan more than God. And men began from that time forth to be carnal, sensual, and devilish. (Moses 5:10–13)

And so it has been in every dispensation where God has sent prophets to teach and warn the people—Satan has been there whispering in their ears, "Believe it not." Unfortunately, the skeletal record we have of mankind's mortal experience testifies that a majority of mankind has "believed it not."

It should be noted that prophets are just men like the rest of us who have been called of God to a special calling. The ancient prophet Amos said: "And **I raised up of your sons for prophets**, and of your young men for Nazarites. Is it not even thus, O ye children of Israel? saith the Lord" (Amos 2:11).

Satan's deceptive ploy has been to characterize prophets as "wild men." Enoch who eventually was successful in getting his people translated was viewed differently by those who did not believe.

> And it came to pass that Enoch went forth in the land, among the people, standing upon the hills and the high places, and cried with a loud voice, testifying against their works; and all men were offended because of him.

> And they came forth to hear him, upon the high places, saying unto the tent–keepers: Tarry ye here and keep the tents, while we go yonder to behold the seer, for he prophesieth, and there is a strange thing in the land; **a wild man hath come among us.** (Moses 6:37–38)

As the people of Nazareth rejected "the prophet" (Christ—see Acts 3:22–23; Joseph Smith—History 1:40), the Savior lamented: "**A prophet** *is not without honour, save in his own country, and in his own house*" (Matthew 13:57).

From the earliest times, the Lord has attached the promise of prosperity to our willingness to follow His chosen prophets. "Believe in the Lord your God, so shall ye be established; **believe his prophets,** *so shall ye prosper*" (2 Chronicles 20:20).

How does the Lord communicate with His prophets? Some seem to have the mistaken idea that the prophet must see an open vision—which many times they do. However, the Lord said: "If there be a **prophet** among you, *I the Lord will make myself known unto him in a vision and will speak unto him in a dream*" (Numbers 12:6).

Nephi further explained how the Lord reveals His will to prophets. In 1 Nephi 22:2 he records: "And I, Nephi, said unto them: Behold they were manifest unto the prophet by the voice of the Spirit; for by the Spirit are all things made known unto the prophets, which shall come upon the children of men according to the flesh" (see also Ephesians 3:5).

One of the most recognizable scriptures linking the doings of our Heavenly Father with His communication to living prophets is found in Amos 3:7: "Surely the Lord GOD will do nothing, but he revealeth his secret unto his servants the prophets."

The Book of Mormon paints an unmistakable picture of a nation who is prospered by the Lord, falls into apostasy, is destroyed, and eventually returns to God only to repeat that cycle over and over again. However, six hundred years before the birth of Christ, Nephi records: "And as one generation hath been destroyed among the Jews because of iniquity, even so have they been destroyed from generation to generation according to their iniquities; and **never hath any of them been destroyed save it were foretold them by the prophets of the Lord**" (2 Nephi 25:9).

As though to cement that concept firmly in our minds, Mormon records the follow two verses concerning those who were destroyed among the Nephites at the death of Christ and those who were spared: "And behold, the city of Laman, and the city of Josh, and the city of Gad, and the city of Kishkumen, have I caused to be burned with fire, and the *inhabitants thereof, because of their wickedness* in **casting out the prophets**, and stoning those whom I did send to declare unto them concerning their wickedness and their abominations" (3 Nephi 9:10).

"And it was the more righteous part of the people who were saved, and it was they who **received the prophets** and stoned them not; and it was they who had not shed the blood of the saints, *who were spared*" (3 Nephi 10:12).

Skeptics question whether we, as Latter-day Saints, are blindly following our sustained prophet leaders, noting the changing times and the advancing age of our leaders. However, following the issuing of the Manifesto abolishing plural marriage, Wilford Woodruff, the prophet at the time, said: "The *Lord will never permit me or any other man who stands as President of this Church to lead you astray.* It is not in the programme. It is not in the mind of God. If I were to attempt that, the Lord would remove me out of my place, and so He will any other man who attempts to lead the children of men astray from the oracles of God and from their duty" (D&C, page 292).

There have always been false prophets and prophetesses in opposition to true prophets. We would do well to give heed to the word of the Lord concerning two of these satanic efforts to deceive. The first came shortly after the restoration of the Church when a faithful member, Hiram Page, found a "peep stone" through which he claimed to be receiving revelations. The Lord revealed:

> But, behold, verily, verily, I say unto thee, no one shall be appointed to receive commandments and revelations in this church excepting my servant Joseph Smith, Jun., for he receiveth them even as Moses . . . And again, thou shalt take thy brother, Hiram Page, between him and thee alone, and tell him that those things which he hath written from that stone are not of me and that Satan deceiveth him;
>
> For, behold, these things have not been appointed unto him, neither shall anything be appointed unto any of this church contrary to the church covenants.
>
> For all things must be done in order, and by common consent in the church, by the prayer of faith. (D&C 28:2, 11–13)

The second warning came when a woman (Mrs. Hubble) proclaimed Joseph Smith to be a prophet but said she was designated to be "the teacher" in the Church. The Lord revealed:

> For behold, verily, verily, I say unto you, that ye have received a commandment for a law unto my church, through him whom I have appointed unto you to receive commandments and revelations from my hand.
>
> And this ye shall know assuredly—that there is none other appointed unto you to receive commandments and revelations until he be taken, if he abide in me.
>
> But verily, verily, I say unto you, that none else shall be appointed unto this gift except it be through him; for if it be taken from him he shall not have power except to appoint another in his stead.
>
> And this shall be a law unto you, that ye receive not the teachings of any that shall come before you as revelations or commandments;
>
> And this I give unto you that you may not be deceived, that you may know they are not of me.
>
> For verily I say unto you, that he that is ordained of me shall come in at the gate and be ordained as I have told you before, to teach those revelations which you have received and shall receive through him whom I have appointed. (D&C 43:2–7)

"The gate," as explained by the Lord, that a man enters to eventually become the prophet is when he is called to be an apostle. Then through a long training and testing period, the man is groomed by the Lord to be His mouthpiece on earth.

The Lord explained to Moses the relationship of the living prophet to the people. Moses was reluctant to take on the task of freeing the children of Israel from their long captivity. He tried to reason his way out of the assignment because of perceived weaknesses. His exchange with the Lord is worth re-reading:

> And Moses said unto the Lord, O my Lord, I *am* not eloquent, neither heretofore, nor since thou hast spoken unto thy servant: but I *am* slow of speech, and of a slow tongue.
>
> And the Lord said unto him, Who hath made man's mouth? or who maketh the dumb, or deaf, or the seeing, or the blind? have not I the Lord?
>
> Now therefore go, and I will be with thy mouth, and teach thee what thou shalt say.
>
> And he said, O my Lord, send, I pray thee, by the hand *of him whom* thou wilt send.
>
> And the anger of the Lord was kindled against Moses, and he said, *Is* not Aaron the Levite thy brother? I know that he can speak well. And

> also, behold, he cometh forth to meet thee: and when he seeth thee, he will be glad in his heart.
>
> And thou shalt speak unto him, and put words in his mouth: and I will be with thy mouth, and with his mouth, and will teach you what ye shall do.
>
> And he shall be thy spokesman unto the people: and **he shall be, *even* he shall be to thee instead of a mouth, and thou shalt be to him instead of God.** (Exodus 4:10–16)

The Lord knew that it would be difficult at times to follow the counsel He gives through living prophets. On the very day the Church was organized, the Lord revealed His commandment regarding the living prophet:

> Wherefore, meaning the church, thou shalt give heed unto all his words and commandments which he shall give unto you as he receiveth them, walking in all holiness before me;
>
> For his word ye shall receive, as if from mine own mouth, in all patience and faith.
>
> For by doing these things the gates of hell shall not prevail against you; yea, and the Lord God will disperse the powers of darkness from before you, and cause the heavens to shake for your good, and his name's glory. (D&C 21:4–6)

There isn't a clearer declaration in scripture that we are commanded to follow *all* of the "words and commandments" of the living prophet than verse 4. In verse 5 the Lord acknowledges that it will require "patience and faith" because we won't always see beforehand the logic or the purpose of the directive.

However, in verse 6 the Lord promises three unparalleled rewards for following the prophet's counsel: 1) the gates of hell (unrepented sin) will never prevail against us; 2) the powers of darkness will be dispersed so that we can see clearly and not stumble when confronted with the "mists of darkness" Lehi and Nephi saw would engulf those striving for eternal life; and 3) the Lord would exert His almighty power—sufficient to shake the entire heaven and earth for our good and His glory—which is our exaltation (see Moses 1:39).

In the very beginning, Adam and Eve's first children failed to recognize and accept direction from their prophet father, Adam. They became carnal, sensual, and devilish, forfeiting the promised blessings had they followed Adam's counsel.

Now in these uncertain times, we are faced with the same challenge: will we believe and follow the counsel of living prophets, seers, and revelators? Ammon, in teaching the people of King Lamoni, said:

> And Ammon said that a seer is a revelator and a prophet also; and a gift which is greater can no man have, except he should possess the power of God, which no man can; yet a man may have great power given him from God.
>
> But a seer can know of things which are past, and also of things which are to come, and by them shall all things be revealed, or, rather, shall secret things be made manifest, and hidden things shall come to light, and things which are not known shall be made known by them, and also things shall be made known by them which otherwise could not be known.
>
> Thus God has provided a means that man, through faith, might work mighty miracles; therefore **he becometh a great benefit to his fellow beings.** (Mosiah 8:16–18)

That "great benefit" evaporates and actually turns to a curse if we turn our back on the Lord's chosen leaders. May we follow Moroni's plea as he witnesses the entire destruction of his people: "Condemn me not because of mine imperfection, neither my father, because of his imperfection, neither them who have written before him; but rather give thanks unto God that he hath made manifest unto you our imperfections, **that ye may learn to be more wise than we have been**" (Mormon 9:31).

POINTS FOR FURTHER CONSIDERATION

Prophet (before times called a seer) (1 Samuel 9:9)

> Beforetime in Israel, when a man went to enquire of God, thus he spake, Come, and let us go to the seer: for he that is now called a **Prophet** was *beforetime called a Seer.*

Prophet—Christ—to be heard in last days or people to be cut off (3 Nephi 20:23)

> Behold, **I am he** of whom Moses spake, saying: **A prophet shall the Lord your God raise up unto you** of your brethren, like unto me; *him shall ye hear in all things* whatsoever he shall say unto you. And it shall come to pass that *every soul who will not hear that prophet shall be cut off*

from among the people (see also Deuteronomy 18:15–19; Acts 3:22–23; 1 Nephi 22:20–21; D&C 133:63).

Prophet of the Highest (Luke 1:76)

And thou, *child [John the Baptist*—see verse 63], shalt be called the **prophet of the Highest**: for thou shalt go before the face of the Lord to prepare his ways.

Prophet of the Lord (Alma 10:7)

Prophet of the Lord; yea, *a holy man*, who is a chosen man of God.

Prophet (who we must hear or be cut off) (1 Nephi 22:20–21)

A **prophet** shall the Lord God raise up unto you, like unto me; *him shall ye hear in all things whatsoever he shall say unto you.* And it shall co me to pass that all those **who will not hear that prophet shall be cut off** from among the people. . . . This prophet of whom Moses spake was the *Holy One of Israel.*

Prophet without honor in own country (Matthew 13:57)

And they were offended in him. But Jesus said unto them, **A prophet** *is not without honour, save in his own country, and in his own house* (see also Mark 6:4; Luke 4:24; John 4:44; JST, Mark 6:6)

Prophetess (Luke 2:36)

And there was one *Anna*, a **prophetess**, the daughter of Phanuel.

Prophets—commanded to search writings of (3 Nephi 23:5)

And whosoever will hearken unto my words and repenteth and is baptized, the same shall be saved. **Search the prophets**, *for many there be that testify of these things.*

Prophets all spoke or wrote about Christ (Jacob 7:11)

And I said unto him: Then ye do not understand them; for they truly testify of Christ. Behold, I say unto you that **none of the prophets have written, nor prophesied, save they have spoken concerning this Christ.**

Prophets as an example (James 5:10)

Take, my brethren, **the prophets**, who have spoken in the name of the Lord, *for an example of suffering affliction, and of patience.*

Prophets (false) condemned

Ezekiel 13

Prophets—Lord reveals to them through spirit (Ephesians 3:5)

Which in other ages was not made known unto the sons of men, as it is now **revealed unto his holy apostles and prophets by the Spirit.**

Prophets mentioned after Resurrection

Acts 11:27; Acts 13:1; Acts 15:32; 1 Corinthians 12:28; Ephesians 2:20; Ephesians 3:5; Ephesians 4:11; James 5:10

Prophet's reward (who receives) (Matthew 10:41)

He that receiveth a prophet in the name of a prophet shall **receive a prophet's reward.**

Prophets see things they are forbidden to reveal (Ether 3:21)

And it came to pass that the Lord said unto the brother of Jared: Behold, **thou shalt not suffer these things which ye have seen and heard to go forth unto the world**, until the time cometh that I shall glorify my name in the flesh; wherefore, ye shall treasure up the things which ye have seen and heard, and show it to no man (see also verses 22–28).

Prophets' words will stand against us on judgment day (Mosiah 3:24)

And thus saith the Lord: **They [words of prophets**—see verse 23] shall stand as a bright testimony against this people, at the *judgment day*; whereof they shall be judged, every man according to his works, whether they be good, or whether they be evil.

Prophets—would that all were (Numbers 11:29)

And Moses said unto him, Enviest thou for my sake? **would God that all the Lord's people were prophets**, and that the Lord would put his spirit upon them.

Prophets write by Spirit and power of God (1 Nephi 3:20)

And also that we may preserve unto them the words which have been spoken by the mouth of all the holy prophets, which have been **delivered unto them by the Spirit and power of God**, since the world began, even down unto this present time.

23

TEACHING WITH THE SPIRIT AND POWER

Likely all of us have sat spellbound by a gifted speaker as he expanded our understanding and enlightened our minds on the subject of his address. What makes one speaker so dynamic and another somewhat difficult to endure? Is there a formula for becoming like the first speaker?

In a revelation entitled by the Lord as "My Law" (D&C 42), a number of laws are outlined. Verses 11–14 contain the Lord's law of teaching. This is the best place to start our investigation of the Lord's law of teaching.

> Again I say unto you, that it shall not be given to any one to go forth to preach my gospel, or to build up my church, except he be (1) ordained by some one who has authority, and (2) it is known to the church that he has authority and has been regularly ordained by the heads of the church.
>
> And again, the elders, priests and teachers of this church (3) shall teach the principles of my gospel, which are in the Bible and the Book of Mormon, in the which is the fulness of the gospel.
>
> And they (4) shall observe the covenants and church articles to do them, and these shall be their teachings, as they (5) shall be directed by the Spirit.
>
> And the Spirit shall be given unto you by the prayer of faith; and if ye receive not the Spirit ye shall not teach. (numbers added)

First, a teacher must be "ordained," or in today's terminology "set apart." In the early days of the Church in this dispensation, the Lord reinforced the concept of there being power associated with the setting apart. "Verily I say unto you, that it is my will that my servant Jared Carter should go again into the eastern countries, from place to place, and from city to city, **in the power of the ordination wherewith he has been ordained**, proclaiming glad tidings of great joy, even the everlasting gospel" (D&C 79:1).

Having taught professionally for four decades, I can testify from my own experience that an additional power is associated with teaching in the Church as contrasted with teaching religion professionally.

The second element of the formula is known as common consent. In a revelation given shortly after the Church was restored, the Lord said: "And all things shall be done by common consent in the church, by much prayer and faith, for all things you shall receive by faith" (D&C 26:2).

Each time a teacher is sustained in sacrament meeting, it is a manifestation that he or she has been called by one who has the authority to issue the call. That simple act is a safeguard against anyone coming in claiming authority but without proper authority.

Third, the Lord makes it crystal clear that we are to base our teaching from the principles taught in the scriptures. Later He expands His command to include apostles and prophets: "And let them journey from thence preaching the word by the way, saying none other things than that which the prophets and apostles have written, and that which is taught them by the Comforter through the prayer of faith" (D&C 52:9).

The fourth element requires our constant attention. We must live what we teach and strive to keep all of the commandments. Two thousand years ago the Apostle Paul wrote: "Thou therefore which teachest another, teachest thou not thyself? thou that preachest a man should not steal, dost thou steal? Thou that sayest a man should not commit adultery, dost thou commit adultery? thou that abhorrest idols, dost thou commit sacrilege?" (Romans 2:21–22).

Some of the most stinging rebukes of the Savior were against those who taught one thing and did another. "Woe unto you, scribes and Pharisees, hypocrites! for ye compass sea and land to make one proselyte, and when he is made, ye make him twofold more the child of hell than yourselves" (Matthew 23:15).

In the Sermon on the Mount, Jesus contrasted the "rewards" of those who walk the walk as well as talk the talk and those who teach others to break the commandments: "Whosoever therefore shall break one of these least commandments, and shall teach men so, he shall be called the least in the kingdom of heaven: but whosoever shall do and teach them, the same shall be called great in the kingdom of heaven" (Matthew 5:19).

The fifth part of the Lord's law of teaching is likely the most challenging. Teach by the Spirit or not at all. "Verily I say unto you, he that is ordained of me and sent forth to preach the word of truth by the Comforter, in the Spirit of truth, doth he **preach it by the Spirit of truth** or some other way? And *if it be by some other way it is not of God*" (D&C 50:17–18).

To the missionaries the Lord gave the following counsel and promise: "Again I say, hearken ye elders of my church, whom I have appointed: Ye are *not sent forth to be taught,* but **to teach** the children of men the things which I have put into your hands by the power of my Spirit; And *ye are to be taught from on high.* Sanctify yourselves and ye shall be endowed with power, that ye may give even as I have spoken" (D&C 43:15–16).

In the years before the resurrected Savior visited the Nephites, Nephi and Lehi (sons of Helaman) were teaching among the Lamanites. "And it came to pass that Nephi and Lehi did preach unto the Lamanites with such great power and authority, for they **had power and authority given** unto them that they might speak, and they **also had what they should speak** given unto them" (Helaman 5:18).

Scattered throughout the scriptures is the injunction that the Lord gave initially to His disciples as He sent them out. "But when they shall lead *you,* and deliver you up, take no thought beforehand what ye shall speak, neither do ye premeditate: but whatsoever shall be given you in that hour, that speak ye: for it is not ye that speak, but the Holy Ghost" (Mark13:11; see also Matthew 10:19).

Some have misunderstood the Lord's charge, believing that their only responsibility is to show up. The Lord clarifies that by saying: "Neither take ye thought beforehand what ye shall say; **but treasure up in your minds continually the words of life,** and it shall be given you in the very hour that portion that shall be meted unto every man" (D&C 84:85).

Treasuring up continually states that studying the gospel continually is what puts us in a position to have the Spirit bring to mind not only what to say but how to say it so that it will have the maximum impact. A few sections later the Lord restates this principle but actually shortens the period when the divine help will be given.

> Therefore, verily I say unto you, lift up your voices unto this people; speak the thoughts that I shall put into your hearts, and you shall not be confounded before men;
>
> For it shall be given you in the very hour, yea, **in the very moment**, what ye shall say.
>
> But a commandment I give unto you, that ye shall declare whatsoever thing ye declare in my name, in solemnity of heart, in the spirit of meekness, in all things.
>
> And I give unto you this promise, that inasmuch as ye do this the Holy Ghost shall be shed forth in bearing record unto all things whatsoever ye shall say. (D&C 100:5–8)

Having taught on a university level for many years, I have witnessed too many religion teachers try to make the gospel so academic that only those with advanced degrees can understand it. This seems to be in direct contrast to what the Lord revealed: "And for this cause, that men might be made partakers of the glories which were to be revealed, the Lord sent forth the fulness of his gospel, his everlasting covenant, **reasoning in plainness and simplicity"** (D&C 133:57).

Returning to a scripture cited earlier in a section where the Lord explains how not to be deceived, He said three things will always be present when the teacher is teaching by the Spirit and the learner is listening with the Spirit.

> Therefore, why is it that ye cannot understand and know, that he that receiveth the word by the Spirit of truth receiveth it as it is preached by the Spirit of truth?
>
> Wherefore, he that preacheth and he that receiveth, **understand one another, and both are edified and rejoice together.**
>
> And that which doth not edify is not of God, and is darkness.
>
> That which is of God is light; and he that receiveth light, and continueth in God, receiveth more light; and that light groweth brighter and brighter until the perfect day.
>
> And again, verily I say unto you, and I say it that you may know the truth, that you may chase darkness from among you;
>
> He that is ordained of God and sent forth, the same is appointed to be the greatest, notwithstanding he is the least and the servant of all. (D&C 50:21–26)

If the student is not understanding what is being taught, either the teacher is not teaching by the Spirit, the learner is not learning by the Spirit, or both of the above.

The second element that must accompany teaching by the Spirit is that both are edified together. To be edified is to be uplifted, motivated to do good, improved, and focused more on godliness. Both the teacher and the learner must experience this feeling.

Third, both the teacher and the learner rejoice together. Both Lehi and Nephi described the fruit of the tree as sweet above all that is sweet and desirable above all that is desirable.

Alma's account of what made the sons of Mosiah such powerful teachers holds several keys to this formula:

> Now these sons of Mosiah were with Alma at the time the angel first appeared unto him; therefore Alma did rejoice exceedingly to see his brethren; and what added more to his joy, they were still his brethren in the Lord; yea, and they **had waxed strong in the knowledge of the truth**; for they were **men of a sound understanding** and they **had searched the scriptures diligently**, that they might know the word of God.
>
> But this is not all; they **had given themselves to much prayer, and fasting**; therefore **they had the spirit of prophecy, and the spirit of revelation**, and when they taught, **they taught with power and authority of God**. (Alma 17:2–3)

Recapping the end result of the teachings of the sons of Mosiah, Mormon says: "And as sure as the Lord liveth, so sure as many as believed, or as many as were brought to the knowledge of the truth, through the preaching of Ammon and his brethren, according to **the spirit of revelation and of prophecy, and the power of God working miracles in them**—yea, I say unto you, as the Lord liveth, as many of the Lamanites as believed in their preaching, and were converted unto the Lord, **never did fall away**" (Alma 23:6).

Teaching by the Spirit is no easy task. It requires that we be people of "sound understanding." The Lord said: "And now come, saith the Lord, by the Spirit, unto the elders of his church, and let us reason together, that ye may understand; Let us reason even as a man reasoneth one with another face to face. Now, when a man reasoneth he is understood of man, because he reasoneth as a man; even so will I, the Lord, reason with you that you may understand" (D&C 50:10–12).

The gospel is 100 percent logical. When it seems illogical it is because we don't understand fully how the principle in question fits into the overall plan of salvation.

The sons of Mosiah did more than a casual reading of the scriptures. They "searched" the scriptures diligently for one purpose: "that they might know the word of God" (Alma 17:2). My experience has been that too many people search the scriptures to get backing for their own opinions. Abinadi warned wicked King Noah: "Behold, the scriptures are before you; if ye will wrest them it shall be to your own destruction" (Alma 13:20).

The Lord explained why He preserved the Book of Mormon for us:

> Yea, and I will also bring to light my gospel which was ministered unto them, and, behold, they shall not deny that which you have received, but they shall build it up, and shall bring to light the true points of my doctrine, yea, and the only doctrine which is in me.
>
> And this I do that I may establish my gospel, that there may not be so much contention; yea, Satan doth stir up the hearts of the people to contention concerning the points of my doctrine; and in these things they do err, **for they do wrest the scriptures and do not understand them.** (D&C 10:62–63)

The sons of Mosiah taught with such power because they added prayer and fasting to their gospel study. The stated result of the accumulation of those activities was that they enjoyed the "spirit of prophecy, and the spirit of revelation" (Alma 17:3). Those terms may be confusing to some or not understood to where we can access or recognize them when we have them. The **spirit of prophecy** is defined in Revelation 19:10: "For *the testimony of Jesus* is the **spirit of prophecy.**" The more of the spirit of prophecy we have, the more we understand the Savior, His attributes, His plan for us, and His willingness to help us.

The **spirit of revelation** is defined by Alma and enlarged by the Lord is this dispensation: "Behold, I say unto you they are made known unto me by the Holy Spirit of God. Behold, I have fasted and prayed many days that I might know these things of myself. And now I do know of myself that they are true; for the Lord God hath made them *manifest unto me by his Holy Spirit*; and **this is the spirit of revelation** which is in me" (Alma 5:46).

"Yea, behold, *I will tell you in your mind and in your heart, by the Holy Ghost,* which shall come upon you and which shall dwell in your heart. Now, behold, this is the **spirit of revelation**" (D&C 8:2–3).

Not only did they teach with power, but those who were privileged to receive the gospel from them "never did fall away." As a parent, teacher, or leader, isn't that what you would pray for all those in your stewardship?

In the great revelation called "the Olive Leaf" (D&C 88), the Lord commands:

> And I give unto you a commandment that you shall **teach one another the doctrine** of the kingdom.
>
> **Teach ye diligently** and my grace shall attend you, that you may be instructed more perfectly in theory, in principle, in doctrine, in the law of the gospel, in all things that pertain unto the kingdom of God, that are expedient for you to understand;
>
> Of things both in heaven and in the earth, and under the earth; things which have been, things which are, things which must shortly come to pass; things which are at home, things which are abroad; the wars and the perplexities of the nations, and the judgments which are on the land; and a knowledge also of countries and of kingdoms—
>
> That ye may be prepared in all things when I shall send you again to magnify the calling whereunto I have called you, and the mission with which I have commissioned you. (D&C 88:77–80)

Following the example of the sons of Mosiah, we ought to give more diligent heed to the doctrine of the kingdom since we are under command to teach doctrine to one another. If we are diligent in our preparation and teaching, the promise is that His "grace shall attend you." Grace is "divine enabling power." Note, however, the breadth of what the Lord commands us to become more knowledgeable about: "theory, principle, doctrine, and laws of the gospel."

Interestingly, the Lord lists academic disciplines we must familiarize ourselves with:

- Things both in heaven (astronomy) and in the earth (geology), and under the earth (anthropology)
- Things which have been (history), things which are (current events), things which must shortly come to pass (prophecies)
- Things which are at home (domestic affairs)
- Things which are abroad (foreign affairs)
- The wars and the perplexities of the nations (international affairs)
- Judgments which are on the land (famines, plagues, natural calamities)
- Knowledge of countries and of kingdoms (geography)

What is the Lord's purpose in commanding us to become knowledgeable? So that as missionaries we can be conversant with topics of interest to a variety of people and then lead them into gospel discussions that "therefore, they are left without excuse, and their sins are upon their own heads" (D&C 88:82).

Finally, "Therefore, **declare the things** which ye have heard, and verily believe, and **know to be true**" (D&C 80:4). There is a power present when the teacher is teaching from personal experience and personal knowledge. Although learning to teach with power and by the Spirit may seem overwhelming, anyone who has ever experienced it will readily testify that the reward is well worth the effort.

24

CONTROLLING AND OVERCOMING DEPRESSION

Before beginning a search for scriptural teachings on how to control depression, I want to emphasize that I am not advocating not taking antidepressant drugs under a doctor's supervision. For your benefit, you might want to Google "antidepressant side effects" and read what the scientific world is saying.

As you would suspect, there are no references to antidepressant drugs in the scriptures. However, there are elements of a formula that can benefit us directly in controlling feelings of depression. With the strongest language I can muster in the written word, I encourage you to watch, re-read, or listen to Elder Jeffrey R. Holland's October 2013 general conference talk entitled "Like a Broken Vessel."

Nothing that I will now outline is in contradiction with his inspired counsel. If I have misapplied the scriptures, consider the source and move on. If you can benefit from my hours of searching, pondering, and study, then the advantage is yours. There is no suggestion or accusation of sin or weakness in what I am writing, just an honest attempt to control the monster of depression as much as is humanly possible with divine help and according to His plan.

First, let us address one cause of depression: sin. Moroni said, "And if ye have no hope ye must needs be in despair; and despair cometh because of iniquity" (Moroni 10:22). Certainly, one cause of discouragement or depression is living below our achievable potential. In a world gone crazy, we would do well to give heed to two Book of Mormon prophets.

Alma said to his errant son Corianton, "Do not suppose, because it has been spoken concerning restoration, that ye shall be restored from sin to happiness. Behold, I say unto you, wickedness never was happiness" (Alma 41:10).

To a nation who had fallen so far that they were ripe for destruction, Samuel the Lamanite said: "But behold, your days of probation are past; ye have procrastinated the day of your salvation until it is everlastingly too late, and your destruction is made sure; yea, for ye have sought all the days of your lives for that which ye could not obtain; and ye have sought for happiness in doing iniquity, which thing is contrary to the nature of that righteousness which is in our great and Eternal Head" (Helaman 13:38).

It should be obvious from everything the prophets have revealed to them for our guidance and from our own personal experience that "you can't do bad and feel good!" Whenever I struggle with depressive feelings, I always begin by taking a huge step back and scrutinizing whether I am falling short in keeping the commandments. If I can't discover an area of needed improvement (I usually can!), then I ask for the Lord's help. He has graciously stated that He will point out where I need to improve. "Let us therefore, as many as be perfect, be thus minded: and if in any thing ye be otherwise minded, God shall reveal even this unto you" (Philippians 3:15; see also D&C 66:3).

Assuming you have addressed whatever actions of commission or omission that would cause the Spirit to withdraw, let us now see what the Lord has counseled us in a positive way.

It is comforting to know that the day will come when world conditions around us will no longer generate feelings of depression and hopelessness. Isaiah prophesied:

> Violence shall no more be heard in thy land, wasting nor destruction within thy borders; but thou shalt call thy walls Salvation, and thy gates Praise.
>
> The sun shall be no more thy light by day; neither for brightness shall the moon give light unto thee: but the Lord shall be unto thee an everlasting light, and thy God thy glory.
>
> Thy sun shall no more go down; neither shall thy moon withdraw itself: for the Lord shall be thine everlasting light, and the days of thy mourning shall be ended. (Isaiah 60:18–20)

It is a scriptural fact that conditions in the world will become darker and darker and more and more depressing as the Second Coming approaches. However, the Lord revealed:

> Mine indignation is soon to be poured out without measure upon all nations; and this will I do when the cup of their iniquity is full.
>
> And in that day all who are found upon the watch–tower, or in other words, all mine Israel, shall be saved.
>
> And they that have been scattered shall be gathered.
>
> And all they who have mourned shall be comforted.
>
> And all they who have given their lives for my name shall be crowned.
>
> Therefore, let your hearts be comforted concerning Zion; for all flesh is in mine hands; be still and know that I am God. (D&C 101:11–16)

Two thousand years ago when the Lord explained the events leading up to the Second Coming, His Apostles were troubled: "And now, when I the Lord had spoken these words unto my disciples, they were troubled. And I said unto them: Be not troubled, for, when all these things shall come to pass, ye may know that the promises which have been made unto you shall be fulfilled" (D&C 45:34–35).

If the mere prophesying of conditions preceding the Second Coming could elicit that kind of response from His ancient disciples, why shouldn't we, who are living during the fulfillment of those prophecies, be concerned? The Lord said: "Therefore, verily, thus saith the Lord, let Zion rejoice, for this is Zion—THE PURE IN HEART; therefore, let Zion rejoice, while all the wicked shall mourn" (D&C 97:21).

It seems apparent that there are two very different conditions among mankind before the Second Coming. The world will be in total commotion, and those in that camp will be "mourning." Among the Saints there will be rejoicing.

Isaiah saw our day and prophesied: "Therefore the redeemed of the Lord shall return, and come with singing unto Zion; and everlasting joy *shall be* upon their head: they shall obtain gladness and joy; *and* sorrow and mourning shall flee away" (Isaiah 51:11).

King David penned a psalm about our day: "Sing unto the Lord, O ye saints of his, and give thanks at the remembrance of his holiness. For his anger *endureth but* a moment; in his favour *is* life: weeping may endure for a night, but joy *cometh* in the morning" (Psalm 30:4–5).

It is challenging to determine the best way to present this material since connections need to be made between the approaching Second

Coming and Satan's heightened efforts to destroy us. John the Revelator saw our day and warned: "Therefore rejoice, *ye* heavens, and ye that dwell in them. Woe to the inhabiters of the earth and of the sea! for the devil is come down unto you, having great wrath, because he knoweth that he hath but a short time" (Revelation 12:12).

Here is one of the most instructive elements of the formula. It comes from Joseph Smith's experience leading up to the First Vision:

> After I had retired to the place where I had previously designed to go, having looked around me, and finding myself alone, I kneeled down and began to offer up the desires of my heart to God. I had scarcely done so, when immediately I was seized upon by some power which entirely overcame me, and had such an astonishing influence over me as to bind my tongue so that I could not speak. Thick darkness gathered around me, and it seemed to me for a time as if I were doomed to sudden destruction.
>
> But, exerting all my powers to call upon God to deliver me out of the power of this enemy which had seized upon me, and at the very moment when I was ready to sink into despair and abandon myself to destruction—not to an imaginary ruin, but to the power of some actual being from the unseen world, who had such marvelous power as I had never before felt in any being—just at this moment of great alarm, I saw a pillar of light exactly over my head, above the brightness of the sun, which descended gradually until it fell upon me.
>
> It no sooner appeared than I found myself delivered from the enemy which held me bound. When the light rested upon me I saw two Personages, whose brightness and glory defy all description, standing above me in the air. One of them spake unto me, calling me by name and said, pointing to the other—*This is My Beloved Son. Hear Him!*" (JS—History 1:15–17)

There was no question in young Joseph's mind that Satan was a very real being and, compared to man's power, Satan had so much power as to make it virtually impossible to stand against him. In the very moment of his despair, Joseph gave us a vital key: "But, exerting all my powers to call upon God to deliver me out of the power of this enemy which had seized upon me, and at the very moment when I was ready to sink into despair and abandon myself to destruction." When faced with our darkest and most depressive episodes, could we do as Joseph did—intensify our prayers?

In the very moment where physical destruction seemed imminent, the "pillar of light" came which "delivered [Joseph Smith] from the enemy." How does Joseph Smith's experience help us in our depressive times? As soon as the pillar of light (defined by living prophets as the Holy Ghost) appeared, Father and Son appeared, he was liberated from the evil influence.

In your moment of greatest despair, the adversary tries to isolate you. You may feel all alone, helpless, incapable of continuing on, and ready to abandon yourself to destruction. Before reaching that point, go immediately and find a spouse, a bishop, a friend, or anyone you trust. Why? Because the Lord revealed: "Verily, verily, I say unto you, as I said unto my disciples, where two or three are gathered together in my name, as touching one thing, behold, there will I be in the midst of them—even so am I in the midst of you" (D&C 6:32).

As soon as the two or three of you together focus on your depressive (sometimes suicidal) state of mind, the Savior promises to be there. When that happened in Joseph's experience, he was immediately liberated from Satan's power.

Time and again this key has been elaborated upon by prophets ancient and modern. Alma, quoting a prophet (Zenos) that we do not have record of said: "And thou didst hear me because of mine afflictions and my sincerity; and it is because of thy Son that thou hast been thus merciful unto me, therefore I will cry unto thee in all mine afflictions, for in thee is my joy; for thou hast turned thy judgments away from me, because of thy Son" (Alma 33:11).

It seems almost inconceivable that we do not turn, in faith, to the Savior and plead for His help. Alma, continuing his teaching, refers to the experience of the children of Israel in the wilderness when they were bitten by poisonous serpents. All they had to do to be healed was to look at the brazen serpent Moses had placed on a pole. Alma said:

> Behold, he [Christ] was spoken of by Moses; yea, and behold a type was raised up in the wilderness, that whosoever would look upon it might live. And many did look and live.
>
> But few understood the meaning of those things, and this because of the hardness of their hearts. But there were many who were so hardened that they would not look, therefore they perished. Now the reason they would not look is because they did not believe that it would heal them.
>
> O my brethren, if ye could be healed by merely casting about your eyes that ye might be healed, would ye not behold quickly, or would ye rather harden your hearts in unbelief, and be slothful, that ye would not cast about your eyes, that ye might perish?

> If so, wo shall come upon you; but if not so, then cast about your eyes and begin to believe in the Son of God, that he will come to redeem his people, and that he shall suffer and die to atone for their sins; and that he shall rise again from the dead, which shall bring to pass the resurrection, that all men shall stand before him, to be judged at the last and judgment day, according to their works. (Alma 33:19–22)

How could the Savior know what that hopeless, life-threatening, depressive feeling is like? In Hebrews 4:15–16 Paul records: "For we have not an high priest which cannot be touched with the feeling of our infirmities; but was **in all points tempted like as *we are*,** *yet* without sin. Let us therefore come boldly unto the throne of grace, that we may obtain mercy, and find grace to help in time of need."

In His hour of greatest trial, Matthew records that Jesus "began to be sorrowful and very heavy" (Matthew 26:37) and according to His own words: "My soul is exceeding sorrowful, even unto death" (verse 38). Luke records: "And being in an agony he prayed more earnestly: and his sweat was as it were great drops of blood falling down to the ground" (Luke 22:44).

One would think that Jesus prayed in total earnestness all of the time (which He did). But He ramped it up even more with the weight of the salvation and exaltation of all mankind hanging in the balance. Instructively the two verses preceding states: "[Praying] Saying, Father, if thou be willing, remove this cup from me: nevertheless not my will, but thine, be done. And there appeared an angel unto him from heaven, strengthening him" (Luke 22:42–43).

Even the Son of God had an angel to encourage or strengthen Him during His darkest hour. No wonder, then, that He said in our dispensation: "Behold, and hearken, O ye elders of my church, saith the Lord your God, even Jesus Christ, your advocate, who knoweth the weakness of man and how to succor them who are tempted" (D&C 62:1). During our mini-Gethsemanes, He can relate perfectly, having gone through the unfathomable in His Gethsemane.

Eighty-three years before the Savior's birth, Alma realized the importance of informing the people of the scope of the Savior's Atonement. He said: "For behold, I say unto you there be many things to come; and behold, there is one thing which is of more importance than they all—for behold, the time is not far distant that the Redeemer liveth and cometh among his people" (Alma 7:7).

Then Alma described the Savior's mission in these words:

> And he shall go forth, suffering pains and afflictions and temptations of every kind; and this that the word might be fulfilled which saith he will take upon him the pains and the sicknesses of his people.
>
> And he will take upon him death, that he may loose the bands of death which bind his people; and he will take upon him their infirmities, that his bowels may be filled with mercy, according to the flesh, that **he may know according to the flesh how to succor his people according to their infirmities.**
>
> Now the Spirit knoweth all things; nevertheless the Son of God suffereth according to the flesh that he might take upon him the sins of his people, that he might blot out their transgressions according to the power of his deliverance; and now behold, this is the testimony which is in me.
>
> Now I say unto you that ye must repent, and be born again; for the Spirit saith if ye are not born again ye cannot inherit the kingdom of heaven; therefore come and be baptized unto repentance, that ye may be washed from your sins, that ye may have faith on the Lamb of God, who taketh away the sins of the world, who is mighty to save and to cleanse from all unrighteousness. (Alma 7:11–14)

Given that Satan's objective is to "destroy the world" (see Moses 4:6) and make all men "miserable like unto himself" (see 2 Nephi 2:27), it seems unfair that a being that powerful is an adversary to puny mankind with such very limited power. The Savior knew that and gave the following solution to the problem:

> I am the true vine, and my Father is the husbandman.
>
> Every branch in me that beareth not fruit he taketh away: and every branch that beareth fruit, he purgeth it, that it may bring forth more fruit.
>
> Now ye are clean through the word which I have spoken unto you.
>
> Abide in me, and I in you. As the branch cannot bear fruit of itself, except it abide in the vine; no more can ye, except ye abide in me.
>
> I am the vine, ye *are* the branches: He that abideth in me, and I in him, the same bringeth forth much fruit: **for without me ye can do nothing.** (John 15:1–5)

Unless we can turn to the Savior, in all faith, we are doomed to marginal success at best in overcoming weaknesses associated with mortality. Those who have or are battling depression, or are trying to assist someone who is, will readily admit that those so afflicted are in bondage more restrictive than a prison cell with bars. Confirming our dependence on the Savior and also giving us a formula to get the help we need, Mormon recorded the following verses:

> Behold what great destruction did come upon them; and also because of their iniquities they were brought into bondage.
>
> And were it not for the interposition of their all–wise Creator, and this because of their sincere repentance, they must unavoidably remain in bondage until now.
>
> But behold, he did deliver them because they did humble themselves before him; and because they cried mightily unto him he did deliver them out of bondage; and thus doth the Lord work with his power in all cases among the children of men, extending the arm of mercy towards them that put their trust in him. (Mosiah 29:18–20)

As noted in the beginning of the chapter, some depression comes because of iniquity. But using the Savior and Joseph Smith as examples, certainly neither of them merited their depressive feelings because of iniquity. So, we are focusing on the "bondage" we or our loved ones face because of our infirmities not caused by sin.

One cannot help but notice that unless we can get the all-wise Creator (Christ) to interpose, we must "unavoidably remain in bondage" (Mosiah 29:19). To interpose is to stand between two opposing or antagonistic foes. The elements of this formula include the following: 1) we must be humble; 2) we must pray mightily; and 3) we must trust in Him. Then He will deliver us. Note carefully: "**Thus doth the Lord work with his power in all cases among the children of men**" (Mosiah 29:20).

Isaiah again sensitively describes what the Savior has done for us: "Surely he hath borne our griefs, and carried our sorrows: yet we did esteem him stricken, smitten of God, and afflicted. But he was wounded for our transgressions, he was bruised for our iniquities: the chastisement of our peace was upon him; and with his stripes we are healed" (Isaiah 53:4–5).

Nephi saw the Savior's day as he was being instructed by an angel who was interpreting Lehi's dream: "And he spake unto me again, saying: Look! And I looked, and I beheld the Lamb of God going forth among the children of men. And I beheld multitudes of people who were sick, and who were afflicted with all manner of diseases, and with devils and unclean spirits; and the angel spake and showed all these things unto me. And they were healed by the power of the Lamb of God; and the devils and the unclean spirits were cast out" (1 Nephi 11:31).

So many in our day (even among members of the Church) are prone to say, "That was great during His mortal ministry, but things are different in our day." Here again, the scriptures contradict that notion: "Thereby showing that he is the same God yesterday, today, and forever" (D&C 20:12). If He did it then, He can and will do it now. Shortly after His resurrection, the Savior appeared to the Nephites who were spared because they were more righteous than those who were destroyed.

Mormon records the following touching event:

> And it came to pass that when Jesus had thus spoken, he cast his eyes round about again on the multitude, and beheld they were in tears, and did look steadfastly upon him as if they would ask him to tarry a little longer with them.
>
> And he said unto them: Behold, my bowels are filled with compassion towards you.
>
> Have ye any that are sick among you? Bring them hither. Have ye any that are lame, or blind, or halt, or maimed, or leprous, or that are withered, or that are deaf, or that are afflicted in any manner? Bring them hither and I will heal them, for I have compassion upon you; my bowels are filled with mercy.
>
> For I perceive that ye desire that I should show unto you what I have done unto your brethren at Jerusalem, for I see that your faith is sufficient that I should heal you.
>
> And it came to pass that when he had thus spoken, all the multitude, with one accord, did go forth with their sick and their afflicted, and their lame, and with their blind, and with their dumb, and with **all them that were afflicted in any manner; and he did heal them every one** as they were brought forth unto him.
>
> And they did all, both they who had been healed and they who were whole, bow down at his feet, and did worship him; and as many as could come for the multitude did kiss his feet, insomuch that they did bathe his feet with their tears. (3 Nephi 17:5–10)

Trying to battle the monster of depression alone has less than optimal results. Yes, we should use all medical and psychological resources available as Elder Holland so eloquently pleaded. However, if we stop there because of our unwillingness to turn and look to the Savior, we are short-changing ourselves. We can even put on a happy face and pretend that everything is all right. Wise King Solomon saw the futility of that approach: "There is a way which seemeth right unto a man, but the end thereof are the ways of death. Even in laughter the heart is sorrowful; and the end of that mirth *is* heaviness" (Proverbs 14:12–13).

There seems to be one element to this formula that overshadows everything else: "Look to God and live" (Alma 37:47).

Putting our depression, trials, tribulations, and afflictions in perspective, the Lord told the imprisoned Joseph Smith and fellow prisoners:

> Know thou, my son, that all these things shall give thee experience, and shall be for thy good.
>
> The Son of Man hath descended below them all. Art thou greater than he?
>
> Therefore, hold on thy way, and the priesthood shall remain with thee; for their bounds are set, they cannot pass. Thy days are known, and thy years shall not be numbered less; therefore, fear not what man can do, for God shall be with you forever and ever. (D&C 122:7–9)

It is comforting to me to know that there is divine purpose in all of our mortal trials. His comparison to the Savior helps me know that my trials, compared to His, are miniscule. Then come His comforting words: "Hold on thy way." I read that as "don't get discouraged, don't give up, don't contemplate ending your own life. "The priesthood shall remain with thee" means that t he very power of God that created and controls the universe is with us. "For their bounds are set, they cannot pass." Don't worry. Limits, or bounds, of the trials, persecutions, or depression that you are facing are set. God is faithful and will not allow you to be tried beyond your capacity to endure ("There hath no temptation taken you but such as is common to man: but God is faithful, who will not suffer you to be tempted above that ye are able; but will with the temptation also make a way to escape, that ye may be able to bear it" [1 Corinthians 10:13]).

"Fear not what man can do for God shall be with you forever and ever" (D&C 122:9). Even in our darkest hours, we must look upward rather than relying solely upon the "arm of flesh" (see 2 Nephi 4:34).

Listed below are some other scriptural verses to ponder. They aren't in any given order but re-emphasize what has been written before. Although not used specifically for this meaning, the scriptures use the phrase "it came to pass" 1,887 times. Does that suggest that our troubles and trials were never intended to "come to stay"?

How are we to act in our daily walk of life? The Lord said: "If thou art merry, praise the Lord with singing, with music, with dancing, and with a prayer of praise and thanksgiving. If thou art sorrowful, call on the Lord thy God with supplication, that your souls may be joyful" (D&C 136:28–29).

First, last, and always, the Savior holds the key to liberating us from the monster of depression or any other mortal weakness. He also determines what part those mortal weaknesses play in the perfecting process. He alone determines how long and to what degree those challenges must be endured before He interposes on our behalf. Be assured He will not cause us to suffer more or longer than is absolutely necessary to prepare us for exaltation.

POINTS FOR FURTHER CONSIDERATION

Discouragement

Elder George A. Smith (1817–75) of the Quorum of the Twelve Apostles reported that once when he was discouraged, the Prophet Joseph Smith said, "I should never get discouraged, whatever difficulties should surround me, if I was sunk in the lowest pit of Nova Scotia and all the Rocky Mountains piled on top of me, I ought not to be discouraged but hang on, exercise faith and keep up good courage and I should come out on the top of the heap" (Quoted in *Memoirs of George A. Smith*, in George A. Smith papers, ms 1322, box, folder 1, Family and Church History Department Archives, The Church of Jesus Christ of Latter-day Saints).

How long wilt thou forget me, O Lord? for ever? how long wilt thou hide thy face from me?

How long shall I take counsel in my soul, having sorrow in my heart daily? how long shall mine enemy be exalted over me?

Consider and hear me, O Lord my God: lighten mine eyes, lest I sleep the sleep of death;

Lest mine enemy say, I have prevailed against him; *and* those that trouble me rejoice when I am moved.

But I have trusted in thy mercy; my heart shall rejoice in thy salvation.

I will sing unto the Lord, because he hath dealt bountifully with men. (Psalm 13:1–6)

For all things are for your sakes, that the abundant grace might through the thanksgiving of many redound to the glory of God.

For which cause we faint not; but though our outward man perish, yet the inward man is renewed day by day.

For our light affliction, which is but for a moment, worketh for us a far more exceeding and eternal weight of glory;

While we look not at the things which are seen, but at the things which are not seen: for the things which are seen *are* temporal; but the things which are not seen are eternal. (2 Corinthians 4:15–18)

And also Zeezrom lay sick at Sidom, with a burning fever, which was caused by the great tribulations of his mind on account of his wickedness, for he supposed that Alma and Amulek were no more; and he supposed that they had been slain because of his iniquity. And this great sin, and his many other sins, did harrow up his mind until it did become exceedingly sore, having no deliverance; therefore he began to be scorched with a burning heat.

Now, when he heard that Alma and Amulek were in the land of Sidom, his heart began to take courage; and he sent a message immediately unto them, desiring them to come unto him.

And it came to pass that they went immediately, obeying the message which he had sent unto them; and they went in unto the house unto Zeezrom; and they found him upon his bed, sick, being very low with a burning fever; and his mind also was exceedingly sore because of his iniquities; and when he saw them he stretched forth his hand, and besought them that they would heal him.

And it came to pass that Alma said unto him, taking him by the hand: Believest thou in the power of Christ unto salvation?

And he answered and said: Yea, I believe all the words that thou hast taught.

And Alma said: If thou believest in the redemption of Christ thou canst be healed.

And he said: Yea, I believe according to thy words.

And then Alma cried unto the Lord, saying: O Lord our God, have mercy on this man, and heal him according to his faith which is in Christ.

And when Alma had said these words, Zeezrom leaped upon his feet, and began to walk; and this was done to the great astonishment of all the people; and the knowledge of this went forth throughout all the land of Sidom. (Alma 15:3–11)

And it came to pass that as I was thus racked with torment, while I was harrowed up by the memory of my many sins, behold, I remembered also to have heard my father prophesy unto the people concerning the coming of one Jesus Christ, a Son of God, to atone for the sins of the world.

Now, as my mind caught hold upon this thought, I cried within my heart: O Jesus, thou Son of God, have mercy on me, who am in the gall of bitterness, and am encircled about by the everlasting chains of death.

And now, behold, when I thought this, I could remember my pains no more; yea, I was harrowed up by the memory of my sins no more.

And oh, what joy, and what marvelous light I did behold; yea, my soul was filled with joy as exceeding as was my pain!

Yea, I say unto you, my son, that there could be nothing so exquisite and so bitter as were my pains. Yea, and again I say unto you, my son, that on the other hand, there can be nothing so exquisite and sweet as was my joy. (Alma 36:17–21)

Many sorrows *shall be* to the wicked: but he that trusteth in the Lord, mercy shall compass him about.

Be glad in the Lord, and rejoice, ye righteous: and shout for joy, all *ye that are* upright in heart. (Psalm 32:10–11)

And this shall ye have of my hand—ye shall lie down in sorrow.

Behold, and lo, there are none to deliver you; for ye obeyed not my voice when I called to you out of the heavens; ye believed not my servants, and when they were sent unto you ye received them not. (D&C 133:70–71)

O then, if I have seen so great things, if the Lord in his condescension unto the children of men hath visited men in so much mercy, why should my heart weep and my soul linger in the valley of sorrow, and my flesh waste away, and my strength slacken, because of mine afflictions?

And why should I yield to sin, because of my flesh? Yea, why should I give way to temptations, that the evil one have place in my heart to destroy my peace and afflict my soul? Why am I angry because of mine enemy?

Awake, my soul! No longer droop in sin. Rejoice, O my heart, and give place no more for the enemy of my soul.

Do not anger again because of mine enemies. Do not slacken my strength because of mine afflictions.

Rejoice, O my heart, and cry unto the Lord, and say: O Lord, I will praise thee forever; yea, my soul will rejoice in thee, my God, and the rock of my salvation.

O Lord, wilt thou redeem my soul? Wilt thou deliver me out of the hands of mine enemies? Wilt thou make me that I may shake at the appearance of sin?

May the gates of hell be shut continually before me, because that my heart is broken and my spirit is contrite! O Lord, wilt thou not shut the gates of thy righteousness before me, that I may walk in the path of the low valley, that I may be strict in the plain road!

O Lord, wilt thou encircle me around in the robe of thy righteousness! O Lord, wilt thou make a way for mine escape before mine enemies! Wilt thou make my path straight before me! Wilt thou not place a stumbling block in my way—but that thou wouldst clear my way before me, and hedge not up my way, but the ways of mine enemy.

O Lord, I have trusted in thee, and I will trust in thee forever. I will not put my trust in the arm of flesh; for I know that cursed is he that putteth his trust in the arm of flesh. Yea, cursed is he that putteth his trust in man or maketh flesh his arm.

Yea, I know that God will give liberally to him that asketh. Yea, my God will give me, if I ask not amiss; therefore I will lift up my voice unto thee; yea, I will cry unto thee, my God, the rock of my righteousness. Behold, my voice shall forever ascend up unto thee, my rock and mine everlasting God. Amen. (2 Nephi 4:26–35)

And now I say, is there not a type in this thing? For just as surely as this director did bring our fathers, by following its course, to the promised land, shall the words of Christ, if we follow their course, carry us beyond this vale of sorrow into a far better land of promise.

O my son, do not let us be slothful because of the easiness of the way; for so was it with our fathers; for so was it prepared for them, that if they would look they might live; even so it is with us. The way is prepared, and if we will look we may live forever. (Alma 37:45–46)

But if he repent not he shall not be numbered among my people, that he may not destroy my people, for behold I know my sheep, and they are numbered.

Nevertheless, ye shall not cast him out of your synagogues, or your places of worship, for unto such shall ye continue to minister; for ye know not but what they will return and repent, and come unto me with full purpose of heart, and I shall heal them; and ye shall be the means of bringing salvation unto them. (3 Nephi 18:31–32)

And pray for thy brethren of the Twelve. Admonish them sharply for my name's sake, and let them be admonished for all their sins, and be ye faithful before me unto my name.

And after their temptations, and much tribulation, behold, I, the Lord, will feel after them, and if they harden not their hearts, and stiffen not their necks against me, they shall be converted, and I will heal them. (D&C 112:12–13)

DO THE FORMULAS WORK?

"Thank you for your advice, Brother Bott. It really worked. My commission was three million dollars. I know I'm only thirty-three years old, but I'm retiring to Florida and just wanted to drop by and say goodbye!" I was stunned and asked for a few more details.

This happened more than forty years ago in Raleigh, North Carolina. I was a young institute teacher who thought he knew everything. I had been asked by the stake Seventy's quorum to present a lunch-time lecture on Doctrine and Covenants 130:20–21: "There is a law, irrevocably decreed in heaven before the foundations of this world, upon which all blessings are predicated—And when we obtain any blessing from God, it is by obedience to that law upon which it is predicated."

We had recently moved from Utah to North Carolina to accept the responsibility of supervising all CES programs in the eastern half of the state. The people were hungry for gospel discussions, so I found myself responding to numerous speaking invitations—the one mentioned above to the Seventies was just one of many.

Not wanting to disappoint them, I spent considerable time preparing my talk. After the formal presentation, they requested a question and answer time. Confident that I could handle any question (I really was naive!) I agreed. The first question was from a dynamic young real estate broker. He raised his hand and asked, "Brother Bott, you say that all we need to do to claim a blessing from the Lord is to determine the law upon which it is predicated." I thought he was restating what I had just taught so I agreed. He continued with his question: "What is the Lord's law for accumulating wealth?"

There was silence in the room. All of the Seventies were relatively young businessmen. It was obvious that they wanted to hear the answer. Stalling for time (because I had never really thought of trying to identify the laws upon which any particular blessing is predicated), I suggested that his question deserved more time than I had available since I was scheduled to teach an institute class within the hour.

Not to be put off, the senior president asked the group if they would like a follow-up discussion at the next month's luncheon. All readily agreed. I was stuck. They asked me to outline the elements of the Lord's formula for accumulating wealth without losing one's soul and be prepared to discuss it in a month.

That next month saw me burning the midnight lights, searching for whatever advice I could find that the Lord had revealed through His prophets. It was an exhilarating experience.

At the following month's luncheon, we had a lively discussion that at least acted as a catalyst to get them searching the scriptures for principles. I thought I had failed miserably since they graciously thanked me for my efforts but never asked me to speak again.

Three months later the thirty-three–year-old Seventy came by my house to say goodbye. When I asked for an explanation, he said he had been working for well over a year on a six-state real estate transaction. Every time all the players were lined up, at the last minute one of them backed out. He then said he had taken the principles I had researched and scrutinized his entire program.

He didn't say exactly what mistake he had been making, but he said it became crystal clear what he needed to do. The month following our second meeting he held a collective meeting with all of the parties, and applying what he learned from the scriptures, they all agreed. His commission was three million dollars.

I almost suggested he pay me a finder's fee, but his jubilation prevented me from putting a damper on his success. Unfortunately, being young with a near photographic memory (at that time—my, how things have changed!), I saw no real reason to keep the notes from my talk. Over time I forgot what I had learned since no one asked that same question for many years.

For nearly forty years I have had in my mind that the Lord has given that declaration of eternal truth not just so we can quote it—which many members can—but as a challenge to discover the laws upon which every blessing is predicated. God's objective is our eternal exaltation, but He is also very interested in helping us make our mortal experience a positive one.

Having just completed my fourth mission, and knowing that I am rapidly growing old, I decided to identify some of the major blessings I want and then see if I can quantify some of the principles the Lord has revealed as parts of the laws upon which those blessings are predicated.

This book is the initial effort to share what I am learning. It comes with a challenge to the reader to continue the quest, apply the laws, and enjoy the blessings.

EPILOGUE

Now, dear reader, as I come to the end of this work, I think it appropriate to add a postscript. I would like to use a story from my distant past that seems to illustrate my final thoughts. Although I will condense and abridge this story, all of the facts are accurately portrayed. I will give this account as best I can remember the details.

I was sixteen years old when my widowed mother permitted me to travel to the tiny island of Tutuila, American Samoa, to visit a friend whose parents were teaching at the local high school. My planned six-week visit had, at their invitation and my mother's reluctant permission, been extended to include my junior year of high school.

In those early days, now more than fifty years ago, there was (as there is today) only one road running the entire length of the island. Unlike today's road, the road in those days was unpaved. In fact, it was better described as one pothole after another, one jig and jog after another. The trip to Pago Pago (the capital city) was a tortuous experience.

The "buses" were two-and-a-half-ton trucks with planks for seats running the length of the bed. A canvas canopy was designed to keep the rain out and the sun from beating mercilessly on us—neither purpose was well served. The buses were often filled far beyond capacity. In addition to the human cargo, each bus served as the only means of delivering the produce, pigs, chickens, and sellable goods to Pago Pago. The non-human cargo was stacked in the middle of the bed between the passengers' feet.

Most often the driver was either unskilled or motivated by racecar movies. He would drive the road as though it were a freeway. Not infrequently upon hitting a pothole I would be projected like a missile across the cargo into the arms of a husky fellow sitting opposite me. Regaining my position on the bench, the next pothole would often find me in the comforting arms of the woman sitting next to me.

Not to be exclusive, just as often I would be the one to catch a woman or child as they were thrown from the far seat into my arms. Making the journey really was a joint effort. By the time we reached our destination, I felt like I had been beaten mercilessly over the entirety of my body.

Why make the trip, you might ask? Once a week a movie was shown in Pago Pago. It was the only movie "theater" on the island at the time. It was a large single-story building with woven mats on the floor to sit on. It had no air conditioning, so when the doors were shut to darken the room, it was insufferably hot. Most often cowboy and Indian movies were shown. The local people would cheer loudly when the Indians had the upper hand. My friend and I (the only Caucasians in the room) would cheer loudly when the cowboys won—which they always did. In addition to the movie, Pago Pago was the only place on the island to purchase ice cream.

In telling this part of the story, I want you to sense the agony of the weekly trip that was overridden by the reward at the end. But the purpose comes not from the trip but from the following experience.

Adjacent to the village of Mapusaga where I stayed was a mountain called the Mapusaga Rainmaker. This fifteen-hundred-foot mountain looked like some angry giant under the crust of the earth had thrust his fist upward, creating the near-vertical sides of the mountain. From the local people, we learned that on the top of the mountain, under a rock, in a glass jar was a piece of paper and the stub of a pencil. Those who successfully climbed the mountain wrote their names on the paper—a prized goal for two sixteen-year-old boys noting how few names were on the paper.

Against the near constant warnings of the people to stay away from the mountain, my friend and I decided to climb. Knowing that it would be a challenge, we trained for over a month. We worked up to one hundred sit-ups, one hundred push-ups, several times up the tortuous rope climb, and we even ran the track in the hot, humid early December weather.

The day after Christmas was a beautiful, clear day. With a canteen of water attached to our belts, we stood at the base of the mountain looking straight up toward the top. Feeling well prepared, we began the climb.

The first few hundred feet posed little problem since we could ascend ape-like, climbing with our legs and using our hands to steady us against the mountain.

About four or five hundred feet up, the incline increased to near vertical. Now the going was much more challenging. In order to ascend, we had to grab one of the abundant vines on the mountain and tug on it. If it dislodged, we knew it wouldn't support our weight, so we would try another vine until we found one that held. Slowly we inched our way up the mountain.

Unlike the lower elevation where we could sit on the mountain to rest, at the higher elevations, in order to take a breather, we had to wind ourselves into the vines with both arms and lean facing the mountain. The sting of perspiration in our eyes couldn't be eliminated by wiping the sweat away because we would lose our grip on the vines. The foliage in our faces and the bugs crawling uncontested on our faces only made the climb more distasteful.

It didn't take us too long to determine that instead of a hundred push-ups and sit-ups we should have done a thousand. Instead of a few rope climbs we should have done dozens. But the preparation time was over. We had to go on. We were too tired to go down (which was just as taxing as the climb up).

Then, as it always seems to happen, the unexpected occurred. Looming immediately above our heads was a small tabletop jutting perpendicularly from the mountain. It wasn't huge—probably only ten feet or so—but we couldn't get around it. It was invisible from the ground and so totally unexpected.

What to do? As we hung there wrapped in the foliage of the mountain, we deliberated. My friend suggested that I go first. If I made it, he would come. His reasoning was, "If you fall and die, it will take two weeks before your mother finds out. If I die, my folks will know immediately." That sounded like reasonable logic at the time.

So, venturing out, I took hold of a vine and a rock anchored in the tabletop. You may be able to sense the increase of strength and adrenaline that surged through my body as my lower body was suspended 1,200 feet in the air and blowing in the wind. Quickly I scrambled to the top of the tabletop. Breathless, I called to my friend to join me. He arrived in short order as well. Then he said, "I could have been killed!" By that time my more reasonable teenage senses had returned, and his prior logic didn't seem quite so reasonable.

We climbed the last few hundred feet without incident. Once arriving at the top, we located the rock, moved it out of the way, discovered the bottle, opened it, put our names on the paper, and put it back in place for the next climber.

That is when I had a revelation. Since there is no pollution in Samoa, on a clear day you can see forever. The view was breathtaking. We visually surveyed the entire island and looked out to where the sky meets the sea. As we sat resting on the top of the Rainmaker, we looked down at the road below.

Contrary to all of the complaining we had done about the senseless jigs and jogs in the road, from our vantage point we could see that each had purpose. We had accused the engineer who constructed the road of being inspired by the devils from hell. Now we could see that the road jogs here to avoid a bog hole we couldn't see from ground level because of the density of the bush. Another jig in the road was to avoid a huge boulder we had never seen. Then a detour around a village or a sharp turn to prevent going into the ocean. From 1,500 feet in the air, everything made perfect sense. And, from 1,500 feet in the air, we couldn't see the potholes.

Such is my story. Now for the application. As we travel through life, events happen that seem senseless. At times, we are thrown at the mercy of others. Another time we are the ones who must catch someone who is struggling. The more we learn to rely upon each other in times of need, the more doable is the journey. Many times, I was tempted to stop the bus, get out, and walk back home because the journey was too painful or the reward didn't seem worth the cost. Many times, our lives may seem difficult beyond our abilities.

I assume Queen Esther had similar thoughts when her uncle, Mordecai, implored her to intervene on behalf of her people (the Jews) at the peril of her life by approaching the king without being summoned. Mordecai's convincing statement to Esther may well apply to you: "Who knoweth whether thou art come to the kingdom for such a time as this" (Esther 4:14)?

There may come a time when your decision to faithfully follow the Lord may be the means of saving untold, unseen, unnamed people from imminent destruction. That may be a spiritual rescue rather than a physical one, but just as real as Queen Esther's.

Or you may be placed in a position when your dedication to the Lord puts your very life in jeopardy as it did with Shadrach, Meshach, and Abed-nego when King Nebuchadnezzar set up a golden image and commanded everyone to bow and worship it. Refusing to comply meant death by fire. Who can forget the courageous reply of these three young men to an irate king who commanded the furnaces to be heated seven times hotter than normal to execute them: "O Nebuchadnezzar, we are not careful to answer thee in this matter. If it be so, our God whom we serve is able to deliver us from the burning fiery furnace, and he will deliver us out of thine hand, O king. But if not, be it known unto thee, O king, that we will not serve thy gods, nor worship the golden image which thou hast set up" (Daniel 3:16–18).

You may not be faced with death by fire but possibly with the fiery scorn of the unbelievers. If you are, how will you stand?

In today's cutthroat world, it would not be unheard of to be set up by those who are jealous of you—much like Daniel in Old Testament times. Unrighteous men convinced the king to sign a decree that anyone worshiping other than the king for thirty days would be cast into a den of starving lions. Because of the arrogance of the king, the decree could not be altered.

Upon hearing of the decree, Daniel went immediately to his house and with the windows wide open so all could see, he prayed three times a day toward Jerusalem. When those evil men reported Daniel's violation of the unrighteous decree, with a great deal of sorrow, the king followed his own decree and put Daniel in the lions' den, hoping against hope that God would spare Daniel.

The next morning the king had the stone covering the mouth of the lions' den removed and with extreme gladness, he heard Daniel answer when he called to him. Then, because "what goes around comes around," the king ordered the evil men, their wives, and children to be thrown into the lions' den. If you haven't read Daniel 6 lately, it is well worth your time.

You may not be thrown into a den of lions, but treachery abounds and God is just as willing to turn their wickedness back onto their own heads as you steadfastly continue your devotion to Christ and His gospel.

Perhaps boldness in the face of overwhelming odds may be your challenge as it was with Elijah when confronting an apostate nation. Remember, there were 450 priests of Baal against one prophet with an unshakable testimony. If you haven't read 1 Kings 18 in some time, now would be a great time to refresh your memory. Then ask yourself, "Am I courageous enough to stand for God-ordained marriage between a man and a woman against the loud, blatant, apostate voices of the masses?" In eternal retrospect, your sterling example of fearlessly defending the Lord's gospel may prove as remarkable as Elijah's defense before the wavering children of Israel when he said, "How long halt ye between two opinions? if the Lord be God, follow him: but if Baal, then follow him" (1 Kings 18:21).

You may feel surrounded as Elisha and his servant were with no possible way of escape. Here is the young servant's question and Elisha's response:

> And when the servant of the man of God was risen early, and gone forth, behold, an host compassed the city both with horses and chariots. And his servant said unto him, Alas, my master! how shall we do?
>
> And he answered, **Fear not: for they that *be* with us *are* more than they that *be* with them.**
>
> And Elisha prayed, and said, Lord, I pray thee, open his eyes, that he may see. And the Lord opened the eyes of the young man; and he saw: and, behold, the mountain was full of horses and chariots of fire round about Elisha. (2 Kings 6:15–17)

The Lord has not preserved you for these troubled times so you will fail. If we could see them, I am convinced that there really are more for us than are against us. Trust in the Lord.

When life seems grossly unfair as trials, tribulations, and temptations bombard you in multiple doses at the same time. Are you up to following the Savior's counsel: "Take therefore no thought for the morrow: for the morrow shall take thought for the things of itself. Sufficient unto the day *is* the evil thereof" (Matthew 6:34)? Don't try to live life all at once. One day at a time, we can overcome the world. I like this trite cliché: "How do you eat an elephant? One bite at a time." That is true of life—one day at a time, one challenge at a time.

The Lord outlined the challenge of mortality when He said, "These things I have spoken unto you, that in me ye might have peace. In the world ye shall have tribulation: but be of good cheer; I have overcome the world" (John 16:33).

Are we ready to join hands with the Apostle Paul, who said, "We are troubled on every side, yet not distressed; we are perplexed, but not in despair; Persecuted, but not forsaken; cast down, but not destroyed" (2 Corinthians 4:8–9)?

Sometimes the challenges of life seem like they will never end. However, now as I stand, as it were, on the last lap of the journey of life, James' observation makes more sense: "Whereas ye know not what shall be on the morrow. For what is your life? It is even a vapour, that appeareth for a little time, and then vanisheth away" (James 4:14).

We are here in mortality to learn the lessons that will enable us to confidently return to the presence of God. Hopefully, the older we get the more Christlike our behavior will be and more Godlike our vision.

When that final day comes for each of us—and it will come—may we be able to say with the Apostle Paul: "I have fought a good fight, I have finished my course, I have kept the faith: Henceforth there is laid up for me a crown of righteousness, which the Lord, the righteous judge, shall give me at that day: and not to me only, but unto all them also that love his appearing" (2 Timothy 4:7–8).

Possibly not until we stand atop our "Rainmaker" after passing into the eternal worlds will we fully realize the purpose of every jig and every jog in our pathway through mortality. And, more likely than not, the potholes that are so troubling to us now will not even show up on the review screen of eternity. So, enjoy the ride, draw near to the Lord, and He will not forsake or abandon you.

ABOUT THE AUTHOR

Randy Bott is married to the love of his life, Vickie (fifty years and counting). They have six children, sixteen grandchildren, and one great-granddaughter.

Brother Bott has degrees from Utah State University (a bachelor's in psychology and a master's in secondary education) and a doctorate degree in educational leadership from Brigham Young University. He has served as a bishop, in two stake presidencies, and as a mission president. He served his first mission in Samoa.

After he retired from BYU in 2012, he and his wife served missions at BYU–Hawaii and in Sydney, Australia. They are currently preparing for another mission.

Brother Bott taught in the Church Education System in Utah and North Carolina for twenty years, and nineteen years at BYU–Provo. He has authored many books and articles. His passion is teaching and counseling. He loves people and loves problem-solving and creating new programs to help people succeed.